THE
MONUMENT

THE
MONUMENT

T. BEHRENS

JONATHAN CAPE
THIRTY-TWO BEDFORD SQUARE LONDON

First published 1988
Copyright © 1988 by T. Behrens
Jonathan Cape Ltd, 32 Bedford Square, London WC1B 3EL

British Library Cataloguing in Publication Data

Behrens, T.
The monument.
I. Behrens, Justin 2. England—Biography
I. Title
942.085′092′4   CT788.B3

ISBN 0 224 02510 4

The author and publishers are grateful to Graham Greene
for permission to reproduce the letter on pp. 243–4; and to
Faber & Faber Ltd and Harcourt Brace Jovanovich, Inc. for
permission to quote lines (p. 21) from 'Ash Wednesday' by
T. S. Eliot, taken from *Collected Poems 1909–1962*.

Printed in Great Britain by Butler & Tanner Ltd
Frome and London

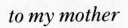

to my mother

Contents

Acknowledgments

The Monument could never have been written without the help of a great many people. The contribution of one in particular, Riri Howse, was so fundamental that without her the book would have taken quite a different shape. I would like to thank her first of all for her generosity in undertaking a task that must have been as painful as it was time-consuming. I am also specially grateful to Kenelm Digby-Jones and Tom Hilton for the very different ways in which they nudged me closer to the truth.

Very many thanks too (in order of appearance) to Fiona Martin, Christopher Moorsom, Bruce Chatwin, Maureen Digby-Jones, Patrick Leigh Fermor, Gianni de Sisti, Eve Molesworth, my mother and father, Annie Frances Sturt, the Rev. R. D. Baird, Hugo Stewart, my brother Jonna, Adam Craig, Betty Morris, Harriet Frazer, Mrs E. H. Carr, Mark and Louise Peploe, Carmen Nuñez and Manuel Vazquez, James Walston, my sister-in-law Beverley, Caroline Dawnay and Graham Greene.

For the account of the preliminary stages of the Hungarian revolution I am totally indebted to Noel Barber's *Seven Days of Freedom*.

The Monument would never have reached completion – let alone found a publisher – without the persistent encouragement and technical assistance of my friend Jonathan Gathorne-Hardy.

In the interests of discretion I have changed the names of a minority of the characters who come into the story.

1

Justin, Ursula and I

I heard that my 16-year-old brother was involved with a most exotic creature, some sort of Hungarian countess, married and probably a spy. Having hardly seen him since his voice had broken, I was curious to know more. We arranged to have dinner in Olwen's French Club. He had grown a lot, and I was impressed by his certainty, his determination, as he outlined the latest developments in the affair. His girl-friend's husband, in what seemed to me a highly understandable last-ditch attempt to save his marriage and prevent a humiliating scandal, had whisked her off either to Rome or Jerusalem, Justin wasn't sure which. All he knew was that he must immediately fly out to both places if necessary and chivalrously rescue her. He was in no doubt that the minute she saw him she'd leap into his arms and they'd live happily ever after. I remembered the picture of Perseus swooping from the sky to slay the dragon, but the idea of Ursula as a passive Andromeda didn't fit in with what I'd already heard about her. I was also sceptical, to put it mildly, of my little brother's ability to compete on such serious, adult ground – even if he managed to locate his friend, which seemed unlikely, considering that his only guideline was a couple of addresses on the backs of envelopes.

I was torn between the desire to encourage him and the responsibilities befitting a brother eleven years older. I gave plenty of common-sense objections to his going ahead with such a crazy course of action, but in the end the enormity of his romanticism swung the balance. I wrote a cheque for his return flight to Rome, and promised him the loan of a room I rented in Kentish Town, so that if he did find Ursula he'd have somewhere to take her. What I didn't yet understand was that he didn't need my, or anyone else's, help – he was perfectly capable of managing on his own.

He didn't find her. He had a frustrating time following up his nebulous contacts, wandering distractedly round an unknown and hostile city. But a few of the Romans he met evidently felt sorry for him, and one of them let him crash out at night in the back of his car. Justin returned to London a week later, starving hungry, exhausted, and more determined than ever. He decided to wait night and day outside Ursula's Chelsea flat until he met anyone who could give him news of her. When finally, a few days later, he saw the light go on in her bedroom window, he rang the doorbell. Ursula came downstairs, not even having had time to take off her coat. He brought her straight to the room in Kentish Town, where I then met her for the first time.

Exotic, Ursula certainly was. Her silky, very blonde hair hung in a sheer curtain, surging into and merging with her silky, very blond mink. She was like a heraldic animal, or maybe an Afghan hound, whose profuse coat set off the smoothness of an extraordinary face. She had hooded, huge, pale blue eyes which in repose were stony – a rare and expensive stone no doubt, but forbidding none the less. She had high, wide Slavonic cheekbones, a fine curving nose a little on the long side, and a thin wide mouth which naturally turned down at the corners. When she laughed her face was transformed – the sapphire eyes sparkled and seemed to deepen with amusement, while her mouth opened wide to show a great deal of sharp little teeth, including unusually pointed canines. I couldn't take my eyes off her. My brother, though glowing with delight at having her back (he stroked her hair and held her hands continually), was even more concerned with administering to her immediate comfort – was she warm enough, hungry, thirsty, would she like a bath? Yes, she would love a bath. I had to leave but arranged to have a meal with them next day. As I went down the stairs I turned to see them kissing in the bathroom doorway like a couturier's advertisement in a glossy magazine.

In the week or two that followed I saw them nearly every day. It immediately became clear that Ursula's appearance, while fascinating, hypnotic even, in its effect on anyone who happened to be present (it has to be admitted that women were noticeably less susceptible than men), wasn't the most impressive thing about her. Although the English language was a comparatively recent acquisition of hers, she spoke it more correctly, more interestingly, and certainly more fluently than the majority of Englishmen. I say Englishmen advisedly – her phrasing had a masculine muscularity. But these perfect, almost architectural sentences rang out in a middle-European accent so unashamed that it seemed at first hearing disdainful, as though, having mastered in such a short time a thousand nuances of the subtlest of languages, she had then decided that it would be gilding the lily to make the effort to pronounce it correctly. Ursula was perfectly capable of such arrogance, such condescension, but as time went by and I got to know her better, I came to another conclusion – that she hung on to her absurd accent for self-protective reasons. If she turned herself into a clown she'd be providing an extra shield for her painfully vulnerable centre. She had several clownish attributes – she had the whiteness and the huge eyes, and more important, she had the traditional compulsion to amuse while inwardly crumbling away with a generalised and inherited melancholy.

When I knew her best, that's to say when she was first with my brother, before the two of them became so exclusive of the outside world, she still retained many traces of the brilliant party-goer she must have been before she met him. She would talk about anything to anyone. She had a most charming and discreet technique for extracting people's life histories. Like a skilful interviewer she'd lay an extra-pertinent question whenever the subject seemed to be running out of steam. She was almost a better listener than talker, and that's saying something. And her intelligence was infectious, you raised your game like some random qualifier at Wimbledon taking a set off the defending champion. Unfortunately you knew all too well that afterwards, with hilarious accuracy, she would explode the pretensions of the sucker she'd just been lulling into self-betrayal. She fed off the amusement of her audience, and usually ended up giggling, till tears came into her eyes, at the ludicrous exposure of someone who was apparently not unlike yourself. I was afraid of Ursula in a good many ways, but one of my chief fears was of what on earth she'd think of to say about me when I wasn't there.

In the remainder of her truncated lifetime, her life with Justin, their increasing interdependence (and consequent rejection of all but one or two friends and acquaintances) left less and less room for these social talents to emerge. And the profound and lifelong unhappiness, which had previously been held in check by some kind of contact with society, submerged the sense of the absurd that had once been such an important part of her.

2

Ursula

After Ursula died, Justin wrote a book about her life which he called *Style* – a title intended to convey in his private language all that she meant to him. This book has been my only consecutive source for the reconstruction of her early life. In spite of exhaustive efforts, I've found it impossible to locate reliable witnesses either to corroborate or refute its evidence. Justin and Ursula spent seventeen years almost entirely alone together and, given that she was more than usually voluble, it's reasonable to assume that gradually she must have given him a fullish account of her childhood. If, as I shall explain later, Ursula had her own reasons for whitewashing certain passages, her analytical mind and interest in her own psychological difficulties would have compensated for the tendency. Justin's own reliability is another matter. Since he considered Ursula to be almost superhuman he was inclined to attribute the grandest possible motives to all her actions. With this in mind I have followed only the factual thread of his narrative, except where I quote directly from his book.

Ursula was born in Budapest in 1938. Her father's family was of Russian descent and her mother was Italian, from the Veneto. They decided to hire a *Fräulein* as Ursula's nanny, so that her first language should be German. Seeing that Hungary fought on the German side in the war and that her father was always firmly on the side of the status quo, this choice can be seen as conventionally diplomatic. But when the war was lost and the Russians took over, and Ursula began at an early age to think for herself, she was humiliated by the connotations of the language she spoke most naturally. She decided to 'forget' it, concentrating instead on a mishmash of Hungarian, French and Italian, the other languages used interchangeably in the household. Then at sixteen she began to learn English and, perhaps because it was the only one she had chosen, she later expressed herself more freely in it than in any other language. Polyglottal both by upbringing and by cultural inclination, Ursula lacked a mother tongue.

Her mother was a beautiful, intelligent, but neurasthenic woman who had never come to terms with the discovery that she had nothing in common with her coarse-grained, horse-loving husband – the marriage was a disaster. She became increasingly melancholy and reclusive with no time at all for her only child. She retreated to her own quarters to read nineteenth-century novels, which reinforced her conviction that fate had treated her cruelly.

Ursula grew up in feudal surroundings on her parents' estate near Budapest. She didn't know any other children. Her companions were the cook, the groom and a succession of governesses. Then there were the gipsies whom her father encouraged because he loved their music, as well as their horses. Every year he held a fête for all his tenants at which the gipsies played and danced and everyone drank himself silly. Gipsy looks and music, exotic, erotic and out of reach, affected Ursula powerfully. The influence was a lasting one – to the end of her life she was susceptible to any approximation of the thrill of danger, a somehow profitable danger, that gipsies gave her.

However, the real passion of her childhood, indeed of her life, was books. At the age of seven she began to acquire a voracious appetite for reading. Ursula was without exaggeration the best-read person I've ever known, and the basis for this superb culture was laid down in the library of her father's house, a huge room walled with books which other members of the household rarely set foot in.

To make up for her mother's continuing neglect, Ursula redoubled her reliance on her father, trusting without qualification his values and opinions, of which there were many. When she was eight, though, he betrayed this trust in an unforgivable way. What follows is Justin's account of how it happened.

Ursula, aged eight, was in the library trying to translate Tasso's 'Lirici Amorosi' into German. Suddenly she heard the sound of her father's heavy boots approaching. When it stopped she looked up: her father, unsmiling, took the leather-bound volume away from her and, after glancing at the title, dropped his arm, which then hung with the little book gripped in his huge hand. He said, 'My dear, I would like you to come for a walk with me', and turning on his heel strode away, depositing the book on a table as he passed. This was unprecedented and sounded to Ursula so improbable that she wondered whether she might not have misheard. In her anxiety to avoid mortification she hesitated, but excitement prevailed, and she followed as quickly as discretion permitted.

Although he moderated his military stride she kept up with difficulty. They went along the avenue and out on to the rutted, dusty track at the edge of the forest, on the other side of which stretched an endless expanse of arable land . . . They rounded the forest as the heat began to slacken. If they followed a certain track they would be back home before dark. But then her father struck out on a path leading to a village about an hour away by foot. They followed the path for twenty minutes until the forest was out of sight behind the tall corn. The sun had begun to set when they came to a clearing made by the peasants. Here her father ordered her to remain until he returned. He departed briskly in the direction of the village. Ursula was absolutely alone, exposed. Night fell, there was no moon, the stars were too remote to give any light. It's hard to imagine what that child must have experienced in the four hours before she heard the heavy, irregular footsteps returning through the dust. Her father was a black shadow smelling strongly of liquor. He laughed and clasped her clumsily by the shoulder. He took out his pocket watch and made it repeat. 'Two-thirty. Not bad, little woman. Now let's be off.'

Ursula's disillusionment with her father was succeeded by fury, which in turn hardened into a hatred intense enough to last her a lifetime. It would even be safe to say that her father used up her entire allowance of hatred, that is apart from the residue that she reserved for herself, particularly the parts of herself that she imagined she had inherited from him.

During her first marriage Ursula wrote an essay entitled 'A Central-European Father'. Written as an exercise in self-examination, it details the ill-effects of her father's influence. In some cases she finds that her tastes and prejudices have been formed in deliberate opposition to his, in others that his precepts have been unwillingly incorporated into her way of thinking. The piece is composed in alternating and contrasting paragraphs, one starting 'He', the next 'I', the next 'He', and so on. With its flat and ironical tone it provides, as well as an interesting insight into the way she saw herself at the time (a view that was to change conspicuously during her years with Justin), a vivid portrait of her father. In the interests of continuity I am including here only a selection of the paragraphs that refer to him.

He is a sturdy man of middle height with a round skull, high cheekbones, swarthy skin, and strong eyebrows. Thick, hairy wrists, two heavy old rings on chunky fingers. Very punctilious about correctness of attire. Always smells the same – of sweetish tobacco and pungent eau-de-Cologne. Rich baritone voice – given to singing snatches of song (Schubert *Lieder* or 'Give me a good horse and a lovely woman') with exaggerated feeling. Invariably followed by the remark, 'Could have been a singer, you know.' Complacently voiced contempt for artists . . .

He has read *The Count of Monte Cristo* and *Les Misérables* twice each. Thinks modern literature indecent. Knows what he likes in sculpture though – Rodin and Michelangelo. Can't tell them apart. Enjoys baiting the supporters of modern painting, which he considers funny. But scientists are clever buggers – that's the thing to be nowadays . . .

He is proud of his indifference to money. The proof – a

disastrous marriage contracted for love. Borrows the stuff
when he needs it. When he's got it takes it for granted . . .
He has a pathological loathing of illness. His own health
is robust. The ill, as well as physically dangerous, are
morally suspect. He walks out of the third act of *La
Traviata* in a state of high indignation – Alfred's hygienic
risk is one of the few things in art which succeeds in
genuinely upsetting him . . .

He gets drunk tragically – fatality, defiance, a grand self-
pity . . .

He agrees with Hitler because he knows from experience
that the troubles of honest landowners always come from
usury. Yet he keeps his one Jewish friend hidden in a false
cupboard for six months at considerable danger to himself
and family ('though between ourselves he's an absolute
bastard') . . .

He thinks that it is the greatest folly to marry for love.
What might he not have done if not bound hand and foot by
wife and child, 'not to mention the obvious hopelessness of
your mother's character'. He thinks I would have made a
better wife for him than my mother – 'my own blood, the
blood of the Khans, don't you know?' But he'd rather have
had a son than a daughter. He is convinced that having
children is the greatest misfortune of all.

In 1944 the Russians seized power in Budapest. There was
fierce fighting in the streets and a sense of indiscriminate
persecution. While the family, along with most of the crippled
aristocracy and many other minority groups, was obliged to
dodge from place to place, never staying long enough in any
one to attract attention, Ursula had her only taste of school.
To keep her out of harm's way her father sent her as a boarder
to a convent just outside Budapest.

Boarding school can be a shattering experience for any
sensitive child, and it was specially so for Ursula who was
accustomed to a degree of freedom bordering on neglect. After
years of the sporadic directives of her disconcerting father, the
time-compressing hours in the library, and the daydreamy
wanderings over the estate with the dogs and horses, she had

to cope with the regimentation of uniform, organised games, pious instruction, and, worst of all, the constant company of her jabbering contemporaries. Her education had up to then been arbitrary. The nuns were astonished to find that this girl, who had such an impressive command of four languages, who knew more European history than they did themselves, and who could discuss with innocent fluency the relative importance of Dante and Goethe, had great difficulty in dividing by two and had never heard of geometry.

When she realised that the authorities mistrusted her as much as the other girls did, she resorted to sabotage – Ursula was anti-institutional to the core. Since her family's denominational religion was Greek Catholic, she had the idea of claiming the right to attend the services at an Orthodox church in a nearby village. She had already found out that if she drank several black coffees in quick succession they made her heart race in an interesting and alarming way. So, after putting in a token appearance at the church, she made straight for the bar, drank the coffee, and ran back to school, where she reported the resulting malfunction to the appropriate nun. By this trick she managed to get herself exempted from team games.

The Mother Superior quickly understood that Ursula was never going to be anything but a liability to the convent, but it took her six months to think of an acceptable way of saying so to the child's father. By this time Ursula's behaviour had become more or less anarchic. The Mother Superior finally solved the problem by writing that the child was obviously frustrated (since her gifts were too prodigious for the school's limited academic resources) and suggested that Ursula would benefit more from private tuition with special attention to the arts. That was the end of her schooling, and her father was again faced with the dilemma of where Ursula should live.

The experience taught Ursula that you can get what you want if you want it badly enough, if you've got enough ingenuity and if you're not too fastidious about bending the rules. When I first began reading the journals included in *Style* soon after Justin's death, I was immediately struck by the sheer volume of her egocentricity. Time and again some sensual or literary insight of great beauty was fed like sand into the churning cement-mixer of her self-examination. Was this a prerequisite of all journal-writing? I didn't think so. Was it unhealthy? If so, she would have been the first to admit it. What interested me most was that, both as a conversationalist and as a friend, she had disguised the habit completely – and I was confronted with the familiar and very uncomfortable feeling that I hadn't really known her at all. When you were with her you talked about the idiocy of Heath or Callaghan, whichever of the two was in power, or the relationship of Proust to César Franck, or how to cook squid in its own ink, or whether it was possible to believe Jesus and Jung at the same time. Often, very often in fact, you talked about yourself – *never* about her. She must have hidden her all-embracing egotism not because she was ashamed of it, but out of a sense of delicacy, of privacy, in the same way as you refrain from talking about things of extra importance to you, such as the details of what you do in bed with your lover. Nevertheless at that first reading of her journals it stared me in the face that Ursula cared less about other people (with the obvious exception of my brother, whom she had half-recognised, half-fashioned, as her own male complement) than one is used to assuming is normal. It seems probable that the need to develop this fierce sense of self was born out of the trauma of the convent. It was there that she first experienced other people *en masse* – finding that she didn't much like them, she was determined from then on to exclude them as far as possible from her emotional priorities.

It was decided that Ursula should live in her godfather's house in Budapest, which he had been allowed to keep because of his usefulness to the regime as a senior biochemist. Ursula was fond of her godfather, who had often taken her to museums and told her which pictures to admire. He had an enormous library and played the cello. The atmosphere in the family was rather strange, but maybe that didn't worry her too much, as it was a strangeness that had something in common with her own.

The family consisted of Tibor, her godfather, Marta his

wife, and a grown-up son and daughter. It could be pigeon-holed by gender – both men were quiet and withdrawn, while both women were liable to bluster. Tibor would return from his work in the laboratory, go straight to his study with hardly a hullo to the womenfolk, and there he'd stay till it was time to go to bed. He had a soft spot for his little god-daughter who, like himself, spoke very little. In fact, she was so affectionately unobtrusive that he gradually got into the habit of allowing her into his study while he was working and giving her the free run of his bookshelves. Ursula found this arrangement ideal because she didn't feel at all at home with either of the women, who were strident, discontented creatures.

Justin has reconstructed an evening in the study:

Sometimes, infrequently, her godfather would rise from his desk and sit himself down in the middle of the room with the point of his cello stuck vigorously into a particular hole in the parquet, and play a favourite movement. After a pause while the last chords faded into silence, he got up from his chair and, standing with his back to the room, arms folded, gazed into the dark garden between velvet curtains the colour of dusky cinnamon, which he had carefully parted by pulling on the tassel of the old gold-threaded cord. Coming then away from the window, he usually took two crystal glasses and a crystal decanter out of a cupboard and placed them on his broad, flat desk, a seventeenth-century piece of great beauty with a leather surface and ormolu fittings. Slowly he filled the little glasses with vintage brandy and set one of them on the table beside Ursula's usual chair in the corner. After selecting and carefully splitting a cigar, he would remain standing, glass in hand, absorbed in his thoughts. Perhaps he might look once more briefly into the garden before closing the curtain and returning to his work.

It was not until she'd passed her thirteenth birthday that Ursula discovered the real reason for the disharmony in Tibor's household. During the war Tibor's son had been in

active combat on the Russian front. The family had no news of
him for two years and he was presumed to have been killed.
But one day, after the war had ended, a pitifully emaciated,
white-haired old man knocked hesitantly at the door – it was
Tibor's son, now thirty years old.

They nursed him back to health, and in a few years' time he
had recovered sufficiently to get married and hold down a
steady job at the university – he had inherited an aptitude for
science and acquired a good degree before the war. He was
naturally close to his father, and they often met for coffee and
a chat in the course of their work. So it struck the son as odd
that, though his father seemed to knock off work at a normal
time of day, it was not until hours later that he arrived back
home. On investigation it turned out that Tibor kept a
mistress, and the son, shocked, felt it his duty to confront him
with the knowledge. Tibor took it calmly, and explained
frankly, man-to-man, how the need for such a state of affairs
had arisen, that these were facts of life, and there was nothing
to get so excited about. He ended by saying that he was relying
on his son to keep what he knew to himself.

The son, however, after his appalling experiences, had
become a worrier, and after some sleepless nights he confided
in his wife. And somehow, the way these things do, it all got
back to Marta, which couldn't have been more disastrous.
Marta, who had been disappointed with her marriage for
many years, needed only this justification to make Tibor's
existence the hell he perhaps deserved. Without difficulty
(since they always sided together on the subject of the
unspeakable behaviour of men) she enlisted her daughter's
help. And every evening as Tibor got home they would greet
him with a deafening, duplicate hullabaloo often accompanied
by physical assault, so that it was as much as he could do to
fight his way into the study and bolt the door.

By the time Ursula arrived from the convent the main fury
had somewhat eased, though the volcano was still only
dormant. Her position was immediately ambiguous. Her
sympathies were with Tibor. At first she had no idea what
the whole thing was about. When she finally discovered, her
attitude was if anything reinforced, since, lacking what's often

called a moral sense, she was naturally uncensorious. What's more, it excited her that her dignified, cello-playing connoisseur of a godfather still had the hot blood necessary for conducting an illicit liaison.

When Tibor was at work, the two women naturally tried to convert her to the cause, seeing that she was the confidante of the villain of the piece. Ursula's nature was pragmatic, opportunistic. Her play-acting skills had been honed in her lonely childhood, when she loved to compose involved scenarios which she then performed in the woods, playing every part in turn. She now needed all these skills to be convincing in the role of the delicate *ingénue* for whom literature was the only thing in the world that counted, while the rights and wrongs of grown-up marital behaviour went sailing over her head.

In reality Ursula, who was thirteen but looked much older, was longing to be grown-up. At that time in Budapest it wasn't easy to be elegantly dressed. She managed with the help of an elderly aunt who passed on jewellery, splendid old dresses, even curtains, which could then be styled by tailors so hungry that they'd work for whatever the client could afford. If she dressed well instinctively she also developed the talent out of ambition – she was already formulating plans. She wanted a magnificent future and saw that to achieve it she also needed a magnificent façade. Budapest was a dead end – she dreamed of Paris, Rome, Cairo, Istanbul. In *Style* Justin describes a visit to Tibor's country house, a journey which gave flesh to the bones of Ursula's wanderlust:

He only went there perhaps six times a year, and she felt most honoured on the occasions when she was to be taken with him. They would leave early in the morning. The child watched the mountains recede behind them until they disappeared and all directions resembled one another, an impression she greatly enjoyed. That moment of disappearance, of disorientation, happened to coincide with their stopping for lunch. Her godfather, who had hitherto been taciturn, became suddenly cheerful as they shared a picnic of hard cheese and sour fresh wine sitting at a rickety table

under a dusty acacia beside a small whitewashed house a
little way off the road. For the rest of the trip he hummed to
himself, drumming two fingers on the back of the passenger
seat. On arrival in the evening she could not sleep for
imagining the thrilling possibility of continuing further and
further south, as if this were only the first stop on a very
long journey. On the way back there was no humming, and
usually a cold wind drove white summer clouds in the
opposite direction.

The Monument is the story of a woman in flight – flight from
her ancestry, her memories, from everywhere she had ever
been before, and in the end from her love and from this world.
Whenever she felt tempted to settle, this fugitive instinct
would intervene and plan some enormous voyage to the
Amazon or Indo-China. One of Ursula's favourite words was
dépaysement, which she used in the positive sense – the
dangerous and delicious sense of being away from, beyond,
out of touch with anything familiar to her. Because familiar
places haunted her, not least Budapest. Here is an entry from
her journal written in southern India in 1970:

I had a bad night thinking of Budapest as a town,
geographically so to speak. Unable to place anything with
precision. Those walks just outside the town beyond the
Hill of Roses, where the woods began and the last Turkish
street led very steeply to the springs, the Planes, the Lukacs
bath; the violets in the spring, the little yellow chapel that
was always shut. The walled orchard of the Franciscans,
Baroness K.'s apartment, the tunnel through which you
came to the Blood Field; the crooked streets of the Palace
Hill, the cathedral, the Ruszwurm for cakes and ices after
Mass; the Summer Pavilion among the chestnuts by the
river, where the concerts were held; the Bar Paradiso, the
chortling espresso machine, the parrots, the huge window
overlooking the square with the Empress Elizabeth's statue,
the bridge, and the terrace of the Bristol, where one wore
sunglasses when the weather was better; the white river
steamers always empty . . . The desolate boulevards, the

cafés full of people on the make; restaurants with gardens, the steam of fish soup and the green light on white tables on summer evenings. My only dinner with my father. He came to meet me after the theatre, *Midsummer Night's Dream?* Or did we meet by chance? His teeth shining in the dark by the news kiosk in the milling post-play crowd, lighting cigarettes. Autumn mist in the Andressy Avenue – I was coming out of the Oriental collection; the empty garden, the creaking leaves . . . the regular rhythms of library, walk, books, music, the problem of money, the problem of life, the problem of my body; hungry, swimming in the steaming, opaque water of the Turkish springs . . . How easy it would have been to sink and how thin the membrane that separates hope from despair. If I was obstinate and brave it was because I had little imagination and less choice; and also determined to ignore anything that was not bearable, shutting my eyes and ears and quoting Baudelaire to myself. Very juvenile, very necessary. And a final picture of myself walking, for lack of transport, across the whole town, which was peculiarly empty, peculiarly silent, all the way from Imre Street to the station, looking at everything quite clearly for the first time and repeating over and over: I shall never come back.

In the end the pressure on Tibor became such that he was obliged to give up his mistress. Ursula noticed not only that he now spoke less than ever but also that his cello-playing had lately become almost crazily strenuous. Several times she was alarmed for his health because of the breakneck tempo he set himself for the most difficult of the Bach suites.

While Tibor's utterances, always monosyllabic, were dwindling into almost total silence, Ursula found a friend. Along with a few other displaced young people she was in the habit of spending her time in an old club which had once been frequented by princes and ambassadors, but which was now practically deserted. It was a rococo palace with shimmering reception rooms, gambling tables, a Turkish bath, and extensive gardens, presided over by a few old retainers with nothing much to do but mull over their memories of the good old days – Ursula and her companions they treated with gentle, nostalgic deference. One day, as she was wandering through the perspectives of this operatic stage, she bumped into a cousin on her mother's side whom she hadn't seen since childhood.

Lorenzo was eighteen, with Italian good looks. Though Ursula was four years younger, her precocious physique and intellect narrowed the gap. She and Lorenzo were attracted to one another – meeting on equal terms, they quickly became inseparable. They shared interests in painting and music, poetry and ideas, but their common obsession was the necessity for escape.

They met in museums. The Eszterházy collection in Budapest contains the finest assembly of Spanish paintings outside Spain. Ursula, who loved painting, was also sensitive to its suggestions – Goya, with his sense of drama, his modernity, his indignation, suggested impatience.

Lorenzo, too, was impatient. That her blood-relation should be equally exasperated by the restraints and uncertainties of Budapest confirmed Ursula's suspicions – she belonged to a doomed caste, a doomed race. The escape she anticipated so eagerly was as much from the shakiness of her racial identity as from the political situation.

Perhaps luckily, since Ursula was still after all only fourteen, circumstances got in the way of their plans. In 1953 there was a round-up of those loose ends of Budapest society who couldn't easily be categorised – all these people were to be exiled to distant villages dotted over the country to work on the farms. Ursula and Lorenzo were sent to different regions and didn't see each other again for two years.

Enforced disruption is much easier to bear when you haven't yet formed fixed habits, and exile is perhaps too strong a word for what was for Ursula a time of new sensations and valuable new experience. She was also lucky in that she had to put up with very little physical discomfort. Because Tibor had provided her with a lump sum on her departure from Budapest, she found herself relatively well off in a community where living was extremely cheap. She lodged with a house-proud widow who cooked excellent peasant goulashes. She was given a room of her own – her bed had an enormous eiderdown over coarse, sweet-smelling sheets that were washed several times a week. There was a huge stove in the sitting-room, beside which she could sit and read in the winter.

The work was a kind of agriculture now nearly forgotten. In the summer you slaved away in the sun from dawn to dusk, and then collapsed on to your bed half-dead with exhaustion, but in the winter there was nothing much to do. The peasants spent whole days singing and dancing just to while away the time. Ursula, on the other hand, was busy with her reading. She had brought a selection of books from Budapest, and when she had finished them Tibor sent her more. He always sewed some money into the binding – the bigger the book the more money there was. So it happened that the largest denomination banknote she had ever possessed was concealed in the capacious leather skin of Marx's *Das Kapital*.

It was beautiful countryside, harsh and melancholy, in keeping with the Byronic dreams of adolescence. Ursula bought a horse from a gipsy and rode for miles each day, cutting switches of basket-maker's willow for her whips. As she rode she rehearsed her reunion with Lorenzo. She imagined the two of them newly arrived in Paris, already leaders of the most brilliant group of poets and thinkers at the Sorbonne. Fame and huge quantities of money would quickly follow.

In 1955 it was announced that all deported people were to be returned to their places of origin. On her arrival at Tibor's house, Ursula was greeted with the news that he had died of an unsuspected heart condition the previous month. It was a true bereavement – Tibor was the only person who had ever really cared for her. She now had no reason whatever for staying in Budapest.

Lorenzo, who had arrived back from the countryside a week or so before, arranged for her to sleep in the house where he had rooms. Ursula felt as close to him as ever, more so perhaps, after Tibor's loss. They immediately set to work on their plans. The atmosphere in the city was panicky, electric. Clandestine anti-regime groups were forming all over the place, and the cousins lost no time in joining up. It was typical of Ursula at that stage of her life to feel that any insurrectionary tendency was to be supported out of principle and then exploited out of pragmatism. The trouble was that Lorenzo, either from a genuine ideological conversion or from cold feet at the increasingly real possibility of escape, had begun to believe in Soviet Communism. He didn't communicate this to Ursula, undoubtedly recognising that such conformity would be unacceptable to her essentially anarchic nature.

The plan was that as soon as the revolution occurred, Ursula and Lorenzo along with four or five sympathisers would start off on the long westward journey in a car belonging to a friend of Lorenzo's. What in fact happened was that at the last moment Lorenzo himself sent a message that he would not be coming.

Ursula never showed any sign of bitterness at this betrayal, and Lorenzo continued to represent for her an ideal of romantic friendship. Later in her life she altogether lost faith in her capacity for friendship – after she had committed herself entirely to Justin she gradually stopped corresponding with all but one or two of the friends she had previously made. Perhaps she already recognised in Lorenzo's action the kind of response that she herself might have made in his place. As if he were saying that friends, like political groups, were there to be enjoyed and used and dropped when convenient.

After the Magyars founded Hungary in the ninth century it was dominated successively by the Turks and the Hapsburg Empire, which was dismembered in 1918. From then until 1944 Hungarians enjoyed the only period of independence in their history. When the Russians took over, Stalin appointed Rakosi as premier and the result was a reign of terror. On coming to power in 1953 Khrushchev, realising that Rakosi had been mismanaging the economy through over-industrialisation, dismissed him and instated Imre Nagy in his place. There followed a brief period of relative freedom – Hungarians could read what they liked, could listen to American jazz all night in clubs. Little shops, closed down by Rakosi's policies, opened up again. But when Nagy became too popular, Rakosi plotted with the Kremlin to get him kicked out and himself restored to power. Since Nagy became a folk-hero in exile, Rakosi's victory could be seen to have been pyrrhic.

Intellectuals – meaning anyone with a reputation for liberal views – were arrested, including Nagy. But Khrushchev, who was committed to a policy of *rapprochement*, took it badly – Rakosi was summoned to Russia and never heard of again. Now Khrushchev, instead of reappointing Nagy, chose Erno Gero, a monster almost as rabid as Rakosi though a less inept politician.

In October 1956 a group of students and intellectuals staged a demonstration outside the national radio station, demanding the right to broadcast a manifesto. They were not advocating a return to Western-style democracy, but rather an end to the perversion of true Communist ideals. The demonstration was noisy and aggressive, and the AVO, or secret police, the most widely feared agents of Soviet oppression in Hungary, responded first by firing blanks, then by lobbing a canister of tear-gas into the crowd. It exploded in the face of a teenager and blew his head off. The crowd managed to break into the building and the AVO opened fire. In the confused skirmishing that ensued the students managed to disarm some of the AVO, and the short-lived but heroic revolution had begun. After a series of tactical mistakes by the government, including a savagely repressive speech on the radio by Gero which alienated the entire population, Russian tanks were called in. The students and their sympathisers, whose numbers swelled by the minute, were by now committed to battle. By means of desperate guerrilla manœuvres they managed to capture weapons, including anti-tank guns, from the Russians and the AVO. Groups were mobilising all over the city, but there was at first no centralised planning and no headquarters.

The population of Hungary was ten million. Of these the names of a million were already on the AVO files, and Ursula's was probably among them. If so, the AVO had got her wrong – Ursula was apolitical and anything but patriotic. All that she had wanted for a long time was to get out, and in the confusion it seemed that at last the moment had come. This attitude, though it might be thought morally reprehensible, served her in good stead, because if she had waited a few more days she would have been part of a mass exodus. There would have been less chance either of escaping intact or of making sympathetic personal contacts in Vienna.

Of the six young people who did begin the journey all were apparently eager to escape the country. But when on their first day the car ran out of petrol, the others all began to reveal various degrees of lack of preparation. One of them thought the border they were heading for was with Yugoslavia, another had left his money on the kitchen table, a third was already homesick. It was as if the whole idea of escaping had been some kind of children's game – Ursula was amazed to find herself alone in actually wanting to put it into practice. By the morning of the third day she had said goodbye to the last of them, and the car was on its way back to Budapest.

She herself had spent the previous weeks in an exhaustive study of large- and small-scale maps. She was also well-equipped for any but the severest climatic conditions. She wore a heavy sheepskin coat over jerseys and trousers, and someone had given her some high snow-boots. In her coat pockets she had enough money for several days' food, a compass, a set of dice, and a small volume of Eliot's poems. She had taught herself enough English to repeat over and over like a talisman the lines:

> Because I do not hope to turn again
> Because I do not hope
> Because I do not hope to turn.

So there she stood all alone facing westward across an endless expanse of virgin snow. There was nothing to do but start walking. Several hours after Eliot's words had lost whatever meaning they had once had, she arrived at a cottage on the edge of a forest. She knocked on the door, which was reluctantly opened by a peasant woman. The husband was sitting smoking by the fire and an 11-year-old boy was laying the table for the evening meal. The couple agreed to feed her and put her up for the night, but became cagey when she tried to elicit information. She simply wanted to find out the quickest, easiest way to the frontier, but very few people those days were prepared to risk their skin to help a possible defector or spy. She decided to use her charm on the boy.

In the morning it was snowing, and Ursula let herself be persuaded that it would be safer to stay another day at the cottage before carrying on. Her efforts to charm Janos, the boy, succeeded only too well. In the course of the day, in the intervals when the parents' work took them out of earshot, she convinced him not only to accompany her to the frontier (for which she promised to pay him), but also to escape with her to Vienna, freedom, and a future.

Early next day Ursula said goodbye to the couple and set off into the snowy landscape. After about a mile Janos caught up with her, having used a short-cut as they had arranged in secret the previous night. Ursula's spirits rose as their footsteps crunched into the deep snow, but Janos became increasingly silent and worried-looking. After they had been walking for three hours, he stopped and explained, in tears, that he couldn't desert his parents. It took all her powers of persuasion to get him to accept the money. She kissed him goodbye, and stood for a long time watching him trudge forlornly back the way they had come.

Before leaving, Janos told her that once she reached the forest that they could just see in the distance, she would be in Austria. So the dream was actually visible. She found that she was walking faster and faster, hardly taking in the far-off, irregular *putt-putt-putt* which, with sudden terror, she at last recognised as rifle-fire. She realised simultaneously that, because of the muffling effect that snow has on all sound, it must be closer than she at first supposed. She rushed on and on. The forest was getting close, and it became clear that the shooting, now much louder, was coming from somewhere to the left of it. The odd thing was that she could see nobody. She began to run, and as she reached the first trees she was conscious of a dull ache in her left thigh and a sticky stream of blood spreading down her leg.

She ran on through the forest and collapsed, semi-conscious from exhaustion, near a road. A passing patrol-car of the Austrian military police spotted her there and picked her up. They took her to their headquarters, where her wound, which turned out not to be serious, was cleaned and dressed. Then she was sent by ambulance to hospital in Vienna. The bullet was extracted and she was treated for frostbite.

3

Ursula and Kenelm

In spite of Ursula's spiritual predilection for the south, she had already made up her mind that England was the safest place to be for someone in her politically precarious position. So, as soon as she was finished with the hospital, she made straight for the British Embassy. After the statutory half-hour hanging about, she was told that the First Secretary would see her. This meeting, though short, was unimaginably lucky. The diplomat, impressed equally by her appearance and the detached modesty of her account of the escape (which if anything served to underline her courage) was prepared to be won over on the spot. He was nevertheless obliged to attend to the formalities. 'But you must have some identification, a driving licence, passport, something of that kind?' Ursula smiled and shrugged to indicate that she had absolutely nothing but the clothes she was wearing, the dice, the compass, the remains of her money and the volume of Eliot. The First Secretary, enraptured, threw up his hands. 'As far as I am concerned,' he exclaimed, 'that little book is worth all the passports in the world.' Impetuously he dialled the number of a friend. 'I've met someone this morning who I think you'll like a lot,' he said into the phone.

This prediction turned out to be correct. The First Secretary's friend was the wife of an American diplomat stationed in Vienna. Their meeting was a delighted exchange of shared literary tastes, and these were more effective for breaking the ice with Ursula than the discovery of a mutual friend. She was asked to stay. If the crossing of the Austrian frontier could be said to symbolise rebirth, she was now also being furnished with a fairy godmother. In a month's time they were waving goodbye at the station. Ursula had luggage, new clothes, papers, money, a ticket to London, and an introduction to the History of Art department at Oxford.

Ursula's first impressions of London were bleak. She found that she had to keep reminding herself that she was free in order to counteract the ugliness she saw everywhere around her – in people's faces, in the dingy sky, and in the ubiquitous dirt. Ursula's sensual antipathy to England was never modified, in spite of the fact that she lived in London for nearly ten years and married two Englishmen, one after the other. I was once with Justin and Ursula on a Channel crossing from Boulogne to Folkestone. After France the smell of English armpits was familiarly depressing. Ursula commented on the English belief in the superiority of English hygiene: 'They use less soap and vater than anyone in the vorld, but to hear them talk you'd think they had invented both commodities.'

Ursula chose England without the slightest idea of what it was going to be like, attracted by the legends of English fairness, protectiveness of the oppressed, and safety from invasion. When she found she didn't like it, she still thought – and went on thinking for eight more years – that its assets outweighed its unattractiveness. This sounds patronising towards England – but it was also honest, and honesty was necessary for her survival.

Ursula went to Oxford to follow up her contact. However, before she could get an interview someone introduced her to Anthony Blunt who, like her, happened to be visiting for the day. Blunt was Director of the Courtauld Institute in London at the time, and one of the most admired art-historians in the world. Ursula told him a condensed version of her story, which interested him in ways that she couldn't have been expected to appreciate. He then proceeded to put her through a searching test. Ursula's grasp of both artistic and historical concepts was exceptionally mature for an 18-year-old, and Blunt was impressed. I imagine he must have experienced something of the thrill of the talent-spotter when a half-fledged but unmistakable star lands slap in his lap and he knows that all she needs is a little polishing up. He set out to persuade her to forget all about Oxford – London was the place to be, and in particular the Courtauld.

Anthony Blunt arranged for her to be found a place there. In those days entrance to universities and art schools was considerably more relaxed than is the case today, and someone with romantic qualifications, rather than the ability to pass exams, could be squeezed in without too much difficulty. At the same moment in the late 1950s I had first-hand experience of the selection procedures of one of the most seriously regarded art-schools in London – I was a fly on the wall at a staff meeting to discuss the next intake. The new students were chosen as often for the photograph they were obliged to attach to their folder as they were for the quality of the work inside it. In Ursula's case, she was also given a relatively generous grant, which took into account her total lack of financial wherewithal, a student card and a room in the student hostel.

It's just like a fairy story. The lost little girl who escapes alone from a Central-European revolution, being shot at and wounded in the process, falls firmly on her feet in a strange country a thousand miles away, through a fortuitous chain of circumstances involving powerful contacts in the very world she is aiming to infiltrate. Or perhaps it's more like Hollywood, since it all happens in the kind of concertinaed time-span you associate with the cinema. Nevertheless, from all accounts it is what happened. So much luck. I'm convinced that throughout her life Ursula had too much luck for her conscience to support – she thought she didn't deserve it.

Anthony Blunt became very fond of Ursula, and the feeling was mutual. He was a civilised man, an excellent teacher, a loyal and compassionate friend. But he wanted his favourite pupil to shine in his field, to become an academic. He misunderstood her and she responded by disappointing him.

Ursula made a splash among the muted colours of the débutantes of the Courtauld, attracting the attention of both boys and girls. She wasn't altogether prepared for this, and it put her on her guard. She found she had to be choosy about whom she ate her meals with, since she was barraged with invitations from all sides. Always sensitive to every kind of stylishness, she also discovered – as I did myself contemporaneously at the Slade which was just round the corner – that the people with the beautiful faces were also, mysteriously, the ones it was most fun to be with. In Ursula's case they also seemed to come from powerful backgrounds – her first real friend was Sonia, a very pretty girl whose father was a Cabinet minister at the time. I don't think that any charge of snobbishness can be laid against her for this. She had to make friends with someone, and that someone was more than likely to be one of the students of her own year at a rather select establishment – it wasn't as if she had the whole of London to choose from.

I make this point only because *Style* consistently implies that Ursula's prime directive at this stage of her life was ambition. He attributes to her a knowing unscrupulousness and a grasp of the weaknesses of the rest of the world (represented as the enemy) that are quite at odds with the probabilities. In trying to convince us that she was superhuman, he makes her nearly inhuman instead. The truth is that Ursula was an 18-year-old completely alone in a strange, cold country, surrounded by largely uncongenial aliens whose motives and preoccupations she had no way of understanding. Possessing nothing in the world but her wits, she naturally tried to use them to stabilise her position.

Through Sonia, Ursula met Fiona, a contemporary who was working at the National Gallery at the time. Recently Fiona and I arranged to meet for the first time over lunch at Bianchi's in Frith Street. I arrived ten minutes early, to discover that the restaurant, an old favourite, had ceased to exist a year before. I recognised Fiona from the air of disorientation with which, on the stroke of one o'clock, she also registered this sad piece of news. Our shared failure to keep up to date with metropolitan changes of fortune seemed an appropriate note on which to begin reminiscing about a dead mutual friend.

As we established ourselves in a second-choice trattoria

down the road, I asked Fiona what she'd thought of Ursula at first meeting: 'What struck me immediately, apart from her charm and intelligence, was the contrast between her and Sonia – it was hard to imagine what they could possibly have in common. The other thing was that she made me laugh, and from then on our relationship was firmly based on a shared sense of humour.'

'How well did she speak English at that time?' 'Not very well at all – in fact I was always teasing her about the strange things she said. But she had a tremendous urge to communicate, and her avid reading extended her vocabulary. In the end, of course, she spoke English marvellously well . . .

'A year later I persuaded her to move out of the hostel in Malet Street and share a flat with me in Chelsea. When we were living there, she had a particularly vivid dream one night, and I heard her spouting off in her sleep in some very strange language – I was most impressed.' 'Was it Hungarian?' 'I don't know.' Two details in this account were surprising – first, that Fiona hadn't asked Ursula in the morning what language she'd been speaking, and second that she should have been so impressed by a foreigner sleep-talking in a foreign language – until I remembered the incuriosity and lack of powers of connection so typical of adolescence. Seen like that, Fiona's recollections of thirty years ago had a distinct authenticity.

Fiona then asked me how old Ursula was when she first arrived. 'Didn't you believe her when she said she was the same age as you?' 'Well, I found it hard to believe, because she was so very much more mature than I was. Having had such a different upbringing, I wasn't accustomed to the extremes and depths of emotion that she showed. She had these terrible black patches, depressions I suppose, although that wasn't the way I would have phrased it then. I didn't believe that real people went through that kind of thing. I thought she must have been influenced by all the literature she read . . . I don't know how she found the time to read so many books. She was good for me, because she broadened my own literary interests. She was the most generous, thoughtful friend I've ever had. After she got married she gave me everything, all those marvellous clothes of hers, even curtains and things like that.'

'Did you ever go abroad with Ursula?' 'No, but I took her to Scotland. At first I was rather nervous about how she'd adjust to all the traditional Scottish ritual and so on, but I needn't have worried – it was astonishing how well she fitted in. Ursula was interested in everything, and she didn't sneer at anything. She was undaunted, uncomplaining, totally intrigued. She could cope with any unexpected situation. You could take her to some awful pub in London, where she was surrounded by a crowd of ragamuffins, and in no time she'd have them all under her thumb. It was the same with the huntin', shootin', and fishin' people in Scotland – she had this chameleon quality. I wanted so badly for her to hit it off there, but in fact something happened that was slightly unsettling for me – she had an immediate and very strong rapport with my father. I know it's common, that kind of thing, your best friend being mad about your father and vice versa, but I didn't know that at the time, and I didn't know how to assimilate it. Anyway it seemed to be quite a serious relationship. They were two wild romantics, whose temperaments suited each other. When he went to work in Africa, it simmered down. But they wrote to each other, I know.'

One of the great advantages of studying at the Courtauld was that you were expected to travel. Month-long stays in Venice or Rome or Florence were laid on every year, and Ursula had the use of a flat belonging to Sonia's family in the Palazzo Doria whenever she needed it. Thus she was able to see at first-hand the many masterpieces already familiar to her in reproduction. Quite apart from her studies, she immediately found Italy as attractive as she found England dreary. It was an attraction that grew with the years, and must, I assume, have had something to do with her being half-Italian. Her preference for Italians over other Mediterraneans was some-thing that I found hard to understand, unless I saw it in that light. Mind you, in the early days her London friends gave her plenty of introductions, with the result that she often found herself in the kind of high-powered company which she then enjoyed. Years later we often argued about it. I found fashionable and well-educated Italians a good deal less interesting than their English counterparts. I preferred the semi-peasant Tuscan families among whom I was then living. She told me that I had simply met the wrong ones, to which there wasn't an easy answer. Even before she first went to Italy from the Courtauld, though, I think she had willed it to be the homeland she lacked. And certainly it's easy to see the appeal to her of the Italian ambience, so graceful and sunny, whose shapes and colours so frequently fit in with a well-modulated ideal of visual hedonism. She was sensitive to history too, and there's hardly a street in the centre of Rome or in the Tuscan cities for which someone with a historical imagination can't provide some vivid corresponding image.

Ursula lacked a homeland. In a sense she had always lacked one, and her escape from Hungary in 1956 must be seen in the light of the fact that, being half-Russian and half-Italian by birth, she was only a second-generation Hungarian. Now the situation was aggravated, and her official status was nothing more or less than that of a stateless person. What's more, she had chosen to put down temporary roots, to resort to a justifiable contradiction in terms, in a country that didn't attract her. Justin writes, 'The condition [of statelessness] irked her, and she was preoccupied with finding a way out of it. It occurred to her that an English husband would automatically give her a nationality.' He makes this sound a most dynamic insight, but it seems more likely that, with her superior mental equipment and instinct for survival, the idea had already been in her mind before leaving Budapest. Be that as it may, an opportunity for marriage was soon to present itself.

Kenelm was a 'mature' student at the Courtauld. He had gone there at twenty-seven, intending frankly to exploit its education to help him get rich as quickly as possible. The dreamier approach to art of the 20-year-olds around him would later have to be severely reconstituted if they were to make a living at all.

Having been born with a hole in the heart, Kenelm grew up

accustomed to the idea that he was at a disadvantage and that his expectations of a normal life were poor. When he was twenty-five he had an operation, one of the first of its kind, which, against the odds, was a success. Although it also stood the test of time, he hadn't then got used to the luxury of treating his health with a certain amount of negligence. Incredulously he learnt to eat and drink as much as he wanted, travel wherever he liked, and generally have the good time which he had always understood was the prerogative of other people. He was quick and amusing – his wit was based on the anarchistic undergraduate tradition that refuses to take anything seriously. To grow up accepting that you haven't long to live requires courage, and his was of the kind that makes a joke of mortality. Along with this romantic fatalism he had impressive looks and was also solidly enough based in what was then called the Establishment to represent a certain security. Ursula liked him very much.

There are rival versions of how their friendship first shook itself free of the inhibitions imposed by fellow-studenthood. Christopher a contemporary and friend of Kenelm's, had a spare room in his flat which he wanted to let. Christopher's version is that Kenelm persuaded Ursula to take it, thinking that he could keep more of an eye on her if she were on friendly territory. Kenelm's is that Christopher knew her first and had already moved her in by the time he himself got to know her better. People seldom agree on the chronological sequence of events that happened thirty years ago.

Christopher, whom I first met at roughly the same time (although it wasn't until eight or nine years later that I first became aware of Ursula's and Kenelm's existence), remembers that Ursula brought out a surprising side of Kenelm. He became a suitor of the old school, the kind who treats a girl as she likes to be treated – to meals in restaurants and a string of compliments whose form is frivolous enough to be laughed at but whose sincerity leaves no room for doubt. 'You could even say he was giving her the big rush,' Christopher added. If Kenelm was in love with Ursula, he was also a businessman by inclination. He could see that she was a great potential asset, with her insight into the art of a wide variety of places and periods coupled to an aesthetic intuition which enabled her to spot a fake blindfold, as it were.

Although the last sentence is a loose transcription of Kenelm's own words, he later thought that he had overstated the case. By nature hostile both to any easy generalisation and to post-mortem sentimentality, he afterwards added the qualification, 'Though later she bought lots of fakes – as we all did.'

While Kenelm talked to me freely and was generous with his time, he affected not to understand why this book was being written – he insisted over and over again that nobody would be interested. 'You mean because nobody has ever heard of Justin or Ursula?' 'I mean because they achieved nothing. They took themselves much, much too seriously, and that made them uninteresting.'

This point of view alarmed me more with each repetition. Obviously I didn't agree, but no writer, however much he bolsters himself with bravado, can ever be completely sure that his original premise isn't the bastard of a misalliance between ambition and delusion. This doubt becomes even more reasonable when the subject of his story is the lives of his brother and sister-in-law.

I'd have liked to argue the case for the extraordinariness of Justin and Ursula as people, in spite of their admitted lack of so-called achievement and the undeniable fact that they took themselves seriously. But I couldn't really do so without going into the quality and intensity of their passion, which would have been not only tactless but banal, since Kenelm of course knew all too much about that already.

In fact I think he was rather enjoying having the upper hand. I was now forced into my second-string argument, which was that everybody is interesting. Although possibly even lamer than the first, it had the advantage of steering clear of personalities. Kenelm countered with ease by refusing to allow that everybody is interesting. I then asked him if he was interested in himself. 'No, I am not,' he replied with great emphasis. 'It's impossible to be interested in yourself if you haven't been expected to live.'

The strain of this conversation had obliged me, at least, to drink more than I'd intended. I went away feeling confused and immediately visited a friend. When I repeated to her everything that had been said, she laterally observed, 'What attracted Ursula to Kenelm was his death.'

Christopher had a bit-part in the first act of Ursula's engagement to Kenelm similar to, though considerably more ethical than, the one I played in her later affair with Justin. One night they were alone together in the flat having a last drink before retiring to their respective beds. Ursula, who had seemed rather preoccupied, suddenly announced, 'Kenelm vants to marry me – vhat do you sink I should do?' 'I think you should marry him.' With an air of gratitude for a response that evidently relieved her, she laughed and slowly enunciated three monosyllables that Christopher knew instantaneously he would never forget: 'Vell, vhy not?'

'She spotted me straight away as a fellow-buccaneer,' Kenelm said. He described with a relish that had survived gradual disappointment, weariness, divorce, and a great many intervening years, their success as a double act. Their marriage was a partnership of taste, their common aim – which is in fact uncommon enough – a civilised level of subsistence with as few responsibilities and as much amusement as possible. They amused each other so much that they took on the job of amusing the rest of the world in tandem. As they built up a reputation for dealing, they found themselves invited every other weekend to grand country houses where, in return for tips on how best to dispose of the Reynolds and valuations of one kind and another, they consumed as much champagne as they could lay their hands on. At the end of the evening they would stagger up arm-in-arm to their guest-room and, throwing themselves on to the four-poster, roll about in helpless laughter at the absurdity of this kind of living and the fraudulence of their own position. As I listened to Kenelm I could hear Ursula's ludicrous accent and ironically drawled circumlocutions with almost uncanny vividness, and felt an acute pang of regret for never having been present at such an occasion.

After they left the Courtauld, Kenelm became Peter

Wilson's assistant at Sotheby's. 'They would have much preferred to get Ursula,' he said, 'but she wouldn't do it.' 'Why would they have preferred her?' 'Because she had real flair. If she'd wanted she could have become a great Byzantinist. I was all right but more pedestrian. Ursula was a scholar, whereas I'm really more of a salesman. I'd sell an old tin kettle for a couple of quid. But mind you, if it comes to that, she would have done too.'

While Kenelm was working for Peter Wilson, he started doing some business on his own account. The opportunities for private enterprise and educated travel that such a way of life suggested appealed to Ursula much more than a job at Sotheby's or any other regular employment. She thought it might provide an outlet for a combination of her skills. They started in a small way, buying drawings wherever they could find them at the right price, and selling them through friends in the network. With their combined taste and contacts, it wasn't long before they began to make money. After a couple of years they had developed a specialised reputation in the trade for dealing in Middle-Eastern antiquities and *objets d'art*. This gradually involved them in a lot of travelling, since the paintings and objects they dealt in were best acquired at source. They had two principal means of disposing of what they bought – they had an arrangement to sell through a gallery, and they dealt by appointment from their flat in the King's Road.

I asked Fiona if Ursula changed after marrying Kenelm. 'Yes, she did – it was her chameleon thing again. Perhaps she changed whoever she was with. Her affairs were landmarks. After she got together with Kenelm we went on being close friends, and used to see each other at least once a week, but she certainly was different. She developed this interest in business, and it turned out that she really had a terrific feel for dealing. She was always on about what was new in the art world, the latest trend for icons, that sort of thing. I felt a bit out of it. What we had in common from the first was History of Art, and I didn't really feel at home with the commercial side.' 'Did you get on with Kenelm?' 'Oh yes, I liked him, but we were so very different. He had a sort of international aura about him that I was completely unused to. I think he was good for Ursula, he was generous to her and they had a lot of fun.'

Bruce Chatwin, who was two years younger than Ursula, also worked at Sotheby's, his position being slightly senior to Kenelm's. I asked him how highly he rated Ursula's talent for dealing. He answered that she was erratic. When pushed, he even went so far as to question whether she had any real feeling for visual art. This divergence of opinion between Kenelm and Bruce may have been simply a difference of degree exaggerated by the passage of time. How do you quantify flair, in any case? If Ursula were brilliant, it would reflect on Kenelm, her husband and discoverer, whereas Bruce, the rival star, would prefer to eclipse her. Puzzled, I consulted a neutral friend. 'It sounds to me,' he said, 'as though Ursula had flair for making people think she had flair.'

Kenelm says that each of them recognised an equilibrium between Ursula's statelessness and his own ill-health. But while Ursula's deficiency was, at least legally, put right by the act of marriage, Kenelm's was unaltered. If their marriage is to be regarded as some kind of deal, which is an impression I've been given by a number of people, it seems that Kenelm, and certainly not only in the respect just mentioned, got very much the worst of it. For a start he loved her. Ursula had never been in love and didn't pretend that she was with Kenelm. Perhaps because this imbalance seemed to her unfair, she gave herself *carte blanche* to conduct her affairs, while always taking care to provide convincing alibis. She did this so successfully that Kenelm was unaware until years later that she had ever been unfaithful to him. 'I was too stupid,' he told me, 'I knew nothing about any of them.' Trust may be called stupidity in the art-dealing world, but it seemed to me rather that he must have stuck his head in the sand to protect his peace of mind. All the same, Ursula's smokescreens (or perhaps better, sandstorms) were ingenious. When she wanted to go to Paris to meet a lover, she told Kenelm that her father had suddenly appeared there from Hungary and insisted on seeing her. Much later, to cover up for her almost

daily lunches with Justin, she invented a whole course of
sessions with her gynaecologist.

As time went by, and without ever becoming what you
could call promiscuous, Ursula gradually allowed herself more
and more leeway. However, Justin writes in his book that
during her marriage to Kenelm only two lovers had any
importance for her, at any rate retrospectively. One was the
16-year-old son of some friends who were visiting the house
that Ursula and Kenelm had rented on the Ligurian coast.
Justin writes:

> Half-Jewish, he was born just after the war and educated in
> the conventional upper-middle-class tradition. When Ursula
> first saw him he was naked to the waist . . . He was beautiful
> but disconcertingly pale. They went swimming and boating
> together, and made love whenever they could in the
> grottoes of the garden.

The second man was:

> a black American jazz-musician called Buffalo Clem whom
> she met in a Paris club three or four years after her
> marriage. This affair was in a completely different key. It
> endured for nearly two years, and was coloured with
> turbulence and a sort of desolate torment. A long nocturnal
> affair conducted sporadically and with difficulty. One
> afternoon she awoke in his Montparnasse flat choking from
> the after-effects of dope and heavy drinking. The long,
> supine, beautiful body beside her would not, she knew,
> come to life for another three hours. She packed quickly,
> left, and never went back.

When I first read these paragraphs I accepted them at face
value, but I'm now reasonably certain that Justin intended us
to read between their lines. He singled out and then described
these two men in such detail because he wanted us to attribute
their significance to Ursula's prophetic sense of her own
destiny. The descriptions are packed with information which
could equally refer to two other men, who were arguably the

most important in her story – Justin himself (who taught her to value her life) and Ali (the innocent accessory to her death). To give some examples, Justin was part-Jewish, born just after the war, educated at public school, good-looking. He was sixteen when he first met Ursula, and their affair was consummated in the grounds of a villa on the Mediterranean. Ali was black, tall, handsome. Ursula's feelings about him were undoubtedly tormented. The affair was nocturnal, sporadic and fuelled by drink and drugs. When she left she never came back.

In making these connections Justin was bending the rules, and perhaps it was as a gesture of apology that he made them so obliquely. Whether Ursula told him her life story all of a piece in the early days of their love, or whether he picked it up bit by bit over the years, it would have been tasteless to cite her previous adolescent boy-friend as Justin's harbinger, and Ursula was supremely taste-conscious. Nor, in spite of her concern with destiny, could she have been expected to predict that another incarnation of her jazz-musician would play such a part in her fate. So Justin was putting his own words into her mouth, thereby giving a very subjective idea of her extramarital preferences.

At first Ursula was happy being married to Kenelm. She liked, admired and trusted him. He made her think and laugh, he gave her a passport and the opportunity to use it all over Europe and the Middle East. Her marriage was far the most rewarding relationship that she had yet formed. Never having been in love, she didn't miss the lack of it. The one thing she did miss was the excitement of danger and it was in order to simulate this that she slept with other men. But at some point or other she began to chafe under the limitations of such a solution, and her lovers were increasingly on trial to give her the extra something that could extricate her from a surfeit of safety.

During her affair with Clem, Ursula often used to stay at the Louisiane, a hotel in the *sixième* famous for being the haunt of the great New Orleans (Louisiana) jazz-musicians, who had a hold on her imagination. Bruce Chatwin, who stayed there as well, went dancing with Ursula, wearing a live python instead of a black tie. He found her exciting, excited, provocative . . . but unattainable. He thought this was because she preferred older men, but a quick glance at her life story shows that in reality Ursula's taste in men was catholic. I suspect that her involvement with the jealous Clem made another lover (as opposed to the kind of fleeting adventure that I shall describe next) a dangerous proposition of the wrong sort.

Ursula managed to spend a fair amount of time in Paris, a city she preferred in every respect to London. The Louisiane was her base, but she also had access to a more literary coterie in the *cinquième*, centred round the poet Jean-Marc Delafont and his wife Monique. Monique was crippled with arthritis at forty, but was still an attractive and mysterious woman whose source of power Ursula never completely succeeded in analysing. She treated Ursula as a protégée and confided in her to some extent. Ursula was guardedly deferential in return. Monique had a lover of Ursula's age, an Italian-Swiss called Gianni, with whose permission I'm giving this possibly apocryphal adventure, both the Delafonts being dead. Having made the qualification, I must say that the story sounds fairly likely to me.

Monique trusted Ursula's discretion, ill-advisedly as it turned out. One February day, after a long session of lunchtime drinking at the Brasserie Lipp, she took Ursula to visit Gianni in his seventh-floor flat near the Gare de Lyon, from whose windows you could see the broad swathe of the tracks and the sun-bound expresses leaving. The connotations of this magnificent view were aphrodisiac. They went on drinking for a couple of hours. Ursula and Gianni established a number of tastes in common – the novels of Montherlant, the Middle East, gossip, Gregorian chant, and the films of Godard, the first of which were appearing at the time. Riffling through *La Semaine à Paris* they discovered that *Vivre sa Vie* was showing that day at a cinema near the Boulevard St-Michel – they decided to go there and then.

The three of them walked arm-in-arm through the rush-hour crowds to the Métro. When they reached the platform there was a train already waiting. Gianni and Ursula leapt on just as the doors were closing, but Monique, who was now a few yards behind them and whose movements were hampered anyway by her arthritis, was left standing there as the train moved out. Ursula and Gianni got off at the next station but one, having brought their growing mutual admiration to a startling climax wedged solid among the rocking mass of sober commuters. After a quick tidy-up they took the next train back to the Gare de Lyon where Monique had had only twenty minutes to wait.

Kenelm brought many improvements to Ursula's life. In addition to the companionship, the security, the home and the occupation, all of which her daemon was so intent on squandering, he gave her a mother – his own. Maureen, after initial misgivings – 'I do think it makes things easier when people marry into their own nationality, don't you?' – welcomed Ursula into the family with the open arms of the truly maternal. Ursula responded with the hunger of the motherless. Long after she had dropped most of her other friends Ursula continued to correspond with this delightful and generous person, who, in spite of her protectiveness of her son, somehow managed not to blame her blatantly culpable daughter-in-law for the divorce. Years later, Ursula even visited Maureen without Justin's knowledge, an unprecedented and unrepeated deception which gives an idea of the strength of the attachment.

In 1961, according to Justin, Ursula had a brush with death. She was a passenger in a car driven by a drunken friend which crashed in icy conditions. She cracked a vertebra and spent the next six months with her torso encased in plaster. Kenelm denies that there was such an accident – what happened, he says, was that she slipped on a bar of soap in the bath and fell backwards violently against one of the taps. Maureen, on the other hand, remembers that Ursula was hit by a car while riding a bike in Oxford. Whatever the truth – and Justin's account, containing no precise location either for the crash itself or for the hospital where she was treated and no identification of the driver, was impossible to check – she was left with the kind of recurrent back condition to which the victims of such accidents are prone.

Justin also says that the experience altered Ursula's sense of life and death. It made her realise that she wanted to get more from and give more back to life – this made it imperative that she should find the proper airspace for her spirit to fly in. She decided that if she hadn't found it by a certain time, an imprecise term for whose definition she trusted her instinct, she would resort to suicide.

I arranged to meet Patrick Leigh Fermor because I took it for granted that he must have known Justin and Ursula as neighbours in the Peloponnese. Since they also shared a passion for literature and exploration I was amazed when he expressed ignorance of their ever having lived there. My amazement was redoubled by the discovery that he had, however, been a devoted friend of Ursula's during her marriage to Kenelm. She certainly knew *he* lived in Greece, indeed his love for that particular corner of it must have contributed, subliminally at least, to her desire to go there in the first place. Her failure to renew their friendship can only be explained by her chameleon habit of matching herself so closely to the colour of the man she had chosen that she was afraid of clashing in any other spectrum, allied to her diminishing interest in the most basic demands of friendship itself.

If my meeting with Patrick Leigh Fermor was a wash-out in one sense, it was thought-provoking in another. Among various affectionate reminiscences he said, almost in parenthesis, 'But she was a most reckless sort of girl – dangerous almost. Her stories about her adventures were most amusing but . . . lurid, would you say? Always within the bounds of possibility though. All the same I used to wonder if she didn't rather . . . heighten them, you know.'

The point was that, the day before, I'd had a long conversation with an old friend of Ursula's and Kenelm's called Marie. This lady, though she admired, even loved Ursula (whom she always referred to as Dolly, perhaps because the nickname was so absurdly inappropriate), also questioned her veracity. So suspicious was she in the early years of their acquaintance that she even went so far as to invite another friend of hers, apparently an expert on everything Central European, to dinner with Ursula so that he could question her and vet her credibility. The verdict he later pronounced in private to Marie was, 'That girl no more comes from Hungary than you or I – she's from Lithuania or Northern Russia.'

Why should not only Patrick Leigh Fermor and Marie, both intelligent and perceptive people, but several others I talked to as well have disbelieved Ursula without being able to produce a shred of evidence in support of their disbelief? I even heard it suggested that she was a hopeless fantasist who, far from having escaped from Hungary like an operatic heroine, had really spent the previous eight years in suburban comfort in Canada. I fell back on an observation I'd often made before – that some people don't give a damn if you're lying or not so long as you don't stand to gain anything by the lie. Nobody seemed to blame Ursula for what they saw as her fantasies; in fact they were on the whole amused, even Marie for whom the inquisition-by-proxy had been a kind of tease.

I saw then that my indignation on Ursula's behalf was the result of a strictly opposed belief – that lying only has anything to commend it when the liar knows he's lying. I was all in favour of Ursula's invention of her father's arrival in Paris, since it was done to protect both her love affair and her marriage, but took as a slur the implication that she lived in a fantasy world.

Personally I never heard her say anything that I didn't believe on either of these levels. It's true that, during the time I knew her, she had neither the desire nor the opportunity for marital infidelity, so fathers and gynaecologists were unnecessary to invent. But a taste for fantasy, for which I have a horror and therefore a more sensitive built-in detector than most, I'd surely have spotted. She was far too fascinated by herself to risk the slightest misrepresentation of her own life story. If she had extraordinary anecdotes to tell, it was because, with her despair and complete lack of interest in personal safety, she was the sort of person to whom extraordinary things naturally happened. She aroused suspicion circumstantially – because she had hooded eyes, impeccable clothes, seductive manners, extreme articulacy and a joke spy's accent, and because she talked freely about a past that seemed impossibly dramatic to anyone brought up in an English climate.

Ursula was uningratiating. While her manners were attentive, she was too arrogant to feel the slightest obligation to try and impress you. In January 1972 she wrote of Maxim Gorki, 'His honesty is his great quality – nothing like it for conveying emotion of any kind.' Her reason for noting it down was that she aspired to a comparable honesty herself. This is confirmed emphatically by a journal entry of the previous year, ' . . . honesty to oneself is the only convenient way of living.'

Nevertheless I'm unwilling to abandon the subject without quoting Bruce Chatwin, who gave me a funny and presumably accurate version of a typical Ursula story: 'It's 1945 and Ursula is seven. We're in a boudoir of the battlemented mansion somewhere in the Hungarian plains. The Mongols arrive – the aristocrats cower in the corner. The Mongol commander, at least eight foot tall with a moustache like the end of a broom, casts round wild-eyed for refreshment. He sees, then snatches, an enormous bottle of Chanel No. 5, downs it at a draught. He crashes to the ground like a felled oak. His minions retreat in disorder – the family is saved.' And it was a standing joke among Bruce's circle of friends that Ursula, on seeing a reproduction of, say, a particularly beautiful early Corot, would be bound to murmur, 'It vos in my muzzer's bedroom.'

The impression I formed from talking to Ursula's friends was that she didn't have enough to do. Her life had settled into a routine that was short of challenge. There's not much point in being continually the centre of attention, unless the attention seems merited by achievements directly related to your personal ambitions. Ursula's ambitions, though fierce, were undefined. She was twenty-five at the time of the incident with Gianni, an age when brilliant promise threatens to petrify into the shape of a mill-stone. Her increasing boredom provoked the desire to take her life to bits and reassemble it in some other form – but it takes superhuman courage to destroy your present security, however unsatisfying it may be, without a very clear vision of what you intend to replace it with.

Ursula came to England in a spirit of conquest. Aged eighteen and sexually still dormant, she saw life as an adventure in the exercise of power. Later, without giving sex any real emotional precedence, she discovered that it could be used as a passport to amusement. But there she came to a halt – she had taken a wrong turning. The reason for this was that she had misunderstood her ambition, misled by the fun of being a woman of the world. With hindsight it's apparent that her real ambition was inner. What she wanted was to live well, in the profoundest sense of that expression. At the time all she realised was that now she was living badly. She had become a 'bad' girl consciously, in the absence of any reference point for 'goodness' that didn't stink of hypocrisy.

I was struck by the determination with which Ursula's old friends pooh-poohed the suggestion that she had had lofty ideals or dreams of a soaring beauty expressible through love. Their attitude was one of distaste that she should have betrayed the healthy, cynical, 'bad' values (to which they themselves still adhered) for something so pious and saccharine. Of course it's only too easy to misunderstand your friends, and the more you love them the easier it is. Ursula, who kept her distance, was capable of being more discerning about hers than they were about her.

Friends are usually chosen for their ability to mirror – and so illuminate – some aspect of yourself. Knowing this, you take great care to disguise the sides of yourself which don't 'belong'. Ursula was adept at this game, and friendship with her could be a risky business. In adolescence, according to Justin, she was disinclined to commit herself to a friend beyond the strict requirements of self-interest. In the journals of her first ten years with Justin there are references to her impatience with the entire concept of friendship. At other times of her life, and it's noticeable that they were times of maximum weakness, maximum disorientation, friends played a more significant role. Now that she was getting lost, she relied increasingly on the company of Max Steiner.

Max was a tall, lissom, po-faced, smooth-skinned apparition, dressed in black from head to foot. Everything about his appearance proclaimed it to be an achievement of the utmost polish, on no account to be taken seriously. You were invited to look on him as an artifice. In fact he was a poet, and had even published a volume or two, but he made a virtue of the admission that his only heartfelt creation was his own persona. One of Max's favourite themes was the incurable tragedy that was his life – he relayed it with all the clear-sightedness and good timing of the natural comedian. But in spite of his narcissism, Max was warm-hearted. His fondness for Ursula was disinterested, in the sense that sexually she wasn't his type. At the most he enjoyed being seen around with her – two *soigné* pedigree dogs, she the silky, pale-gold Afghan, he the dark and burnished greyhound.

They would meet at carefully selected points of rendezvous – often the Ritz, where Max and his wife, an elderly Middle-European princess, had a suite – to pick up the thread where it had been dropped at the end of the last instalment. They communicated by means of a running, alternating examination of the hopelessness of their situations, accompanied by a great deal of laughter on both sides. To give an example of the spirit of tragicomedy in which they approached one another, Max arrived one day with a present, which he gravely presented to Ursula after kissing her hand. It was a little package, very expensively wrapped – a Cartier necklace, perhaps. When opened, it was found to contain a lethal dose of barbiturates. 'It's just as well to keep some always in your handbag,' he said, 'you never know when you may need it.' Ursula, although she laughed at the time, took the present as seriously as it had been intended, carrying it about with her until some time after she became involved with Justin.

Another friend on whom Ursula depended increasingly was Bruce. He had become disillusioned with the art business as a result of a piece of chicanery in which both he and Ursula had been unwillingly involved. He made a trip to Sudan from which he returned a changed man. He stripped his flat of its treasures and painted it the colour of mud bricks. He remembers asking Ursula, 'Don't you absolutely long for "nothing"?' The question intrigued her and she began spending more and more time with him in the empty flat.

It was in 1963 that Ursula first met Eve Molesworth, later to become her closest female friend and one of the few people with whom she ever really let down her guard. Thirty-five years older than Ursula – and, like her, determinedly childless – Eve gradually took over from Maureen in filling the gap left by her mother's withdrawal in her childhood. Eve is a small, talkative, enthusiastic person, full of energy and kindness, whose lack of ceremony about speaking her mind has been known to get her into trouble. Here is her account of their first meeting.

'I had continually been told about Ursula, the beautiful, intelligent Hungarian whom I should meet. We did finally meet at a dinner party. I noticed her immediately – one could hardly fail to. She was certainly beautiful, but with a somewhat forbidding, cold expression. Dinner over, the ladies rose to go upstairs to the drawing-room for the usual nose-powdering retreat, while the men remained at the dining-room table for further drink and gossip. Such dinners are rarely stimulating – I had found this one rather worse than most, and was in no mood for making polite conversation to the various wives and mistresses surrounding me. I noticed an *Evening Standard* on a table, picked it up, and sat down to read it. Hardly had I done so when the paper was removed from my hands. Ursula was smiling at me. She sat down beside me saying, "I shall not allow you to escape behind that paper." We were soon deep in a fascinating conversation. I was leaving the next day for a short visit to Holland and Belgium – I told her that I had not seen the museums there. She knew them well, and gave me an inspiring pre-tour. Her knowledge and appreciation were quite exceptional. A boring dinner had ended with an hour's magic and the beginning of a close and precious friendship, lasting and even growing until her tragic death. I shall always miss her.'

The friendship was slow to develop, though, and meanwhile Ursula sank further into depression, drinking too much and simultaneously conscious that drink made her unhappier than ever. Adept at disguising any but the most extreme distress, she carried on as usual. She had dinner with her friends and champagne with Max, she started a new love affair, she went on buying trips with Kenelm, in the accelerating conviction that unless something drastic were to happen her life would be over. It was in this context that my brother made his appearance.

4

Justin

We were three brothers. I was born in 1937, Jonna in 1946, and Justin in 1948. My parents come from the same kind of stratum of the upper-middle-class, but with the difference that my father is half-Jewish. This was a technicality in the sense that it didn't affect the fairly liberal, agnostic conventions of our upbringing, but of considerable importance to each of our adolescent sensibilities. We all three had problems of one kind or another in getting through the difficult years between fourteen and twenty, and, like all fellow-sufferers, were keen to find a convenient hook on which to hang our 'differentness'. The consciousness of even such diluted Jewish blood was ready-made for the job. Justin's rejection of England is an example. He could allow himself wholeheartedly to embrace Ursula's antipathy to the place because of his 'Jewish' understanding that he was a true citizen of nowhere in particular. Later he even went so far as to adopt a noticeable, if unplaceable, foreign accent, and always referred to himself as a 'European'.

My parents bought a big red-brick house overlooking the Thames and surrounded by parkland and farmland, when I was ten, that's to say around about the time when Jonna and Justin were babies. This meant that my two brothers' childhoods were very different from mine. Whereas I, as a virtual only child, had grown up rather solitary and bookish, my brothers learned early on to pass their time in tree-houses, on rubbish-tips, on the farm, in the garage, and later (though not later enough to be, strictly speaking, legal) in the pub. They fished in the river and shot in the fields. By the time they were eleven and twelve they could not only drive the banger which would otherwise have been left to rot in its shed, they could take it to bits and put it together again as well. They could sail and row and ski, they were all-conquering swimmers and divers. They were healthy, noisy, athletic, attractive, and adept at a vital side of existence which I, late in adolescence, knew nothing whatever about. In other words, I found them a bit of a threat.

My baby brothers' day-to-day life was supervised by Nanny, a paragon of her profession who still lives on in the house. Not having any more babies to nanny, she enjoys nothing better than reliving the babyhood of the old ones. Justin, who was the last that she cared for full time, plainly left her with a niggling sense of something imperfectly understood.

'He was a lovely little boy until he was four or five, and then he suddenly changed. It was about the time they started playing with that Charlie Simpson, who was a real little terror. All of a sudden Justin had it in for me. I know I was silly to let myself get hurt by a little boy like that, but the trouble was it didn't stop, it went on maybe three or four years until he went to that first boarding school. You mustn't think I wasn't patient with him, I tried and tried, but nothing was any good. He'd get cross and as soon as I tried to comfort him he'd rush out of the room, throw himself on to the bed and lie there face down. He'd never tell me what was the matter, however much I tried to wheedle it out of him. He never told tales on Jonna either, although Jonna did bully him. He was a very *proud* little boy. Something went wrong, that's all. I don't think it was anything *I* had done, because your mother always used to say, "Don't worry, Nan, he's just the same with me." It wasn't that he'd throw a tantrum like some children do – he *always* seemed to be cross, quietly cross, and whenever he did say anything it was rude.

'When he went to boarding school and came back home for the holidays, he changed again. He was nice to me then, but he wasn't *mine* any more. I hardly saw him really, he was always out in the woods, shooting and that. One thing I must say though, because it sounds as if I'm going on about what a little pest he was, he was always kind to children younger than himself.

'After he married Ursula, one of the first times they came back here it must have been, I asked him straight out, "Why were you always so horrid to me when you were little?" Do you know, he went all quiet. So I never did find out. But the funny thing was that from that day on he was wonderful to me. He and Ursula both were, but specially him. He'd bring me back presents from wherever it was they'd been, and sit and talk to me for hours. He did tease though.'

Several people I talked to about Justin as a child remembered a sort of generalised anger, already hinted at in Nanny's remarks. Since, at the time of publication, I have been able to find no explanation for it whatever, it will have to go on record as an accident of nature. With hindsight I imagine that he suffered, not so much from the discontent that comes from being spoilt, as from the home-bound frustration of the determined little adventurer who, in some other period of history, would have stowed away on a trading vessel and been taken on as a cabin boy when discovered. However, in the absence of a flourishing modern tradition for that kind of thing, he was obliged to go to prep school and public school like everyone else of his class, his anger unexploded.

At the ages of eight and nine, my two brothers started out on the long stretch of single-gender incarceration which until recently was considered the only serious education for the children of Englishmen who could afford it. Unfortunately the prep school chosen for them went bankrupt half-way through their stay, which meant that another one had to be found. Although both brothers adjusted well enough to the replacement to make the soccer and rugger teams and win prizes for diving, they suffered academically, finally passing into public school with marks that didn't do justice to their capabilities. In spite of the disruption, Justin was relatively happy at prep school, and found there sufficient outlet for his competitiveness to soothe, at least temporarily, his mysterious anger.

Justin's competitiveness was also remarked on at public

school. His housemaster there, now retired, wrote to me that:

> Justin was a good athlete and particularly good at the
> breaststroke . . . He had amazing physical determination,
> and, although he was lazy about doing proper training,
> during competition would force his muscles into such rapid
> and violent exertions that he frequently actually tore away
> lumps of bone where the ligaments attached. He knew
> about the need for training, but considered that he was
> special, and that there was no need for him to undergo the
> normal training (not only physical but also academic and
> social) which other people found essential. He was ambitious
> and wanted to take short cuts.

I've understood that the purpose behind the cruelty and
hardship of the public school system was the toughening of the
characters of the inmates – and indeed with different timing it
might have had that effect. But the equation of the age of entry
with the onset of adolescence was surely overdoing it. All but
the strongest were in some way broken – certainly neither of
my brothers survived intact.

If Jonna survived better than Justin, it was because he
managed to channel his instinctive mistrust of the system into
delinquency. Apart from routine smoking, drinking, and
bounds-breaking, he achieved a great theatrical moment of
defiance – or rather of defiant intentions which turned into
slapstick. Having been reared on the river, he had developed
into a skilful oarsman, and in due course it was announced that
he was to be awarded his 'boats'. To get your 'boats' meant
that on one level or another you were qualified to row for the
school but, more important, it represented a tremendous
rise in social status. On the day of the awards ceremony he got
drunk, which wasn't considered disgraceful in itself, since the
ritual contained an element of blooding, of coming of age. The
trouble was that he went too far. The Captain of the Boats, a
huge figure, unbelievably powerful in every sense of the word,
on noticing Jonna lurching unco-ordinatedly around the boat-
house, remarked to a passing minion, 'Get that animal out of
here and sober him up.' Jonna, who also boxed for the school,

staggered over, took a terrific swing, but missed completely – whereupon the Captain of the Boats disdainfully knocked him cold. Well, that was the end of Jonna's 'boats' – he was immediately stripped of the honour he had been only minutes away from receiving, and later beaten. Through the medium of the school grapevine, though, which thrived on Chinese whispers, he also earned himself a certain amount of respect.

Nor was Justin always law-abiding. According to a friend, 'He had an entire cocktail cabinet full of drinks, which he planted in a hole in the ground in the Leas (a grassy stretch of riverside used by the boys for watching the boat-races). The hole had a lid made out of a square of turf which fitted almost invisibly.' Although it seems unlikely that the supply could have lasted long in such an exposed and vulnerable position, I'm inclined to believe the story – Justin enjoyed such ingenious contrivances, and always referred to his flat in Rome, which was small and neat and hidden away, as 'our box'.

On the whole he found public school even more difficult than Jonna did. Jonna rather lost touch with him, in the way that brothers often do in such places, but remembers that Justin became lonely and withdrawn. Tom Hilton, later to become one of Justin's closest friends, insists that Justin had a great horror of public schools in general, and of his own in particular, which he didn't modify even at the end of his life. In any case, when he was fifteen it all got too much. He had a nervous breakdown, in the course of which he ran away from school. He was sent back, and then made a suicide attempt, perhaps serious only as a warning that he was far from happy and something had better be done about it, but none the less upsetting for that. My parents responded instantly by taking him away.

Two years later Justin wrote a story about a schoolboy who has a nervous breakdown. The hero, who is at the moment of exacerbated sexual curiosity that immediately precedes the discovery of what sex is all about, finds himself face to face with an exhibitionist while wandering about alone on the school playing-fields. The boys have already been warned about this flasher, who is known to be dangerous and has in fact already served time for an offence committed at another public school. Highly disturbed, the pupil goes back to his room and pretends to be ill. Tucked up in bed (with the matron's permission) he masturbates for the first time. The experience is accompanied by visual images so nightmarish that he actually vomits with disgust. He becomes genuinely ill, and the horrifying visions persist. Meanwhile he is visited by his housemaster, and in a precociously handled scene of farce that still makes me laugh aloud, succeeds in blurting out what really happened, only to realise that the housemaster has misheard him. Recovering two days later, he gets out of bed to open the window – the flasher is leering at him from a bench conveniently placed on the opposite side of the street. Convulsed with terror, the boy loses control. He collects his money, rushes out of his room, out of the house by the back entrance, into the street, across the fields and away. He runs to the nearest railway station and takes a train to his home town. But once at home he finds that his escape has been an empty gesture, because the nightmare images still won't let him alone. Convinced that he's mad, he tries to kill himself with an overdose of pills. The story ends with his discovery, still alive, by the maid.

Justin showed me his story soon after he wrote it. It seemed to me, as it still does, to be a work of talent, even brilliance. It was completely lacking in the pretentiousness which is normally unavoidable in even the best adolescent writing. Direct, observant, in turn supremely horrifying and very funny indeed, it provided an insider's view of a kind of teenage sexuality that I'd never seen attempted by any writer before. I was deeply impressed and said so to Justin. While we were talking I threw in – as if it were too obvious to be worth discussing – that I realised that the story was autobiographical. Justin frowned severely, and in a clipped, displeased tone of voice quite different from the one in which he had just been acknowledging my praise, muttered, 'Not at all, of course not. I got the main idea from a newspaper cutting and imagined the rest.' This was typical of Justin's secretiveness, and by laughing I let him understand that I didn't believe him.

The story was never published, nor to my knowledge did Justin ever show it to anyone but Ursula and me. He seemed curiously uninterested in it, as though it were merely something he had needed to get out of his system and then forget. But the powerful effect it had on me at first reading stayed in my memory, and I found the poems he wrote later in his life stilted by comparison. He was probably the kind of writer who needs the stimulus of real characters and events – his life with Ursula was rather short of either, despite being full of physical movement and strong emotion.

The sequence of horrifying visions are a *tour de force* of the story. One occurs in the train which is taking the hero homewards – he finds himself unwillingly concentrating on the syncopated rhythm of the wheels:

All the momentum, the weight and brutal power of these continually repeated reports disturbed him increasingly. He imagined the great oily discs racing along the shiny steel rail, and felt that he was getting unpleasantly close to the hammering mechanism that was really not more than a couple of feet below him. As he sank towards it, it rose towards him, so that after a while he was scarcely an excruciating millimetre out of its reach. Suddenly his wrist was caught in a joint of the see-sawing lever-arms and his sliced-off hand was instantly crushed to pulp, leaving a dripping, tattered stump. There was searing pain. The wheels and cogs and pistons churned on all around, and the noise was now actually inside his head. The pulp of his severed hand was being flicked and batted about from wheel to piston, piston to lever. Finally some random activation splatted it back up into his face. Now he dropped bodily into the works: the pistons shot up and broke all his teeth, while the mechanism hurled him around like a doll in a washing-machine. The appalling agonies his body was suffering were transferred to his sensory organs. He choked on lumps of metal, his hair was chewed out in great hanks, his skin was entirely flayed until he was nothing but a mass of bloody gristle. Upside-down, round and round he was whirled, each new impact ripping away a new chunk of flesh . . .

Passages like this are so immediate that they give the impression of having been transcribed directly on to paper from still-fresh memory and, in spite of Justin's disclaimer, I'm in no doubt that he himself underwent such waking nightmares. Whether or not his crisis was precipitated by a confrontation with a flasher needed investigating. Jonna and other contemporaries could remember nothing about it, but Justin's housemaster was more helpful. At first, being understandably anxious to avoid any possible charge of negligence towards Justin, he was inclined to resist the flasher hypothesis, mentioning only that there had been a pederast around at the time, who had wormed his way into one of the houses and seduced a boy – everyone had been warned against him and in the end he was caught. I wrote back asking if this man had exhibitionist tendencies. The answer was illuminating:

> . . . I am fairly certain that our Mr A. was not an exhibitionist but a performer . . . I have been in contact with one or two people and they confirm this view. [But] from time to time children, when returning from the town across the playing-fields, were confronted by a man (not always the same man over the years) exhibiting himself . . . I do not recall ever having this difficulty . . . If you think of it, a boy returning from the football fields would normally be in company with twenty-two others, and it would take a brave fellow to attempt to 'flash' them.

These playing fields were exactly the setting that Justin chose for his hero's encounter with the flasher, which takes place when, wanting to be alone, he wanders off from his team-mates after a football game. So there is some slight circumstantial evidence for believing that Justin's breakdown was provoked by a nasty experience of the kind. If so, the association would help explain his fierce and lasting hatred of public schools.

Justin was sent to work on the management side of a factory in Newcastle, with which my family had business connections – he lodged with the family of one of the executives. This was a temporary arrangement to find out if he had any aptitude for business. In the three or four months that he was there he came home several times for weekends. On the first of these my mother was relieved to find that he was much calmer and more cheerful, even seemed to be enjoying himself. The old anger was still noticeable, as were other symptoms of tortured adolescence – the lowered head, the growled, inaudible mutterings when other people were talking – but she thought that he was slowly emerging from the tunnel. He was full of stories about the Geordie factory workers, complete with accent. One old boy he knew smoked 'eighty cigarettes a day – always have. I'd smoke more if I had the time.'

Teenagers are always worrying their parents with a discontent that they wouldn't dream of revealing to their contemporaries. Hugo Stewart was a month younger than Justin and one of his best friends for a two-year period around the time of his leaving school – the impression he gave of Justin then was considerably more robust: 'I first got to know him on a skiing holiday in Austria with a group of other kids – we must have been fifteen. Justin had longer hair than any of us, and he was always trying to pass himself off as a member of a new group called the Treatles – but I don't think anyone believed him. What I remember best about him that winter is his daring. On New Year's Eve, at the stroke of midnight, he put on his skiing boots and went clumping up the mountainside. We had all tried to persuade him not to, because he was absolutely plastered, but there was no stopping him. He went very high up the mountain and then skied down in the moonlight. Afterwards the locals were furious – he could have broken every bone in his body. But Justin was a very good skier, and as it turned out he was perfectly all right. The main thing was that he achieved his ambition – he wanted to be the first man in 1962 to do the run.'

'Did you see him regularly when you got back to England?' 'Well, by good luck we were later both sent to the same crammer. Justin had just passed his driving test, and he often used to go around in a red Mini – I think it belonged to your mother, didn't it? Looking back on it, the things he did in that car in the middle of London were hair-raising. He used to

roar down the street and then suddenly put it through a
180-degree turn on the handbrake. That makes him sound like
a show-off or a tearaway, which is misleading. The main thing
was his charm and his sense of humour. He had an ebullience
and self-confidence which were very infectious – I always felt
really good when I was with him, we were always laughing.
But our friendship didn't include confidences, and I always
knew that he had a thoughtful side that was nothing to do with
our relationship. I respected his reticence – for instance he
never talked to me about Ursula and I never asked him. But
one day he took me round to her flat in Chelsea when she
wasn't there. I'd no idea what we were supposed to be doing
there, and Justin didn't explain. He just let us in with a key
and poured us a drink.'

I wanted to find out how much Justin had had to do with
girls before meeting Ursula. For a gauche 16-year-old to take
on someone so widely admired, with the physical allure and
social poise to attract strenuous competition from grown-up
men, argues an exceptional amount of sexual confidence. I
asked Hugo what he knew. 'Well, I was so impressed by him
myself that I took it for granted that any women would fall flat
at his feet. I know for certain that he had a fiery affair with
Vicky Kennedy – brief but fiery.' But Vicky herself, a
childhood friend of Hugo's, told me, 'I met Justin at Hugo's
flat, I think. After a noisy evening there I went back with him
to his room – though it might just as well have been any of
those boys I ended up with. I'm afraid I was all over the place
in those days. We did get into bed, and then there was a lot of
fumbling about, but nothing very serious happened – you
know what it's like at sixteen.' So it looks as if Justin may have
been showing off to Hugo.

Tom Hilton remembered, 'We were walking down Charing
Cross Road one day, and we passed a bookshop where you
could buy postcards of naked girls – it was the soft porn of the
era. As I was sheafing through them without, I'd have
thought, an abnormal degree of interest, Justin glanced at me
curiously and asked, "Are you a lonely boy?" It was semi-
facetious, but I took it to mean that he thought I was less
experienced than he was. And he used to describe these parties

near where you lived, where everybody screwed and the boys passed round used Durexes. Even I found that pretty revolting.' Again this sounds like a piece of childish bravado.

Finally, here is Jonna's account of what happened, or rather didn't happen, in the summer of 1963 at a house my parents had taken in the south of France. 'Jilly and Emma were invited to keep us occupied, and they certainly did, though not in the way we wanted. The poor girls were under constant attack from us two randy bastards. We were determined to lose our virginities and they were determined to hang on to theirs. I was mad about Jilly, but in the end her extreme chastity got a bit much, so it wasn't the end of the world when Justin pinched her off me. But I don't think he got any further with her than I did.' Another friend, Adam Craig, thought Justin had an affair with a girl in Aix, but he couldn't remember her name, and nobody else I talked to knew anything about it.

Justin had never been short of female company, thanks to his place in the entourage of his elder brother, Jonna. But it looks as if his relations with girls were more limited than he liked to pretend.

5

Ursula, Kenelm and Justin

Ursula and Kenelm had known my parents for some time, having been introduced originally by a mutual friend. Kenelm had then sold my father a pair of eighteenth-century cupboards. If I myself had never met them, it was only because my work, my children, and the hoo-ha of London life seemed to leave little room for weekends in the country. But it was not at all surprising that they should have been staying at the house the next time Justin came home. No one can remember on whose initiative – and probably no one even noticed it happening – but somehow, on Saturday morning, Justin and Ursula went on a long walk together, and didn't come back till lunchtime. After dinner, when everyone else had gone to bed, they stayed up together, drinking and talking, long into the night.

Justin aroused in Ursula a sensation that it took her a long time to understand. She realised, of course, that it resembled a sexual attraction, but since he was sixteen, and in some ways young for his age – he had a sort of incoherent brashness mixed in with his obvious sensitivity which didn't fit in with the mental qualities she was used to expecting from a lover – she didn't allow herself directly to recognise it as such. My mother, in the course of a conversation with Ursula soon after this fateful weekend, asked her why, when she seemed so happily married and lived so comfortably, she showed no interest in having children. Ursula replied, 'The only person I've ever felt faintly maternal about is your son.' So that was how she rationalised it – at any rate publicly. The only role she thought it either appropriate or dignified to assume, from that first Saturday until various social and emotional knots were loosened, was that of protectress-cum-educator.

The conversations they had that day were about art – Justin asked the questions and Ursula answered them. He must have had a thirst for such things that he hadn't even known was there, because he drank in everything she told him as if his survival depended on it. She was astonished by the depth of his ignorance and delighted by the authenticity of his interest – in people of any age a genuine concern for art, as opposed to a superficial attraction to its romance, is rare enough for its symptoms to be recognisable to the initiated.

Justin, unlike Ursula, was in no doubt what had happened – he had fallen in love. Before their nocturnal conversation came to an end it was already established that Ursula and Kenelm had been invited by my parents to stay in the south of France for a week or two during the coming summer. The prospect of another possible meeting emboldened Justin to kiss her. The kiss was a frontier through which he passed into territory from which he had no return ticket. The metaphor sounds exaggerated but my brother's character was romantic to a degree that's rarely met with nowadays. When after Ursula's death he wrote, 'Our love was *willingly* doomed', he was speaking above all for himself.

When Ursula finally went upstairs to join her sleeping husband, Justin snatched a piece of paper from my mother's desk, and scrawled on it in capital letters I LOVE YOU. It was four in the morning. He ran up to Ursula's room – the door was shut, but he could hear her moving around inside. He slid the piece of paper under the door, and rustled it. Nothing happened, so he shook the door till it made a gentle knocking noise. This achieved results – he felt the paper being pulled from within, and then heard Ursula's quiet laugh.

The capacity to love another person so exclusively, so unswervingly, so self-effacingly as Justin did Ursula is one of the rarest talents in the world – it would be ridiculous to suppose that it had remained entirely hidden until that day, because of course it had always been a component of his nature. Justin had been a passionate, all-or-nothing sort of child. My mother remembered, when he was six, inviting a little girl-friend of his for tea. Half an hour before she was due to arrive, her mother telephoned to say that the girl didn't want to come after all ('Why the hell don't you smack her bottom and tell her to do as she's told?' thought my mother with irritation). The result for Justin was not just the rest of the afternoon, but two whole days – a lifetime when you're six – of inconsolable tears, tantrums, fasting, and moaning in his sleep.

Justin went back to Newcastle with a lot on his mind. On that first long walk with Ursula he had told her about his experimental business apprenticeship. She evidently wasn't very encouraging, because one of the first indications of her influence was his decision that business was not for him – he had previously shown both application and a certain amount of promise. Now he took the risk of writing to Ursula. I still can't get over the sheer nerve that was needed for this 16-year-old boy to write what was nothing more or less than a love-letter to the 26-year-old wife of a family friend. It paid off, though, because Ursula wrote back. She and Kenelm were planning to use their invitation to the south of France as the first step on a business trip by jeep to Syria, Lebanon, Jordan, and Iraq. Justin's delight in having a page of this magical handwriting for his own was redoubled when he realised that the dates of his stay in France would coincide with theirs. He was to spend the summer with a family near Aix-en-Provence, to 'improve his French', in preparation for starting A level work at a London crammer in September.

Justin's friends had always tended to be family rather than school connections. One of these was Adam Craig whom he was seeing regularly at the time he first met Ursula. They had arranged that as soon as Justin had settled into his Provençal family life, Adam would drive down in his newly-acquired car to give him moral support. 'I meant to drive there slowly and look at France the way you're supposed to, but somehow I couldn't cope with it – maybe I was just lonely – anyhow in the end I drove as hard as I could and got there in sixteen hours. Justin seemed to have become an urgent objective. Our meeting was quite dramatic. I found the place at last, it was in beautiful country near Mont-Ste-Victoire. I was driving slowly up a steep dirt track – the final leg – when down roared this guy on a beat-up bike and screeched to a halt. It was Justin. He was just as pleased to see me as I was to see him, because he was bored, you see. He was stuck out there, it was some kind of summer camp for him and four other kids, including two bosomy American girls, who were both all moony about him. It was a lovely house in lovely country, but the set-up was wrong – you can imagine the authority of the household, conversation in French after dinner, that sort of thing. Justin fixed me up with this little room in Aix, where he'd had some girlfriend, I think. I used to drive out to his place – there was a summer-house with big windows overlooking the valley. I'd paint a bit, and after lunch Justin would escape with a plateful of food for me. There was an old wind-up gramophone, and we'd sit there playing Supremes records and drinking and smoking Gauloises . . . Then we drove out to Cassis with a couple of girls. No, *not* the American girls, I think they were English, some connection from home maybe, but I can't really remember. We had a great time. 'Did the difference in your ages matter?' 'No. When I first met Justin, he must have been thirteen, but he seemed tremendously grown-up to me. He was sophisticated, he could drive, he was always getting into jams. But at the time I'm talking about, he'd turned into a thoroughly lovely person, tough and funny and fun. He was a wild boy, he wanted to be free. You know, I wasn't surprised that Justin never had a career. I always thought of him as a larger-than-life character, who didn't need one.'

The bike on which Justin had nearly collided with Adam belonged to Billy, an American student whom Justin had met in Aix. In the middle of June, after Adam had left, Ursula and Kenelm were due to arrive at the house that my parents had taken on Cap-Ferrat – and Justin had to find a way of getting there. Billy had often lent Justin his bike for a day at a time, but a trip of nearly two hundred kilometres was another matter. In the end they arranged that Billy would drive him there in return for two comfortable nights on the Mediterranean, with swimming and plenty of food thrown in. When the time came, Justin rang my parents, both to confirm that this met with their approval and to check that Ursula had arrived. Two days later, when the family and the other guests were having their siesta, Billy and Justin clanked through the gates with a loud back-firing report. Ursula, with whom Justin had managed to talk on the telephone the night before, was waiting for him on the lawn. Billy, briefed in advance, strode over to the parapet overlooking the sea and, whooping like an Apache, galloped down the stone steps towards the jetty.

Ursula, wearing a light, loose-fitting dress, was sitting reading on one of those swinging garden-seats with a canvas shade. Justin, in T-shirt and torn jeans, was covered with grime from the journey. He approached her with a rather serious smile, squatted beside her, and repeated in a low voice what he had written a few months earlier in the note. To Ursula's surprise her eyes filled with tears. I suppose it's embarrassing for a sophisticated and fundamentally reticent person to be caught out in the emotional gestures of the heroine of a Mills and Boon novel. Ursula was toughish, at any rate with regard to the façade she presented to other people. She had always been in control of her love affairs, whether she wanted to be or not. On first meeting Justin she had been puzzled by the force of her feelings and hoped that they would later fall into some kind of recognisable order. So her present reaction, allied to the fear that Justin might misinterpret it, was particularly disturbing.

Two days later, Billy rode back to Aix. Justin stayed another five days at the house, taking every possible opportunity to be alone with Ursula. Kenelm made no difficulties – he was unsuspicious by nature, and anyway Justin couldn't possibly be considered a serious competitor. After the rest of the party had gone to bed, Justin and Ursula would set off in the jeep to do the night-spots. Ursula, having never herself learned to drive, entrusted the job to Justin – he had never before been accepted on such equal terms by a grown-up. It appeared to be *he* who was taking *her* to drink and dance in clubs. Even her unthinking way of handing him the money to pay the bill, as though money were merely some boring detail to be dealt with by whoever happened to have it to hand at the time, did nothing to dispel the illusion.

Although there were plenty of opportunities in the grounds of the house, they didn't immediately make love – another novelty for Ursula. Usually, if a man she was interested in didn't make a pass at her at the beginning of the acquaintance, she'd take the initial steps herself, not so much from force of appetite as from boredom with the conventions of courtship. It would have been perfectly natural, in this case, for her to have assumed the role of the experienced older woman with a duty to cut short the painful hesitancy of the beginner – but she didn't. She was content to let the affair develop slowly, or rather at a speed it seemed to be dictating of its own accord. This argues, I think, that the gentle, even deferential, dominance noticeable later in Justin's treatment of Ursula was mysteriously there from the start. In spite of her extra ten years and the wealth and variety of experience they contained, in spite of her superior education and intellectual lucidity, she knew that it had to be he who did the seducing.

They used to meet at seven-thirty in the morning on the smooth rocks near the jetty. Although the sun wasn't yet hot enough for the procedure to be strictly necessary, she would lie face down on the stone, a signal for him to rub her with suntan oil. He massaged her silently, concentrating on movements designed to give the greatest pleasure.

If this is a potent love story, it is because of the rare balance between the characters of the lovers. Justin and Ursula lived together with such corresponding aims and such a sharing of tastes that they used to tell each other that their marriage was like a fruit perfectly joined from two component halves. The old image of 'the other half' occurs regularly in their writings. Yet, as far as their natures, their talents, went they were as opposite as Tarzan and Jane – and this double stress was surely what made them so unusual. For instance, Justin was the giver, Ursula the taker. The pleasure of giving relates directly to the pleasure given – a woman who gets the intensest pleasure from being made love *to* causes the intensest pleasure in the maker of the love. No amount of 'reciprocal' giving can compare with this simple recipe, but the chances that a man who is good at giving will find a woman who is good at taking are a hundred to one against.

Anyway, by means of the ritual of the suntan oil, they arrived gradually at a consummation on the night before Justin's departure. Then, lying in the moonlight, they were struck by a coincidence that neither of them had previously noticed – while she was naked except for a Byzantine coin on a chain round her neck, he wore nothing but an ivory monkey similarly placed. These they ceremoniously exchanged.

Ursula and Kenelm had originally planned to drive on eastward after leaving my parents, but some business came up which necessitated a return to London – this meant a fortnight's delay. Ursula was by now in a state of acute inner confusion. Like everyone else she had always wanted to fall in love, but in the course of time she had almost stopped hoping for it to happen. Of course it's a truism that forced feelings give poor returns, and another that marvellous strokes of luck only come when you've given up expecting them. But why did it have to be someone so tremendously unsuitable, someone it would be so humiliating, so risky and possibly destructive to run away with? She made an effort to put the whole Justin business out of her mind. But she felt so unhappy, and missed him so much, that she rang him in Aix to suggest a meeting there on her way back to London.

They met for breakfast in a hotel in Aix. Kenelm made business calls to London, while Justin and Ursula sat, in some restraint, on the terrace. Afterwards Ursula wished she had never made the arrangement. She and Kenelm drove back to London more or less in silence. At one point Kenelm, concerned about her obvious distress, asked her what was the matter. She told him that she couldn't understand what was happening to her, that the Justin business was an absurdity, but that nevertheless it was all she could think about. Kenelm was sympathetic and tried to reassure her – everything would be all right as soon as they started travelling. She must try for a little composure.

The insatiable appetite for travel that Ursula was later able to indulge to the full was far from being an indiscriminate

wanderlust. She gravitated to three clearly defined points of
the compass – south-eastward, as in the present case, in the
rough direction of India and beyond, south-westward towards
Mexico, Colombia or Brazil, and southward through Egypt to
Central Africa. In spite of her involvement with the literature
of certain countries – Russia, Poland, the United States – she
showed not the slightest curiosity about them as places to visit.
This was less odd when you remembered that Ursula was a
creature of compartments. The imagination she used to read
Dostoievski operated by means of a different mechanism from
the one she used when heading for the Sahara. The first was
harnessed to her brain, the second to her instincts. And her
instincts were migratory, like a bird's. 'But not beyond the
Equator,' she wrote of her southward pull. If you had asked
why not, she would have shrugged her shoulders.

In her confusion Ursula had forgotten the powerful
excitement of travel in one of her given directions, an
excitement that was heightened whenever there was an
element of danger. They got lost in the Syrian desert, with a
shortage of petrol and an inadequate reserve container. She
found herself separated from Kenelm in the midst of a
labyrinthine Jordanian souk, surrounded by silent men with
incomprehensible eyes.

She felt like deliberately provoking the danger that could
provide such stimulation, but she was constantly being pulled
up short by reminders of the Justin business. The letters from
him that she collected at various prearranged poste restante
addresses undermined her pleasure, which was of an imper-
sonal kind. She almost wished she hadn't succumbed to the
temptation of corresponding with him. His letters frightened
her in a less acceptable way than the hazards of Middle-
Eastern travel, as if some kind of nemesis were lying in wait
for her when she returned to London.

The self-occupied state of mind that I've ascribed to
Ursula at this time is based on the account she gave of it to
Justin afterwards. Reality intervened. Kenelm became ill –
and Ursula, who was much more compassionate than she
pretended, was relieved that she was now forced to give him
some overdue consideration. Like a reprieved alcoholic who

discovers, in the teeth of popular opinion, that he can after all drink socially in the normal way, Kenelm had become used to taking the partial restoration of his health for granted. In fact, the slightest fever was still potentially dangerous. Since they had been invited to stay with friends in Istanbul, they decided to drive there as quickly as possible. By the time they arrived, he was in a state of collapse and had to be taken straight to hospital. His condition quickly deteriorated, and Ursula was told by the doctors that he might easily die.

It had been agreed that the balance of their marriage depended on a strict adherence to certain tenets of toughness, style, and individual survival. Each one for himself. When in trouble, you don't bring the other down with you. Whenever Kenelm was seriously ill, he didn't betray these principles, but became withdrawn and unapproachable. This time he went further – although Ursula visited him two or three times a day, he gave no sign of recognising her.

Ursula had no doubt that his attitude amounted to an act of generosity towards her personally. Simultaneously she discovered that, for the first time, she was unable to go on believing in the articles of faith on which it was based. Part of the magic of falling in love is that you have the illusion of escaping from the stranglehold of your egotism, and then there's the period of sheer exaltation, when your new-found expansiveness of heart overspills beyond your loved one on to everyone within reach. Although Ursula didn't quite dare to admit that she had fallen in love with Justin, she understood that he was playing a part in the terrible pity she felt for Kenelm. Feeling that this pity was belittling to him, she was overcome with guilt. So she concentrated on her admiration for his courage, which was more in tune with the complicity natural to 'fellow-buccaneers', as she prayed for his survival.

Kenelm survived. As soon as he was strong enough to travel, they flew back to London leaving the jeep with its cargo of recent acquisitions to be driven home at a later date.

It was September 1965. Justin had moved, along with a friend of his own age, into the house of some friends of my parents in Drayton Gardens, off the Fulham Road. The idea was that they should keep an eye on him during his three-month period at the crammer. It was a fortunate choice from Justin's point of view. The Morrises, my parents' friends, had always been fond of him, and were amused by behaviour that would certainly have irritated most of the older generation. Betty Morris has one image imprinted on her memory. 'I came home one afternoon to see this outlandish figure, with the long hair and fringed, bell-bottomed jeans they all seemed to wear, actually shinning up the drainpipe. I suppose he'd forgotten his key or something, but, honestly, what a thing to do in broad daylight. Typical of him, really.'

As soon as Ursula got back to London, she telephoned Justin. They met the same day outside the Victoria and Albert Museum, a rendezvous appropriate to Ursula's educational responsibilities. Justin repeated once again that he loved her. This time Ursula, dazed and nearly choking on the smell of burning bridges, replied that she loved him too. But she couldn't just leave it like that, she wanted to warn him. 'Listen . . . ' she started off, but was unable to carry on. There would have been far too much to say, and none of it worthy of the solemnity of the moment.

In the following weeks poor Ursula was tormented by doubt – she couldn't make up her mind whether she'd done the silliest or the most sensible thing in her life. Whichever it was, there was plainly no going back on it.

Max, Ursula's closest confidant, and of all her friends the one who had least to do with her marriage, entered into the spirit of the adventure by lending her his *pied-à-terre*. This was a flat on the top storey of a block near Sloane Square station. The two rooms had thick, white carpeting and walls of smoked mirror-glass. The bed was huge, and had black linen sheets. In this strenuously decadent setting Justin and Ursula ate gulls' eggs and drank champagne.

The crammer brought Justin two A levels, an O level, and a lifelong friend. Tom Hilton was a young photographer, who had already done a year at film school. His radical and creative approach to things was immediately attractive to Justin. Tom taught him the rudiments of photography, which he practised more or less continuously from then on. It served him both as a travel sketchbook when on the move and as a means of formal experimentation when at home. Although they saw little of each other during the Ursula years, the friendship was important to Justin as the only one he contracted until after her death that had no connection either with her or with the family.

The two boys set out to have a good time at the institution's expense. From Tom's description of their behaviour it seems extraordinary that they were allowed to stay the course. 'I've no idea why they put up with us, because we must have driven them mad. For instance we had a mattress on the roof, where we drank bottles of wine while the others were working. We did things like set fire to newspapers and fill the room with smoke. Once we were standing at the top of the stairs, and Justin muttered to me, "Rub your fist as though it hurts." Suddenly he crashed down the stairs, tumbling head over heels as if I'd thumped him.'

'Did you see much of him outside school?' 'Oh yes, I introduced him to the Notting Hill crowd I went around with. He had a quality people instantly responded to. I'd hate to call it charisma, but you know what I mean? He had an emotional honesty, a natural sense of right and wrong. People who had only met him once wanted to see him again. The quality I loved most was his absolute wildness and freedom. He had fantastic energy and a massive sense of humour and fun.'

I asked Tom if he'd known Ursula then. 'Yes, but I always felt that she only accepted me on sufferance as a friend of Justin's – she was stiff. I sometimes used to go to the King's Road flat. The atmosphere was extraordinarily static – the three of us sat there like a still life. In fact, that's why I can never drink whisky with ice and water to this day. The conversation was of a diplomatic kind of which I had experience from my childhood. We talked about jazz, which we were both interested in, but we were both only really going through it because it pleased Justin – our relationship wasn't important. Whether I saw her as yet another out-of-touch adult or she saw me as another scruffy, precocious little boy didn't matter – we both came from backgrounds where the concealment of feeling builds the structure that becomes the reality.'

Ursula spent more and more time with Justin, often staying most of the night with him in Max's flat. As a consequence she began to neglect the business, whose running had always been shared by her-and Kenelm. Now that she wasn't pulling her weight, Kenelm was having to cope on his own. The resentment this naturally caused him was exacerbated by my brother's apparently full-time presence in the background. On one occasion she took Justin back to lunch at the King's Road flat, and Kenelm turned up unexpectedly. Although he was perfectly polite, there was an obvious feeling of tension. Perhaps Kenelm should have adopted a dominant, avuncular role towards Justin, hoping at best to neutralise, even ridicule, Ursula's maternal one, at worst to retrieve some control of the situation.

Justin's work was also falling behind. My mother rang up the principal of the crammer's to find out how he was getting on. 'He'd be all right,' was the reply, 'if only that blonde of his wasn't always taking him off in taxis.' The implication was that public transport would have been a more stimulating educational aid.

In fact Ursula, 'that blonde', was busy providing him with an education that no institution could have approached. Like many self-taught people disdainful of the conventional authorities, Ursula had an urge to communicate her discoveries. Friendship is unsatisfying in this way – somehow your intellectual equals never take you quite seriously enough. Justin, as a more receptive, hotter-hearted Bosie, must have been rewarding to Ursula's distinctly Wildean sugar-mummyhood. But the gulls' eggs and champagne, rather than a languid, *fin-de-siècle* indulgence, were part of an overall, if only semi-conscious, plan for refining his sensual and aesthetic responses.

Ursula's appreciation of art was both eclectic and rounded. She was equally alive to musical, verbal, and visual forms of expression. She was tremendously well-informed and very discriminating. She had favourites – among others, Petronius,

Musil, Donatello, Proust, Billie Holiday, Mozart, Dante, Goethe, the carver of the Colossi of Memnon, Homer, Borromini, Juvenal, Goya, Céline, Tacitus, and Titian. Although she was expert at justifying her favouritism intellectually, it was always sensual in origin – this was something she proclaimed and for which she never apologised.

Before he met Ursula, art had never impinged on Justin. My parents collected painting and sculpture and beautiful objects, but Justin had no time for such things, being far too busy with his gun or car or fishing rod. None the less his outdoor activities instilled in him something more potent than an awareness of art – a finely developed capacity for the observation of the outside world, which is its raw material.

I don't think I've ever met anyone more naturally observant than Justin. As a result – when the circumstances were right – it was delightful to be with him. Occasionally, too rarely for me, we used to find ourselves walking ahead of or behind our wives in some unknown city. He continually pointed out details of far more interest and subtlety than those I'd have noticed without his help. He had the gift of noticing, in one apparently casual glance and with only a minimal movement of the head, the decorative refinement of first a stork's nest perched on a distant chimney, and immediately afterwards of a scrunched-up ten-franc note wedged into a gutter. Justin was naturally competitive, yet he certainly didn't exercise this talent to score points off an elder brother. It was more that he didn't recognise that it *was* a talent. And I, generally bristling with rivalry where anything 'creative' is concerned, conceded with relatively good grace that I had a lot to learn from him in the field.

So the ground that Ursula was fertilising with the seed of art was already promising. But a fertilising process was also, though less obviously, at work in the reciprocal direction – Justin was making her susceptible to the pleasures of day-to-day observation. He encouraged her, by example, to balance her intellectual habits with a simpler, more outdoor, attention to detail. Justin had no gift for rational discussion, and we often used to wonder why, since Ursula chose to live with him in such isolation, she didn't appear to miss the fun to be had from its exercise. The reason was that, under his influence, she stopped attaching so much importance to 'good conversation'. The spiritual and sensual intensity she replaced it with struck her as a great improvement.

In May 1966 Justin was due to take his A level exams. The idea was that he should then take a year off to travel around and decide what he wanted to do in life. It was agreed that, if he failed to arrive at any feasible alternative, he should go into my father's business, which was banking. All this was discussed one weekend, when Kenelm and Ursula were also staying with my parents. I should point out here that nobody except Kenelm and Max had any idea how deeply Justin was already involved with Ursula. My parents naturally assumed that she was merely being kind to the poor boy, who plainly had a crush on her. At some point in the conversation Kenelm, perhaps anxious to appear disinterested, suggested that Justin should start his travels as an extra driver in their Land Rover – they were planning another trip to the Middle East. He would be free to cut loose whenever he liked.

But Ursula saw to it that the plan was changed – Justin and Tom Hilton would drive the Land Rover to Athens, Ursula would fly out to meet them there, and Kenelm would join them three weeks later.

When Tom saw Justin after Ursula's death, he was struck by how frequently and urgently he referred to that trip. For Tom it had been just one episode in the more or less continuous adventure that was his life in those days. For Justin it was the end of one era and the beginning of another. Justin was often intuitive almost to the point of prescience, and although he couldn't, of course, have *known* how cleanly the journey was going to slice his life in two, there's an explosiveness in Tom's account of it that has all the signs of the consciousness of impending climax.

'We didn't sleep at all for three days, we just drove on and on, keeping ourselves going with drink. We tried to go straight through Switzerland from north to south, but of course there are no direct roads, so we kept getting hopelessly lost. You know how, when you haven't slept for a long time, you can get hallucinations round the edges of the headbeams? The strange thing was that we were getting the same ones. There'd be hundreds of people approaching us, and then they'd suddenly turn into a bush or a rock. When a massive stag appeared in the middle of the road, we thought it was another of these joint hallucinations, but we slowed down just to be on the safe side. He rattled his antlers on the bumper to warn us, and we drove on. Justin said he'd chased us out of his territory. Then there was a hooded figure like a monk sitting just behind our shoulders. We were too tired to be frightened, we just pulled into a lay-by and passed out. We didn't dare discuss it till next day.

'Justin and I both had our hair half-way down our backs. You've got to remember this was 1966, and although there were quite a few men with long hair in London, on the Continent it was practically unknown. I mean, people came down the street after us actually trying to touch us. One time, I think it was in Austria, we stopped at a late-night café – we'd only been there a minute when a bunch of truck-drivers came at us with clenched fists. We got out pretty quick. We'd heard there was a bar in a square in Rome where they served coffee laced with heroin. The trouble was there were lots of bars in the square, and we ended up drinking about fifteen cups of espresso, by which time we were so speedy that we wouldn't have known if they had heroin in them or not. We got into the Land Rover, and Justin drove off at great speed straight into a parked Fiat 500, bounced it into a doorway, and concertinaed it into a thing about a foot long. We ran for it. We didn't stop driving till we got to Monte Cassino, where we watched the dawn outside the monastery, and finally fell asleep.

'Justin was expecting a letter from Ursula in Naples, so we stayed in a nearby village for a bit and waited for it to arrive. We used to park the Land Rover by a terrace of café tables, open up the back, and put some modern jazz on the record player – in no time there'd be forty or fifty people round us. One day this character came up and very formally announced that he was the head of a fascist organisation, whose duty it was to exterminate us "because you are existentialists". We laughed, until we noticed that all these guys had knives and really meant business – and they'd been drinking our wine for the last hour. We leapt into the Land Rover, but they clambered all over it and tried to smash it up with rocks – somehow we managed to shake them off and get away. Then Justin, who had this habit of driving on the left, ran into a bus – full of irate passengers. By this time the Land Rover was beginning to show signs of wear and tear. We picked up a hitch-hiker, a French guy, who came with us on the boat to Piraeus and then to Athens. He kept telling us he was going to kill himself and showing us the razor he had for the purpose. We met Ursula in Athens as arranged. I remember a rather awkward meal with the four of us – Ursula was superior, almost irritable, and Justin went all silent and internal. And – well – that was the end of that. Next day the French guy and I landed up in prison. Why? Well, apparently we had set a hillside alight.'

So Justin and Ursula were now completely alone together for the first time. They spent a couple of days sightseeing in Athens, and a few more driving round the Peloponnese, including the beautiful southern tip, where they were later to build their house. But for most of the three weeks they stayed in a small hotel on an island in the Bay of Nauplion called Bourdzi. They ate and drank and swam and lay in the sun with a total lack of apprehension for the future that anyone who has ever been ridiculously in love will recognise.

When they met up with Kenelm in Athens they were immediately back in the familiar anguish of *ménages-à-trois*. Ursula was confirmed in a new determination to commit herself irrevocably to Justin, but in the meantime there was business to be done in Jerusalem – so the three of them set off in the Land Rover. At the frontier of Syria with Jordan they were stopped, the police refusing to let them through because of Justin's long hair. At this point Justin's and Kenelm's accounts of what happened begin to diverge, though both agree that Ursula flew into a rage.

Justin writes that he offered to get his hair cut, but that Ursula wouldn't hear of it – her anger was directed against a country whose authorities could lay down such arbitrary and absurd regulations. Kenelm says that Justin refused to cut his hair and that it was because of his stubborn vanity that she got so cross. I asked Kenelm what happened next. 'We just drove back to Greece the way we had come.'

According to Justin, Ursula was so fed up with all this haircut nonsense that she changed her mind about the attractiveness of Jerusalem, insisting that they could do their buying in Palmyra without crossing the border. There was a rare marital disagreement from which Justin himself – the cause of the trouble – tactfully abstained. Ursula won, the visit to Palmyra was a success, and in spite of not reaching Jerusalem they arrived back in Greece with their mercantile mission to some extent accomplished.

As the trip progressed Justin and Ursula had been increasingly reckless, making love in the open whenever the occasion arose, as if inviting the show-down which for some reason still refused to materialise. Now Ursula, past caring about finesse, saw that it would have to be forced. She announced in Smyrna that she and Justin were going to stay on Rhodes – Kenelm could go back to Athens, where they would meet him in a fortnight's time.

They crossed to the island, took a room, and settled into a relaxation that had never been more necessary – the whole farcical journey had got on everybody's nerves. Ursula was interested in deceit only when it was demanded for the protection of the status quo. She disliked inflicting pain, most of all on Kenelm – her priorities were sensual. She realised that the trip had been clumsily arranged and that the responsibility for that was hers. Her only excuse was that, at the time when she had organised the journey, her private decision hadn't yet been made. She was now going to ask Kenelm for a divorce.

This is where the difference between the rival versions becomes crucial. Kenelm says that the visit to Rhodes never happened but that the three of them went back to Athens together. 'Ursula and I stayed at the Grande Bretagne, which irritated Justin because he couldn't afford it. He wanted us to move into his own little hotel, but I refused on the grounds that the Grande Bretagne was the only place that would do the washing. He did laugh at that, I must say.

'Ursula never wanted a divorce,' he went on. 'It was I
who divorced her three years later. Indeed Ian Murray
[Kenelm's solicitor] told me afterwards that if I'd given him a
different brief the whole story might have turned out totally
otherwise. It suited Ursula being married to me. She loved
your brother and she didn't love me – there's no denying that.
But I don't think she would have wanted to marry him if I
hadn't made it possible for her – and once I had, of course, she
couldn't very well get out of it. I hope this doesn't drive a
coach and horses through your story.'

But the story isn't mine, it's Justin's and Ursula's. Both of
them are dead, and part of my job has been to find out why.
Justin left behind him a book that purported to be a kind of
biography of Ursula, in which he included a fair amount of
factual detail. Sometimes that detail has turned out to be
inaccurate, but the book is still the most solid base I've been
able to build on. So, without casting doubt on Kenelm's
memory or good faith, I shall also give Justin's version of
how the divorce was initiated – he agrees that it was finalised
only three years later. The difference rests in the events in
Athens in 1966. The obvious referee, Ian Murray, is also
dead.

Justin and Ursula arrived in Athens refreshed and full of
resolution. Justin waited in his little hotel – he also mentions
that Kenelm was staying in the Grande Bretagne – while
Ursula went off to deliver her bombshell. A surprisingly short
time later she was back. Everything was arranged. Kenelm
had agreed to a divorce, and promised to instruct his friend
and solicitor, Ian Murray, to fly to Athens with the relevant
papers. If Ursula, who hadn't quite known what to expect,
was moved by this generosity, Justin was euphoric. He was to
be co-respondent, an honour which sounded to him far more
dignified than a knighthood. Apart from liberating Ursula to
him, the divorce was endowing him with a degree of grown-
upness which put new demands on the strength of his love,
the strength of his character. Ian duly appeared and met them
in a spirit of professional and sympathetic neutrality – after
all, he was as much Ursula's friend as Kenelm's. The papers
were signed. Kenelm was giving her £1,000 a year until

such time as she could support herself or be supported by
Justin.

But divorce is seldom so civilised – it seems to dredge
up from the innards of its antagonists the most painful
and uncontrollably see-sawing emotions. This case was no
exception. When Kenelm had been back in London for a while
he became depressed by the loneliness of his new life, the
embarrassment of having to explain things to acquaintances,
and the sheer pain of missing Ursula. She had given him the
address of a hotel in Luxor. He sent her a telegram there
asking her to have a drink with him in Shepheard's Hotel in
Cairo.

Meanwhile Justin and Ursula had bought an old Volkswagen, shipped it to Alexandria and driven it up the valley
of the Nile to Luxor. They wanted to make a thorough study
of ancient Egyptian art, and Luxor was a convenient base,
being the centre of a circle a few kilometres in diameter which
contained Karnak, Thebes, and the Valleys of the Kings and
Queens. Ursula was just beginning to sink into her favourite
state, the absolute acceptance of the sensuality of the present
moment, when the telegram arrived. There was nothing for it
– they would have to drive back to Cairo.

Kenelm told Ursula that, because of currency restrictions,
she was going to have to come to London for the first
instalment of her money. He gave her a return air ticket, dated
for three weeks' time, and £300 in cash to be going on with. If
this generosity was a bait, it was laid with considerable
cunning – his intuition told him that Ursula must be worried
about money.

He was right. Although she was now sure that she was in
love with Justin and that being with him was her main
priority, she too had had moments of severe depression since
Kenelm left. She was faced with the prospect of returning
to the poverty that she had so successfully and enjoyably
clawed her way out of. Kenelm had promised her financial
support, but until the promise was fact she and Justin were
obliged to live very carefully. On the other hand, she was
determined not to revert to a city-based, dealing life and the
banal restrictions it would impose on her vision of freedom,

once amorphous but now at last decidedly taking shape.

Justin thought such anxiety was unworthy of her. On the last of several occasions when she lay slumped on the bed with her face to the wall, he leapt on top of her, bouncing her up and down and tickling her till she was out of breath. Having softened her up, he reminded her of what she had outlined to him before – the attitudes of mind she had found necessary for survival when she first arrived in England. Then she had understood that if a girl had enough style, everything else would fall into place. This style was based on simplicity, an existential habit hard to acquire but which, once acquired, carried you along in its own momentum. Ursula laughed, reassured by the irrefutable wisdom of her own words and flattered by how well her pupil had understood his lessons.

When the time came, Ursula flew to London and Justin stayed in Cairo to wait for her. She was to write to him care of American Express. Ten days later a letter arrived. It was to say goodbye. Kenelm needed her, his health was bad, he would probably die without her, she couldn't risk that possibility. Besides, she realised at last how much she owed him. He had given her a passport, a career, a *raison d'être*, the reliable warmth of his companionship, and financial security. She had been mad to want still more. The whole thing had been a wonderful dream, but now it was over. He must carry on without her. She loved him, but the circumstances were wrong.

Whether or not Justin was intended to believe this, he didn't. He had just enough money for the plane fare to London. He left the car in the hotel car-park and went without paying the bill. When he arrived at Heathrow, he rang the King's Road flat but there was no answer. He then rang Max, who told him that Ursula and Kenelm had gone away for a month. My dinner with him at Olwen's French Club took place shortly afterwards.

If Kenelm was blackmailing Ursula, it was a form of blackmail with which anyone who's been left for someone else will sympathise. All's fair in love and war, and you've simply got to use whatever weapons come to hand – morality, in those desperate circumstances, hardly seems an issue. Although I was in the opposite camp, so to speak, I secretly admired the guile and tenacity with which he fought the losing battle to keep his hold on her.

For Ursula it was a month of despair. The letter she wrote to Justin in Cairo was far from reflecting her real feelings – it was written conscientiously, and his scepticism was justified. For once she thought she was doing the decent thing – atoning for the deceptions of the past by sacrificing her future. In other words, it was a histrionic gesture – and extremely uncharacteristic of her. As soon as she was alone with Kenelm she realised how impossible it would be to sustain for someone of her temperament. It made it worse that she and Kenelm were travelling, a mode of existence she now associated with her love for Justin. That she felt the reality of her responsibility to Kenelm was true – the mistake had been in thinking herself capable of keeping it uppermost in her heart.

She felt no animosity towards Kenelm – on the contrary, she was moved by the intensity of his need for her. But she had suffered a defeat which seemed absolutely final, and was incapable of any reaction other than silent, incessant weeping. So when she found Justin waiting like a chevalier outside the house on her return to London, it was a reprieve. From that moment on until the last weeks of her life, when she went through a crisis of ten times more hideous desperation, she never left his side for more than an hour or two at a time.

I was excited by Justin and Ursula. The little brother to whose existence I'd given so little thought was suddenly involved in a scandalous adventure with one of the most original women I'd ever met. I would have liked them to stay within easy range, so that I could contact them whenever I liked – I didn't yet take their nomadic aspirations seriously. But they were now determined to go back to Luxor as quickly as possible and carry on from the point where they'd been interrupted. I can't remember how the idea came up that I should visit them there, and at first none of us really thought it was going to happen. However, when I had driven them to the airport and was yelling breezily after them through the departures gate,

'See you in a fortnight', I knew all at once that I meant it.
Driving back to London and imagining what the experience
would be like, I realised that, if I were to avoid the risk of
playing the tedious role of the third who crowds the company,
I should need a suitable companion. By the time I reached
Hammersmith I was thirsty, and stopped at the first pub I
saw. Sitting at the bar was a fairly pretty girl – I asked her if
she would enjoy a short holiday in Egypt. To my amazement
she answered, in a strong French accent but perfectly serious
tone of voice, that she had always been fascinated by the idea
of Egypt, was fed up with London, and thank you very much.
After we had exchanged telephone numbers, she said goodbye
and left.

6

Justin and Ursula

A fortnight later, I was sitting in an aeroplane next to a total stranger – and wondering whether I mightn't have made a mistake. In a taxi from Cairo airport to the railway station, I suggested a drink before catching our train to Luxor. 'I don't drink,' she answered. 'What were you doing in that pub then?' 'Waiting for a friend.' 'Oh.' This wasn't encouraging, but worse was to come. As the train wandered interminably up the valley of the Nile, I tried to expand the previous dialogue: 'Who was the friend you were waiting for?' 'She's the girl I live with.' 'Have you known her long?' 'We've been lovers for five years, since we left school in fact.' 'Do you like men too?' 'Not very much.' I still hadn't seen her smile.

It was February 1967, and beautiful weather. Justin and Ursula were in the process of moving from their hotel in Luxor to another, cheaper and more attractive, across the river in Thebes, near the temple of Medinat Habu. This hotel was run by a picturesque character called Sheikh Mohammed, who was rumoured to have made a fortune out of grave-robbing. Whether or not it was true, his place was certainly conveniently located, at the foot of the mountains which encompass the Valleys of the Kings and Queens, and which separate the narrow, fertile strip alongside the Nile from the desert. The building was long and low, old and ramshackle, with an untidy garden of cactus and palms. Over a squat garden-wall you could see the Colossi of Memnon and the Nile in the distance. The armies of doves that woke you at dawn and then chortled all day long were also the basis of Sheikh Mohammed's cuisine.

Justin and Ursula were decorating their room. They were hatching ambitious travelling plans for the future, but in the meantime Sheikh Mohammed's was as good a place as any to call home. They seemed to have a fair amount of stuff. They spread some kelim rugs on the floor, and filled a sizeable shelf with books. A miscellaneous collection of archaeological *objets trouvés* – stones and statuettes and fragments of Egyptian relief work – stood on tables, while the walls were hung with icons and Persian miniatures. It was a big room, light and sunny and suffused with the atmosphere of their compatibility. Later, when Justin showed me photographs of other rooms they had lived in, I realised that they re-created this atmosphere wherever they went. It was a compound of simplicity, austerity almost, with comfort and fastidious, if idiosyncratic, taste. There was also an element of the shrine – you felt a little intrusive there, as if the love that shone out from every choice were too private and ritualistic for others to understand.

Falling in love is one of the mechanisms designed by evolution to facilitate the choice of a mate. In periods such as the one in which Justin and Ursula met, when it was no longer fashionable to regard it as the lowest common denominator of sexual selection, people frequently resort to other methods, including the roulette wheel. A friend of mine once wrote, by the same post, to three more or less randomly chosen girls, asking all of them to marry him. One was away on holiday, the second had unfortunately died in a road accident the previous week, but the third accepted. While it hasn't been the perfect marriage, the fact that it still survives gives a certain stylistic justification to the technique. Justin and Ursula chose each other against the social grain in many respects, not the least of which was their reversion to a system of choice so outrageously romantic that it could have come out of a nineteenth-century novel.

But the enigma of their relationship is the question why, having made the choice, they should both have found it necessary to change quite so fundamentally. Anyone who knew either of them 'before and after' this change is still shocked by it twenty years later. Allowing for the differences in their age and social context, the way they behaved 'before' was strangely similar. Trading on a degree of magnetism vivid enough to impress their contemporaries, both drank a great deal to encourage their natural flamboyance, both were melancholic enough to be attracted by the idea of suicide, both were engaged on a so far unsuccessful quest. Both were excessive. Yet they themselves seem to have been largely ignorant of the similarity, because both had a good reason for not revealing the extent of their excessiveness to the other – neither of them was at all proud of that side of their character. The Ursula with whom Justin fell in love was surely incapable of fucking a girl-friend's boy-friend on a crowded train, in the same way that the sensitive child whom Ursula took it upon herself to educate bore little resemblance to the public-school hooligan scattering pedestrians in his souped-up Mini.

I heard it suggested that they idealised each other to the point where they were each obliged to *become* the ideal of the other's imagination. But this sounds an unstable base for a structure as close-knit as their relationship. It was less a matter of idealisation than one of recognition. If Justin had idealised Ursula he would hardly have forced himself on her either at the beginning or when she wrote him a goodbye letter in Cairo. Instead he recognised with absolute certainty, as if he were in the possession of secret information, that she needed him for her survival. And Ursula, although it took her longer to commit herself – which wasn't surprising considering her comparative lack of freedom – finally did so in the same spirit of absolute recognition.

And it was Ursula's recognition of Justin that carried more weight. Certainty, though more difficult to achieve the older you are, once achieved is that much more impressive. In other words, she had more to lose. The nugget she recognised in him that justified the risk, the responsibility, was the vision of her younger, 'uncorrupt' self before leaving Budapest – she wanted to remake herself as she was before taking what she'd come to regard as a series of wrong turnings.

Now it can be seen that her choice of Justin, in so many

ways a masterstroke of intuitive recognition, was also typical
of the flaw in Ursula's character. Her malaise, her occasional
but regular bouts of depression, her nightmares, were
symptoms of the fear that slowly poisoned her spirit – the fear
of growing old. By living constantly side by side with someone
still in the process of growing up she secured for herself a
second youth by proxy. From then on she systematically
avoided spending time with her contemporaries, the lines in
whose faces reminded her of her real age.

In the end this fear rubbed off on Justin too. Even if she
didn't talk to him directly about her longing for death, her
journal mentions it frequently, and Justin read it. Sentences
like 'I shall have to die fairly young, because I won't be able to
live with the infirmities of old age' (December 1969), 'Five
years would do me very well' (August 1970), 'I wonder if I am
about to die' (September 1972) must have accumulatively
built up in him a terror of losing her. I always smelt fear on
both of them, particularly Justin. At first I diagnosed it as
being comparable to the fear the rich have of losing their
money. Later I realised that there was also an element of
sexual insecurity in the mixture. Only when it was too late did
I have the information to see that its main component was a
matter of life and death.

I was impressed by Egyptian art in its natural habitat, but my
admiration was qualified, rather like my admiration for Justin
and Ursula themselves. They looked wonderful, yes – but
wasn't there something a bit worrying about so much stylised
stillness, such an unquestioning belief in a rather limited
rightness? I felt ashamed of my doubts, which smacked of
wounded vanity – I suspected that I could no longer be of any
use to them. Their apparent disapproval of anything messy
was directly opposed to my lifelong antipathy for anything
well ordered. My unfortunate choice of Marie-Thérèse as a
travelling-companion was a case in point. Our first evening
meal at Sheikh Mohammed's was distinctly sticky – it seemed
difficult to find a conversational ground that would include
her. As soon as she went to the lavatory, I explained how she
happened to be there. Though Ursula seemed guardedly

amused, my brother frowned, as if, having got that kind of
frivolity out of his system, he refused from now on to allow his
imagination to encompass it. Next day, as we walked through
the sweet-smelling fields towards the Nile (Ursula having
taken on Marie-Thérèse and having succeeded, I noticed with
a good deal of awe, in actually making her laugh) Justin gave
me a lecture – wasn't it about time I grew up and took life
more seriously?

Our relationship, only really a few weeks old, never got over
this set-back. What I didn't understand until much later was
that my carelessness with regard to my own marital responsibilities threatened him profoundly. He knew Ursula wasn't
exactly a stranger to casual affairs, though I imagine that she
must have fed him a slightly expurgated edition of her case-
history, both from natural delicacy and from an instinct for
sexual self-preservation. So how could he be sure that, seeing
such an affair taking place, albeit abortively, before her eyes,
she wouldn't be tempted to revert to her bad old ways?

Justin's cocooning protectiveness of Ursula over the years
wasn't without an element of self-interest. His intuition made
him suspect, however often she assured him that he was the
only one she had ever loved, that other men, particularly of a
certain type, were potentially dangerous. This suspiciousness,
being correct, wasn't quite the same as jealousy, which is
essentially unreasonable. Later that year an incident, slight in
itself but serious by implication, put him for ever after on his
guard. They were in a dance-hall in the Turkish quarter of
Limassol. Ursula was invited to dance by a middle-aged Turk
with a gold tooth and a curling moustache. She seemed to go
into a trance. Eyes closed, she pressed the length of her body
against the man's, and swayed to the slow and plangent
Oriental music. The man was of the 'particular type'. She
associated certain Turks, Afghans, and even, at one remove,
Sudanese Arabs later on, with the memory of the gipsies on
her father's estate and, more sinisterly, with the awful
attractiveness of her father himself and his pernicious insistence that her blood was 'the blood of the Khans'. When she
walked back to the table in a daze, Justin was standing stiffly

beside his chair. He told her that he would leave her if she ever did anything of the kind again. Ursula, wide awake now, was shaken by the experience, and agreed with contrition that he would be justified in doing so.

Marie-Thérèse and I took a train to Cairo, and then flew back to London. Our departure occasioned a certain amount of relief on all sides – on Marie-Thérèse's and mine because it marked the end of an absurd, if quixotically intentioned, co-habitation, on Justin's and Ursula's because our stay had helped them understand finally that they had no desire to know anyone in the world but each other. The odd passing contact, yes, but close friends, confidants, brothers, decidedly not. Luckily for me, I had no idea of this – I would have been extremely hurt. The equalising blood I shared with my newly grown-up brothers seemed to me the most promising basis for friendship I had found so far, and I thought about it frequently. True, I didn't find Justin easy, but that made no difference to the emotion, sentimentally conceived but genuine, that I invested in our future communications.

Soon afterwards they drove to Abu Simbel to see the temple. Having got that far, they decided on the spur of the moment to leave the car and take a boat to Wadi Halfa. From there they went on to Khartoum by train. It was their first taste of Sudan, a Utopian country, or so it seemed to them in those pre-famine days, which was later to lure them back with such a siren attraction. They travelled by bus across the desert to Kassala on the border with Ethiopia, and stayed there for a month, finding it hard to drag themselves away from that remote and beautiful place, whose hospitable inhabitants operated to a leisurely rhythm so in tune with their own.

Ursula was full of ideas for still more ambitious journeys. She particularly wanted to go to Mexico – they had already procured Mexican and American visas before leaving London. But, having all the time in the world, and in Justin a companion who was open to any adventure, impervious to discomfort, and amenable to whatever she suggested, she was determined not to force the pace. She knew that she now had the ingredients she had always been looking for, which made it of vital importance not to make a mess of the cooking. There must be no constriction, no inhibition, no hurry, nothing but a sensual, graceful continuum, set in motion by the power of their love.

So they went back to spend another week or two at Sheikh Mohammed's, before driving up to Alexandria, where they booked a passage on a Norwegian cargo boat from Rotterdam to New York. Then they put the car on to a Russian ship bound for Limassol, where they arrived in April 1967. They stayed the summer in Cyprus. Justin wrote:

The early spring went straight to Ursula's head. It was a period of the intensest love. She lay through the long warm afternoons in scented, olive-shaded grass, with me beside her so desiring, so desired. She read or I read to her. She shopped in the market, and ate and drank as if appetite were a new discovery. One night on the waterfront a handsome gipsy danced angelically with a red-haired dwarf whore . . .

The paragraph defines, or at least illustrates, the stance that Justin and Ursula tried, for the most part successfully, to maintain in relation to their fellow-humans. The lovers are self-sufficient with their books in an Arcadian location, peopled by a cast of more or less picturesque characters, who can be observed or not, according to mood. The Cypriot landscape is close in spirit to that of Nysi, the corner of the Peloponnese where they were later to build their house. There was a dwarf there too, as well as a man who owned the air above his shop and proposed to build on it.

Ursula found it as hard to leave Cyprus as she had Sudan. In fact, leaving anywhere she had been happy was a perennial source of anguish to her – she dreaded the possibility of not returning. But they left and shipped the car, hopping from island to island, as far as Brindisi. In Rome, according to Justin, 'We walked round night and day, imagining in which part of this beautiful and profoundly natural city we would choose to live, if the opportunity arose.' That was for a future too distant to take seriously – they parked the car in a back-street and took the train to Rotterdam.

Ursula, who seemed able to cope perfectly well with the monstrous material inequalities of cities like Cairo and Istanbul, drew the line at New York. In addition to being morally outraged, she suffered simultaneously from both claustrophobia and vertigo. Her allergy to America and everything American infected Justin – he bought a rusty Oldsmobile for next to nothing, and in it, with blinkers rigidly adjusted, they roared down to the Mexican border. Once over it they relaxed slightly, but didn't begin to recover the slow-moving equilibrium that they had come to value so highly till reaching San Miguel, not far from Mexico City.

They got out of the car, stretching legs which ached from days of incessant driving and nervous tension, and looked around them. They saw an attractive town with a well-stocked public library for Ursula, a splendid botanical garden, and a cheap flat, which they promptly took for a period beginning the following month – their plan had been first to explore the country, then to settle down somewhere convenient and set up house for a while. In the meantime they checked into a hotel.

Travellers, who spend an appreciable amount of their time in hotel rooms, are usually sensitive to their atmosphere. Justin and Ursula preferred them to be decaying but elegant, generously proportioned, and capable of surprise. Ursula often described them in some detail in her journal, from which there follow a few examples:

MEXICO
Mérida
It was cool and spacious, with dark old furniture and ghosts of our favourite writers.

ECUADOR
Riobamba
Our hotel room spacious, ceiling painted with art nouveau motifs, wooden floor, slightly peeling wallpaper, good wooden doors and shutters, bedside tables, lurid red light coming in through the window and falling on the red satin cover of the disordered bed.

ECUADOR
Cuenca
The hotel is called Londres and has all the right qualities –
spacious, empty, and elegant in a localised, run-down, and
somehow memorable way. Wash-stand, white furniture,
pleasant colours. Comfort, peace, and a drink of aguar-
diente by candlelight.

As for the element of surprise, she wrote of a hotel in Casma,
in Peru:

The bathroom is full of huge snakes – the charmer is
analysing a couple in his room. There is trouble with the
hotel-keepers. Next day the doctor and his snaky patients
are waiting on the roadside for the morning bus.

Over dinner in a refreshingly un-American restaurant they
reassessed their situation. Although by now the habit of thrift
was becoming ingrained, travelling is by its nature expensive. If
they were going to last out, they would have to find some way
of making money. 'Why not writing?' one of them suddenly
asked. It's ironic that Justin and Ursula, two writers who sit
up and beg to be classified in the unfashionable but historically
respectable subspecies of dilettantism, should have begun
their careers with the brainwave that they could write pot-
boilers.

The brainwave was upstaged by a windfall. When he
married Ursula a month or two later, Justin wrote to my
parents announcing the news. My father, for whom the
elopement had caused considerable anxiety and embarrassment (he was, after all, a friend of Kenelm's) had evidently
come to the conclusion that it was time for a *rapprochement*.
He wrote back that Justin was due to come into a small private
income at the age of twenty-five. However, seeing that he was
now a married man and would be twenty-one next year, he
had made arrangements for the first instalment to be predated
to coincide with Justin's birthday.

Justin and Ursula collected my father's letter at the central
post office in Mexico City, and immediately subsided into a

bar to digest the implications. They worked out that, along with the money that Ursula was still given by Kenelm, the amount ought to be enough to support them adequately. So they never became professional writers. They remained amateurs, not only in the sense that neither of them ever did much more than go through the motions of submitting the occasional story for publication, but also in the more vital one that it would have seemed absurd to either to put writing before pleasure. Nevertheless the idea, conceived that evening in San Miguel, that they should, to some extent, think of themselves as artists, was destined to stick.

Next day they carried on southward, staying in Mexico City just long enough to collect their mail before winding their way down to Puerto Angel on the Pacific coast. It was a very primitive village, set in beautiful, lush, almost jungle landscape, dominated by the mountains behind – obviously a place to stay in. There was no hotel in the village, but they managed to find a room in a peasant house near a deserted cove. They spent the days on the beach. Justin made a hammock, which he hung between two trees. While Ursula was having her siesta in it, one of the ropes came undone and she fell awkwardly. Her back had never fully recovered from her accident in 1961, and any jolt, even one much less severe than this, could cause problems. She was in agony for three weeks. Justin was worried – their way of life was exposing her to unnecessary physical risk. He resolved to look after her better. Ursula was irritated by his concern, which struck her as patronising. Her horrified fascination with mortality made her particularly sensitive to the subject of her own, perhaps incipient, corporal decline. She had to be either perfect or dead. She insisted that there was nothing wrong with her that couldn't be cured by sun and swimming. She slowly recovered her strength.

One day Justin, with the ostensible purpose of presenting her with a coconut, but really to let off a bit of the steam that the constant awareness of physical incapacity dams up in the young and healthy, shinned up a tall palm. Putting all his weight on a frond that wasn't strong enough to withstand it, he fell from housetop height to the ground. Since he was naturally athletic, he succeeded in making a smooth landing and escaped unhurt. But Ursula was terrified, which made her furious. Justin later wrote:

> The shock made her understand the monstrous aloneness I was exposing her to. She saw me as childish and ridiculous, this male displaying his maleness in feats of daring, imperilling her hard-won freedom for the most idiotic of trophies – a coconut. She turned away in scorn.

It was difficult to imagine Justin and Ursula having a row, but that they sometimes did is confirmed by both of them in their writings. The passage from *Style* which follows illustrates both their differences and their similarities:

> Arguments, it's true, sometimes arose, usually as a result of the contrast in our earlier training; for instance, her principled attitude towards other people conflicted with my instinctive one. I was capable of unconsidered remarks and impetuous gestures, and if I was angry I didn't bother to disguise it. This anger distressed her, even though it was seldom directed at her personally. She felt hurt by the mere fact of being within earshot of it. And try as she might to dismantle the reflex, she couldn't prevent herself from memorising my offences, however slight. One either attacks openly at each recurrence, or one keeps quiet, hoping perhaps to correct the fault by contrasting example. The second was Ursula's approach, and though I always recognised the tactic, she sometimes doubted that I had. One's behaviour in love is determined in early childhood – Ursula knew only too well that her own training risked deforming the instincts that are at the base of all passion. So even when I wounded her, she realised that she was only really offended by the honesty of my manner, which was as natural to me as circumspection was to her. But afterwards I felt ashamed, thinking anxiously that I should change myself by curbing my impetuosity. On the other hand, I had a sense of my own passion that made me fear the consequences, were I ever to find myself unable to release

its excess . . . Perhaps what she regarded as my harshness was a necessary, if temporary, outlet for an energy which neither of us had yet learned to control. Perhaps it never could be absorbed sufficiently except in death. But I didn't wish to admit that, not to her at any rate; I merely understood, and continued more or less blindly to offer myself and to plead for continuity. I made her love her life to the limits of her capacity. The truth is that we were planted equally, complementarily in one another. Both rootless, volatile, we found stability together. At fifteen years old, that is before meeting Ursula, I had already assimilated the conviction that the world was in a state of precipitate decline, and that suicide was a logical personal antidote; finding that Ursula went so much further in a similar conviction enabled me to fight more vigorously for life, both hers and mine, so as to lay a solid foundation for the eventual conclusion of our story.

My father's letter wasn't the first good news to come their way poste restante in Mexico City. Calling there on their way back to San Miguel, they were handed a bulky envelope containing the official confirmation of Ursula's divorce. Their reaction was to drive straight to Guadalajara, where they were married in the Town Hall the following week. So when they moved into the flat at San Miguel, the first place they had lived in that they could legitimately call home, it was as a married couple.

A place of one's own is a liberating agent for even the most passionate addict of hotel rooms. They laid down their rugs and hung up their pictures in much the same spirit that I had observed at Sheikh Mohammed's, but here they had a front door key. They were both surprised at the difference this made – it seemed to confirm their slightly unwilling admission that they needed a proper base from which to operate. They immediately started to work out a routine – reading, writing, walking, cooking, photography – for filling the days with as much pleasure and variety as possible. But the routine was quickly interrupted by a liberating agent of a more specific kind.

While walking in the splendid open country outside San Miguel, they found some mushrooms. Ursula, probably mistaking them for some European species of similar appearance, included them in the risotto she was making for the evening meal. After supper they couldn't stop laughing. At first they put this down to the absurdity of their wonderful life, but soon there was no escaping that something unusual was going on – it was absolutely imperative to make love. Of course, that wasn't in itself unusual, but the persistence and violence of the sensation immediately afterwards certainly was. From then until dawn they were sailing on an enormous wave of lust – uninhibited, inventive, and interrupted only by occasional gales of helpless laughter.

At last they went to sleep – till late afternoon. When they awoke and reviewed the phenomenon, they decided, with the mixture of puritanism and common sense that allowed these two reformed desperados to keep all branches of their sensuality within manageable limits, not to eat any more of the mushrooms, but to try and find a way of achieving the same results without their help. They bottled the remaining specimens, intending to have them properly analysed in Mexico City. However, perhaps because they failed to dry them properly, the bottle was found, on opening, to contain nothing but a buzzing colony of bright green-gold flies.

Though sex undoubtedly loomed large in their early mutual attraction, it would be quite wrong to assume, as some biased outsiders do to this day, that Ursula, subtle and serpentine voluptuary, had pounced on the teenager she'd earmarked as most likely to satisfy her, just as it would be wrong to assume that she was after his money. In fact she was late in realising her sexual potential, and was afterwards apt to discount her experiences before meeting Justin as so much preparation for the real thing. As for Justin, his youth at the beginning of the affair surely precluded any real understanding of sex, which needs time and love, experience and imagination, trial and error for the disclosure of its secrets. So their sexual relationship, like that of many couples, only gradually developed. With reference to the mushroom incident, Justin wrote, 'After that we made love with ever-increasing ingenuity and no diminution of passion; the drug had done its job by casting a searchlight on our erotic territory.'

In the public library of San Miguel, Ursula was planning their next adventure, an ambitious Far-Eastern voyage of exploration. At the travel agency Justin was researching the cheapest way of getting to London, their next intermediate port of call. After a last trip, via Oaxaca to Mérida in the Yucatan, they embarked on a Dutch boat with a cargo of coffee and tobacco at Belize. They arrived in England in the spring of 1969.

The first thing they did in London was get themselves married all over again at the register office of Chelsea Town Hall, with Max as witness. It might be thought that such conscientious double-checking would run counter to their romanticism – but that would be to underrate the combativeness in Justin's nature. Aware of being at odds with the bureaucratic world, he was always careful not to give it a chance of catching him with his pants down. He also had an intuitive understanding of the way the controlling forces worked – if he'd been dealt a different hand, he might have made a brilliant shop-steward, say, or even a film producer. Just as he wouldn't have dreamt of setting out on a Saharan crossing without two spare tyres, a gun, three days' supply of water, and a medicine chest, he came to know the languages of civil law and accountancy, at any rate as far as they concerned him personally, like the back of his increasingly muscular hand. The possibility of their Mexican marriage being invalid might have had unfortunate consequences for their finances.

These were now, in fact, even healthier than they had expected, my father having prudently understated the case in his letter to Mexico. Justin, who had attained his majority rather queasily in mid-Atlantic on board the cargo boat, met my father to sign the final documents. As well as a parental blessing, which contained an element of forgiveness, and the first instalment of his income, he was given the money for a new car as his birthday present. His choice, a Citroën 2cv van, showed Ursula's influence – aesthetic considerations should always go hand in hand with utilitarian requirements.

If there's anything more stimulating to the spirit than a shiny new car, it's a fat cheque. Heading for Paris in the one and stopping to eat an unusually self-indulgent Norman lunch on the strength of the other, Justin and Ursula felt light-headed and -hearted in equal measure. On arrival they took a room in a hotel in the Rue-St-André-des-Arts, which represented a move up the social scale. Then something happened which checked, if only momentarily, their euphoria – that something, unfortunately, was me.

I had heard that they were in Paris and, since I was passing through at the time – though travelling in the opposite direction – I rang them up and arranged to meet them in their hotel. It was April but cold, and Ursula was still in her winter feathers – soft leather boots and blond fur-coat. Cold weather suited her. When she smiled to show all her pointed little teeth, the effect was as sparkly and invigorating as that of icicles in the sunshine. But as we sat down to dinner in a restaurant, small, warm, and extremely well-chosen by Ursula, I quickly understood the cause of a niggling anxiety that I had registered, though not diagnosed, in Egypt – I wanted to talk to each of them in a different conversational form. Ursula was wonderful company, with her lucid delicacy of expression and eager sense of the ridiculous, but I felt inhibited from enjoying myself as much as I'd have liked by Justin's rather glowering presence beside her. On the other hand, it was him I was so keen to find out more about, to get closer to – and my concentration was distracted by the effervescent atmosphere she created. They seemed to function in antithetical cerebral areas – Ursula was strong on classification, generalisation, Justin on slanted comment and detail. This was a superficial distinction – ignorant of the central spring of their mutual attraction, I was simply fumbling for the slightest available insight.

Most of all I wanted to separate them for a moment or two. I suggested to Justin that we should have a drink alone together next day. He declined with the utmost brusqueness – the idea apparently struck him as being in the worst of taste. I said goodbye to them regretfully, with a feeling of frustration and wasted chances.

* * *

During the heady period of their Greek honeymoon at
Bourdzi, Justin and Ursula had put in a few days' travelling
round the Peloponnese – they were particularly attracted to
the area of Koroni, on its south-western tip. They now
modified their original plan, deciding to spend most of the
summer there before setting off for India. They rented a little
house in the town, and spent the days swimming, walking,
and reading. Justin bought a Greek grammar, and practised
what he had learnt on the locals.

Ursula, without really being a linguist, had spoken five
languages with varying degrees of proficiency at one time of
her life or another, whereas Justin's knowledge of languages
was confined to schoolboy French. He had a natural ear
though and, just as important, a hitherto latent taste for
sustained application. So it was he, not she, who worked at
mastering Greek. In fact, after meeting Justin, she gave up
bothering with languages, having always been conscious
anyway that her multilingualism was a threat to her fragile
sense of racial identity. She also enjoyed the adjustment in the
balance of power that resulted from his increasing competence
as mouthpiece and interpreter – she needed him to be
dominant, and encouraged this whenever she could.

It interested me that Ursula, who hardly ever made a direct
reference to herself in conversation, even to the extent of
frequently using the pronoun 'one' when 'I' would have
seemed more natural, would sometimes remark, 'I'm a
peculiarly lazy person', or 'Industry, as you know, isn't exactly
my forte.' She would say it with a good-humoured mixture of
pride and regret – pride, as I understand it, because idleness
fitted in with her own very idiosyncratic idea of what's meant
by aristocracy, and regret because she knew that she would
never do the great things for which she was otherwise
equipped. But that doesn't explain why she should have
broken her rule of reticence to draw attention to her own
qualities. One explanation is that her remark was a reference
to Justin, the final clause of a half-spoken sentence that might
have run: I shelter behind Justin's vitality, perseverance, and
all-round capabilities, since by preference 'I'm a peculiarly

lazy person.' The omission would have been prompted by tact – if she was naturally private, so was Justin, and it would have seemed an unnecessary exposure to praise him in public.

Although her protestations of laziness may have been made in this ulterior spirit, you could also see what she meant. Her laziness, far from being a source of guilt, was a luxury almost, a style. It gave her intense pleasure to lie curled in the boat while Justin was battling against the elements. But apart from this obvious, feline sort of laziness, she was also lazy in a long-term, existential sense. She liked to formulate a rough plan of action, so that she could then go dreamily through the motions of its execution, with no other purpose in mind than that of living through the days in the agreeable (a favourite word, that) way she had chosen. This was because, cursed with an analytical mind, she preferred, if possible, not to use it.

I was told (by the architect Chris Leeming) that Rossini was so lazy that he did all his composing in bed. One day, just as a closely notated sheet of manuscript-paper was nearing completion, some over-industrious movement of his wrist caused it to flutter to the floor. Rossini, rather than get out of bed to pick it up, wrote the entire sheet over again, meanwhile making significant melodic improvements on the first version.

Suppose he had dropped his pen? Rossini wrote some very good music. If he had been differently constructed, he would probably have written either no music at all or enormous quantities of rubbish. The anecdote, apocryphal or not, shows among other things that his laziness was necessary to him.

Ursula's life, I think, was a kind of success story. She achieved every goal she set herself – a great deal of laughter, of euphoria, of exploration, the fruition of her intelligence, a tremendous love, and an early death. The things she failed to achieve – publication, procreation, a serene old age – were things she had never wanted. And if she suffered some terrible pain, particularly at the end of her life, she understood that it was the price she had to pay for going consistently against the grain of conventional standards. Her much-vaunted talent for laziness was one of the cornerstones of her 'success'.

The stay in Koroni had an uneasy purpose – househunting. One side of Ursula wanted a home to settle down in like everybody else, another rebelled violently against the idea. She and Justin later resolved this split by trying to get the best of both worlds. As you read through the journals year after year, however, and compare the insatiable delight that Ursula took in their house in Greece with the uncertainty and pessimism that often seems to emanate from the pages on Asia or Africa, it's hard to suppress a feeling of anguish. Suicide in early or middle life inevitably leaves the survivors with an aching sense of incompletion and an unending list of 'if only's on the tip of the tongue.

Ursula was the best-disguised of all the gifted neurotics I've known, many of whom, in spite of handicaps apparently ten times more crushing than hers, have managed to survive. If only she could have seen her life in the context of theirs, she would have realised that her strength outweighed her weakness. If only she'd had a means of measuring her capacity for happiness against theirs, she wouldn't have dared undervalue it. If only she'd understood that her beauty, her physicality were the least part of her claim to immortality, she wouldn't have overvalued them. If only she'd confided her impatience to some spiritual equal other than Justin – who was far too involved to be of much use – she might have been convinced of its futility. If only she had humbled herself to the extent of undergoing psychoanalysis, she would have been one of the likeliest beneficiaries of that maligned service – all that was needed was the building of a slender philosophical bridge for negotiating her imaginary chasm between youth and middle-age. If only she had built and crossed that bridge, there would have been less and less need for the periodic testing of courage, endurance of hardship, forcing of vitality implied by the journeys to Asia and Africa. She could have lived happily with Justin between Greece and Rome, if not for ever after, at least until some natural cause intervened.

But these whines of impotence, whimpers of desolation, are no help at all in deciphering the network of contradictions that is the map of an individual's destiny. We, the survivors, by voicing them, were merely lamenting that she wasn't someone else, when we should have been searching for clues about who she was. Ursula's wanting, and simultaneously not wanting, a place of her own is such a clue. Here are two journal entries, from January 1970 in Bangkok, and March 1979 of the flat in Rome, respectively: 'One longs for a house, a flat, a room.' And 'We return here as if to a favourite hotel . . . Given plenty of money we would in any case surely live in hotels.' In May 1978 she wrote of Nysi, the home she had built with Justin, 'I am getting dangerously attached to this place.' And in August 1979, again of Nysi, 'I want to go and yet I want to stay.'

Meanwhile they looked at every empty house in the neighbourhood of Koroni, half-longingly, half-satirically weighing up pros and cons. In early September they packed up and set off for Asia with no decision having been made.

They drove unhurriedly to Istanbul, along the coast of the Black Sea, then down to Bayburt and into Iran. The first entry of Ursula's journal was written in Isfahan. She perhaps intended it to be little more than the log of one particular journey, but the habit persisted, with the result that the document records her life with Justin, in an almost uninterrupted flow of observation and reflection, from September 1969 to a few days before her death in March 1981.

Justin included some 250 pages of the journal in *Style*. What he didn't include he burned. He sensibly thought that its quality and autobiographical interest would represent her better than any reconstruction he could write of the period it covers. While I too was extremely impressed, I found that, read consecutively, its bulk was impossible to digest, although I still agreed with Justin that, handed a day-to-day résumé of Ursula's thought-processes on a plate, her biographer ought to rely on it as an essential source. I decided to make a drastic selection. Afterwards, finding that a certain monotony of tone still persisted – no fault of Ursula's, since she wrote without any idea of publication – I began to divide the journal into sections corresponding, loosely speaking, either to the length of one of their voyages of exploration or else to a year or so of ordinary living, and then to punctuate the sections with elucidatory passages of my own, whose prosaic nature contrasted with the obsessional and poetic diction of much of the journal.

My selection was based roughly on these principles: a pruning of the repetitiveness unavoidable in a spontaneous record of this kind, the exclusion of commonplace-book quotations from Latin, Greek, French, Italian, and Arabic poetry, and the omission of references to bit-part players, mentioned only once or twice, whose names would sound arbitrary to the reader.

Then there was the question of editing. The journal was, for the most part, rapidly written and left uncorrected. The spelling mistakes, haphazard punctuation, and constructions that were occasionally muddled or else left trailing were all quite easily remedied. What was more difficult was that Ursula didn't always write English as correctly as she spoke it. You'd be excused for thinking that for a foreigner to make the odd grammatical error when writing a language not her own is not only natural but touching, even picturesque. But, knowing the sharpness of Ursula's speech, I found it increasingly hard to accept – until finally I was obliged, with a minimum of alteration, to anglicise her language occasionally, while remaining faithful to her style and tone of voice.

7

Ursula's journals

IRAN
Isfahan. September 1969
The further the better. The stranger the landscape the lighter
the heart. No responsibilities, no attachments, no belongings.
The secret delight of having no identity – the foreigner, the
traveller, of no fixed address.

To be fortunate, to know one is fortunate. Often one is not
quite equal to knowing it, yet trembles on the verge of
knowing it completely, superstitious with regard to one's own
good fortune.

In the afternoon, just as we get to the first stretch of good
road, there is a smack on the windscreen, which shatters with
a finely modulated sound into a sheet of patterned crystal. An
odd, cold, fatal feeling. How easy it is to smash a whole into
fragments, how sudden. Is one ready to die? I almost think so,
may my presumption be forgiven.

A group of mud huts in the middle of nowhere. Our host is
an extravagantly handsome, aristocratic old man, who also
speaks English. The men are magnificent – tall, sabre-nosed,
prophetically bearded, with brilliant teeth. Dressed in huge
turbans, cloaks, voluminous trousers, and equipped with guns
and daggers. The younger men wear skull-caps embroidered
with shiny stones and bits of mirror – lovely oval faces,
beautiful hands. They hold hands amorously with the bearded
warriors.

PAKISTAN
Baluchistan
Exactly the feeling I hoped for – camels, goatherds, rifle-shots
echoing in the dry hills, men dressed in purple and yellow,
horses, women loaded with jewels and veils walking with the
swaying gait of camels. Lavender fields in the hills.

Lahore
The sadness of decay is hidden by the dusk – the beauty and
luxuriousness emerge. Something beautiful in this homeless-
ness – a man can bed down anywhere.

INDIA
Agra. October 1969
The really poor camp in the garden of the royal tomb,
crouched between little piles of personal belongings and
mounds of public rubbish.

This misery, the direst I ever saw, affects me quite
differently than I thought it would. I feel no charity, I am
frightened. I never get rid of the feeling 'There, but for the
grace of God, go I.' Everything is possible, not just in theory
either. I am sure of nothing, least of all my own character.
How one might end up is a matter of chance. I can understand
pushing others out of the boat.

There is something about moonlight that I don't like –
something uncanny, mocking, odd. Like moving under water
with limited breath.

Fatehpur
Looking at the view, waiting for a line of smoke to shift
position, I travelled over a year of my life, approaching it from
this and that angle. In ten minutes the smoke was diffused all
over the village, and now I'm ten minutes older.

I am reading Fielding and am plunged into the frame of
mind this particular period of English literature always
produces – a robust, secure enjoyment. Not at all secure in the
permanent sense, just in the fleeting one, which seems to me
more important.

Chunar

Woke in the cool dark to the swishing, crumpled sound the sweeper was making with the fallen leaves outside. I thought we were somewhere in Burgundy, and that it was a dark autumn morning. The country in the mist before sunrise was like an illusory Burgundy too – an old forest of oak-like *ficus*. Some disease has eaten away the fleshy leaves, so that they are a silken gold, autumnal. But the hopping, long-tailed monkeys and wizened black women with their wizened dugs and cruel anklets soon brought me back to India. Nevertheless I went on thinking about my house and garden in Burgundy.

Benares

There is an unparalleled indifference. Youth, beauty, age, disease, horror and death all side by side with no attempt to separate, salvage, escape. Will it help now and then to have seen it, grasped at it even? To know that, when it's your turn, it's all the same, it makes no difference. The corpses turn transparent on the pyre – when they are rotated, they throw off sparks, like logs. Meanwhile the skulls and bones are cracked, to hasten the dissolution – a sharp, explosive sound.

Calcutta

Quite as bad as one imagined and even greyer. Desolate faces crouched over rubbish heaps, fingers turning over the putrid matter very slowly. Rickshaw drivers in a row with blank, ugly, exhausted faces. A form of hypocrisy, surely, prevents one from taking a rickshaw. I think one is also ashamed of being pulled along by someone whose body is so under-nourished. Dirt, neglect – a town petrified since the war. A man on the pavement absolutely naked – thin legs, bowed head, neck outstretched. Beggars without legs, without arms, or without eyes, one after another creeping towards the door of our car.

THAILAND
Bangkok. December 1969

We sit among heaps of withering flowers left over from some religious service yesterday evening. Out of one heap crawls a dog, soundless and slow. His hindquarters are smashed – he pulls out the mangled meat and bone behind him patiently. There is no one to put him out of his misery, though the Thais are kind to animals. Only two steps away a woman is feeding some cats on rice. But you can't kill a dog, you haven't the wherewithal, and besides it would be shocking. The first nausea, indignation, and desire for immediate action subside. One of a million, not one's job, etc. It would be as well to remember that train of thought while lying in the gutter oneself.

Two round-headed, round-eyed, long-armed monkeys clutching each other desperately in a box in the market. One has been sold, but it's impossible to separate them.

A short night, full of false awakenings, in a bus, riding through still towns before dawn. Anaemic lights and dustbins – chilly and mysterious.

CAMBODIA
Phnom Penh
Can't get that little boy out of my mind, the one who howled so desperately last night, lost on the street corner. Why does one never do anything?

In the narrow hall, under blazing neon light, seven people sleeping in a row, completely covered in ghostly white.

I woke up feeling very ill – hot and cold, sweaty, searing stomach, tremulous weakness. It went on all day. When I'm ill I feel oddly moved by everything I see. Things are more uncertain, and so more precious. Funny little boys selling lottery tickets and chattering, a beautiful old woman. I observe my metabolism with anxiety and devotion – my character is quite distorted by illness of any kind.

Royal festivity – a regatta. Long, elegant barges with turned-up prows, rowed by dozens of men in red and yellow sarongs, swaying backwards and forwards like a field of corn in the wind. All the royal barges are out – the distant curve of the Mekong river is spiky with them, as in an ancient battle-scene.

Angkor
Bicycling through the jungle. The ruined palace with its

completely wild garden. A bird cries, exciting, tense. A pause, then the answer comes. Strange noises in the undergrowth and in the treetops. Whenever I stop I tremble with utter exhaustion, though I didn't feel tired at all when moving along. I loathe my body's shortcomings. I shall have to die fairly young, because I won't be able to live with the infirmities of old age.

Lying on the stone platform, thinking rather aimlessly of my past, my present, and again my past. Fragments, nothing but fragments. I wasn't even I, just a succession of indifferent mistakes made by myself. God save me from being judged by them.

A boat up the Mekong river to Kratie. We are leaving Cambodia tomorrow – we shall probably never return. How many times do I have to know this?

MALAYA
Penang
I should like to see Fellini's *Satyricon*, go to a concert, see Shakespeare on stage, eat a light French dinner with good wine. And wear a new dress, professional, immaculate. How petty I am. An overdose of travel? But I'm still afraid there won't be time for all the things I like best.

THAILAND
Chumphon
Watching the rice fields passing from the train, I thought about my childhood. Does it bother me still? Will it always? It doesn't surprise me, but I'm hoping for a miracle, I suppose. The rain crashes down.

Bangkok. January 1970
Read *The Economist* on the troubles in Laos. Just as well we travelled by train. How ridiculous I am with my infantile Spartanness – can't help feeling vaguely guilty when I choose the safer, more comfortable way. Do I still need to test my courage? Certainly it's years since I've had an opportunity of being brave in the conventional, physical sense. Yet if I

imagine the gun, the suicide pill, the pain, I know I wouldn't flinch. More a matter of pride than courage.

Little spells of summer morning cool. Yes, I miss Europe.

Too weak to get up this morning. My heart pumped and I felt dangerously empty. It is now 2 p.m. I am alone and nearly normal, but don't feel as well as I would if J. were here. My dependence is now complete. I question my body but never my love.

The museum in the morning. The quality I now look for in visual art is repose – specially if there is any chance of ownership. We bought a gilt monk, heavily patinaed, on a base of red wood – a simple, handsome object and an honest piece of sculpture. One longs for a house, a flat, a room.

INDIA
Calcutta
At Nizam's we had a long talk about our need for each other. Is this dangerous? Is it too simple a thing to talk about so much? Be that as it may, I feel so peaceful now that I have staked everything on one card.

Puri. February 1970
Travel with open, dispassionate eyes – take it all in, absorb, try to remember. Has my overburdened retentive system got room for more material? Have I ever had any talent, any ambition, other than the ability to retain? Every day must yield its quota, because there's nothing to be gained from the past.

Hyderabad
The dreadful pity I feel for the humble, the ignorant, the obliging – and the dreadful impatience that accompanies it. But I do my best, and on the whole manage to be polite, even tactful.

Srirangapatna. Scott's bungalow. March 1970
An adequate house. We may rent it for the summer. A big, lovely rainfall – everything smells magnificent. The river is pale and whipped. Rivers smell differently from anything else,

a clear smell, full of memories impossible to define. Something odd about this midday light, something altogether uncertain about the time of day. Monkeys balance on branches above the muddy water. An eagle hovers overhead, lit through by the sun and greenish-white.

J. is building a temporary garage, the consistency of which changes. Most of the materials prove unsuitable sooner or later and have to be changed. A lengthy, sometimes annoying task.

I lie half-awake for half an hour under the mosquito-net, moving my fingers over the familiar contours of the brown body beside me, shoulders, back and neck. How natural this happiness has become.

May 1970
An immense storm in the evening. Afterwards the bamboo screen on the terrace is adorned with white beads of water. The sky a sombre violet-red, the grass squelching underfoot, the channels overflowing.

The room we spend most time in is cool and low, thick-walled. The deep, black-shuttered windows are nearly always closed for privacy. Two solid white pillars, dark-grey polished granite floor. Our odd collection of books on the shelf – Penguin classics and Greek primers, *Guides Bleus*, paperbacks from the Rive Gauche. The Greek torso I bought in Istanbul such a long time ago props up a manuscript stolen from the winter rooms of the Friday Mosque in Isfahan. The splendid, vigorous little bronzes from Hyderabad, a Rajasthan horse silhouetted against the whitewash, and two miniatures – the man in the red kaftan, and the drawing of two heads, which I think identical and J. quite different. A long white table with a basket full of limes and a wooden lime-squeezer from the bazaar. Another table with a mirror, my old bottle of Hermès, and the prehistoric wooden comb from Mexico. A bamboo bed, a mat, a lantern, and our suitcases – from Athens, Rome, Oaxaca. We fit into them, which is gratifying.

June 1970
The cemetery – obelisks, urns, and quasi-Roman mausoleums like tents under the feathery palms and mangoes. Springy,

undulating turf, and a hazy view of the river, blue and curtained by heavy trees. The funerary pyramids in the foreground – Agnes McGregor died in 1800 aged thirty-three, and someone else who died while discharging his duty during an epidemic. I should like to be buried somewhere warm and still. But I'd prefer to be a handful of ashes cast over the sea.

Always head for the south as if by instinct – but not beyond the Equator. I always have a map of the world in my mind when I think of my life.

A long grey snake is sunning himself on the rocks – we sun ourselves too. Each instance of desire, of wild comprehension makes me remember how little time there is left. After sunset J. reads Yeats to me. We sit in the English cemetery, J. smoking a cigar.

July 1970
I am conscious of feeling well, both on the surface and in my bones. Lying on the tomb where F.F. died aged twenty-six, under a mango tree.

J. is learning to sing Don Giovanni's serenade. I read my typescript of his poems, which are visibly improving.

A letter from J.'s nanny in reply to his. She is happy to hear he had a happy childhood, in spite of the influence of one Charlie Simpson.

A stupid argument, the result of my old fears – but reconciliation. I love him so perfectly that each little crack in the structure opens up a vista of total annihilation.

August 1970
Five more years would do me very well, but I said that five years ago. Cowardice? It's absurd to speculate about the future.

Bundi. November 1970
After a squabble over the best approach to buying a chicken, we talked about my bouts of horror. I am still too proud to show him the chinks in my armour, but sometimes all the ghosts converge to overwhelm me. They come more rarely now, but it's time they went away entirely. I have everything,

and while I still have it, it's blasphemy to feel that old desperation.

Goa, Aurangabad, Ellora, Ajanta, Mandu, Bajasthan, and other stops that I'm sure I've forgotten. Back towards Europe.

December 1970
We were offered the chance of riding in a forest. I was thrown by a stallion, and now I have an aching back.

Bikaner
The Moghul palace – flimsy architecture, magnificent carpets. Marble terraces with cushions, moonlit trees, and lovers gazing into one another's eyes. I feel very peaceful, splendidly idle. Propped up at night, my back is improving.

Delhi
Car trouble – the mechanics of existence. We don't suffer from them much, and so resent them all the more.

Peshawar
J. is in a high fever. I read to him – Rousseau, Tacitus, Apollinaire. One might be in Tsarist Russia here. Pale, bearded faces, skull-caps, necklaces, cartridge-belts. Fat businessmen of Semitic aspect – red hair, Astrakhan caps – counting money and drinking green tea from china cups. Tea-houses with long daisies growing from rotting wooden verandahs. Grinning sheep's heads by the trayful. I sometimes feel a nostalgia for a past I never knew.

AFGHANISTAN
Through the Khyber Pass. Teutonic attitudes among the police. Tribesmen with guns, louts in uniform. Then paler, Chinese-featured people in striped kaftans and skull-caps. A few camels in the stony desert – then the climb.

Herat
I couldn't sleep. Often my brain continues to buzz long after I have forgotten what got me going in the first place – for

instance, the name of a garment worn by the shepherds in
Hungary.

IRAQ
February 1971
Three ivory statuettes from Minrud. A plaque of a lioness
overpowering a young negro. What an erotic idea, to be made
love to by a lion.

TURKEY
Down towards the sea over mountainsides covered in narcissi.
Rainbows over the brilliant green slopes. Tarsus for lunch –
excellent *fasoulia*. Up again into the mountains, olives silver
in the wind. Sturdy horses. Rocky terraces, white villages.

Istanbul
The strange, familiar feeling of wandering round the empty
rooms of museums. Through the windows glimpses of the
world of trees and smells and temperature – inside nothing but
the dead world of frozen faces and gestures.
   I got depressed in my insane, ungrateful, petty way. J.
again got me out of it. Dinner on the bridge. We'll be in
Greece tomorrow.

* * *

*I mentioned earlier that Ursula's journals reveal, almost to the
point of obsession, an egocentricity that I never glimpsed in the
course of a fairly close acquaintance. I was equally surprised
by the extent of her preoccupation with death. Anything could
remind her of it, not only obviously morbid images – a
cemetery, the Ganges at Benares, a mutilated dog, the
vicissitudes of her own health – but apparently healthy ones
too. The snake which suns itself beside her on the rock suggests
to her how little time there is left. And 'I love him so perfectly
that each little crack in the structure opens up a vista of total
annihilation.' Health and love and happiness had to be seen in
unremitting juxtaposition with death, in order that she
shouldn't be caught unawares, shouldn't waste time. If Ursula
hadn't finally cracked under the strain of sustaining the near-
perfection that she discovered with Justin, her constant need to*

*make the connection between the beauty of life and the omni-
presence of mortality would have appeared as a philosophic
strength. But suicide, rightly or wrongly, suggests weakness,
with the result that these reiterations strike you as fruitless,
unhealthy. However, the feeling obtrudes only in the Asian
journal, written before the pattern of her new life was properly
established, and while her earlier depression and sense of
futility were still fresh in her mind. The sections that follow,
written in Greece and Rome, leave different tastes in the
mouth. I'm not implying that her consciousness of death ever
left her for very long – only that, tamed somewhat by her
happiness, it retreated for substantial periods to the background
of her mind. Sometimes she mentions it cursorily, but the
mention sounds superstitious, only for the ears of certain gods,
to whom she owed the odd placatory gesture.*

    *Justin and Ursula chose to divide their living – as opposed to
their travelling – between Greece and Rome. It sounds naive,
but I never, until this moment of writing, made the 'Glory and
Grandeur' connection. Justin, and particularly Ursula, must
surely have done so from time to time, but they never referred
to it, either in conversation with me or in any of their writings.
They weren't at all interested in following in historical
footsteps. In fact, their failure to relate their lives to the
historical continuum contributed to their undoing. Ursula
chose the two places purely because of the contrasting and
complementary opportunities they offered for her requirements.
I say Ursula, not Justin and Ursula, because, although the
balance of power between them evened out in ways that I shall
explain, it was always she who made the geographical choices,
she whose every move was made with 'a map of the world in
my mind'.*

    *Ursula's requirements. She had discovered that the fulfil-
ment of her spirit depended on the paring down, the refinement
of her needs. It wasn't that she and Justin followed any
specially Spartan regime, in spite of the proximity of Sparta to
their headland at Nysi. After all they had a house, a flat, a car,
they ate and drank well, they travelled. It was more that she
had weighed up what she needed, and discarded everything
that she thought superfluous or wasteful. But the sloughing*

of her thriving social life and her habitual extravagances didn't make her a nun – she still needed an outlet for two highly developed but opposed facets of her nature: sensuality and urbanity. Hence the need for two properties, one to accommodate each.

By 1971 Ursula understood her requirements in all their depth and simplicity – that's unusual enough. That she could then translate this understanding into the invention of a set of rules for living, which she followed rigorously for the next ten years, was a major achievement, and one of the justifications of this book. But without her habitual luck, she wouldn't have been able to do it. She fell in love with a boy who turned into a man with precisely the qualities she needed, and who also had enough money to devote himself to her physical and spiritual comfort, without any extraneous commitment, or even interest, getting in the way.

It's been suggested to me that Ursula, the calculating adventuress, banked on Justin's money from the start. This can be discounted for two reasons – first, that she had already married the indigent Kenelm, with whom she hadn't even pretended to be in love, and second, that Justin, in contrast with many of her rejected suitors, neither had, nor was ever likely to get, more than a rather moderate inheritance. If Kenelm and Justin had divided their combined, unearned, annual incomes in half – if you'll excuse the bizarre hypothesis – the resulting sum would just about have paid the wages of a hard-working bricklayer. Calculating and adventurous she may have been at various stages of her life, but gold-digger she was not. Nor, when she met Justin, was either calculation or adventure controlling her moves – Ursula eloped with him desperately, almost involuntarily. That's why I call it luck that it should have been Justin that she found.

GREECE
Athens. April 1971
All our usual hotels are full, and in consequence we find the best one yet. Dinner in Monastiraki – barrels, marble counter, workmen, tarts, all the same as ever. But they have pulled down our little wine-shop.

Koroni

Our old friend, the lady with the straw hat, has the perfect house to rent. We are welcomed everywhere as old acquaintances – and potential suckers in some quarters. After giving us coffee, she shows us the inside of her delectable house, and compliments *me* on my grasp of Greek. Ah well, nature compensates the blind.

I am reading Chateaubriand, alternating each passage with a long look into the gentle blue sea, quite unlike the sea of his stormy childhood. How moving his sonority is, quite like music. Certain sentences fill my eyes with tears.

Being haunted, as I am, by change, by ugliness, I am incapable of staying permanently in my own back garden. I need virgin landscape, *terra incognita*. It's something in my metabolism – my Asian ancestors' mania for space? But to live in a really great city would equal living in the wastes of Guatemala. I would like to go to Brazil. And the austere nostalgia of Borges reminds me of Argentina as if I had already been there.

I painted the window-frames in the morning, and J. carried on after lunch. Something fell with a crash in the night, and afterwards I couldn't sleep for thinking about the wit of my interrupted dream, which took the form of an analysis of love. I was someone like myself but not so fortunate.

May 1971

We quarrelled and made it up. Our quarrels result chiefly from my dissatisfaction with myself, which flares up into exaggeration, both verbal and emotional.

We suddenly heard a Turkish song on the radio – a morose, virile voice declaiming to some plucked instrument, the cadences almost Indian. What a voice, and how those associations move something very low down in me.

More maid's work. I feel domesticated in the extreme.

One dislikes the idea of anyone coming to disrupt the perfection of one's privacy. Life goes by, but it's marvellous to be conscious that one couldn't be spending it better.

The bay is empty, the water choppy. I remember that month at Bourdzi, the first time I was in Greece with J., as being neither in the past nor in any recognisable time-scale – the archetypal summer of luxurious freshness and burning heat, immense stillness punctuated by the slight, recurrent noises the little fish made in the mornings, while we ate our breakfast alone on that stone terrace, surrounded by that immaculate blue. Peaches, toast and honey. Floating in the cool water afterwards, feeling one's happiness as one feels one's skin. The hot, mad wind in the afternoon and falling from the iron ladder into the great salty waves.

Siesta, love-making. Velvety nights when fish jump into one's lap as one is carried ashore. Greece is paradise on this imperfect earth.

The villagers look stupid and uncomfortable in their Sunday best. I am very pleased that for me Sundays seem to have sunk, along with most other trappings, to the bottom of the sea.

Thunder at first, then a few big drops of rain, then the sun again. I can feel one of those oncomings of enlightenment which constitute my principal way of atoning for my selfishness, my happiness. But I haven't really any ethical instincts. My desire to be taken for myself isn't ethical but temperamental – I can't be honest in any other way, and honesty to oneself is the only convenient way of living.

Long swim, heaving water. White-crested waves in the middle of the bay. I stretch and pull like an oiled machine. I, who get exhausted so easily on land, am indefatigable in water.

June 1971
The old man next door is gardening as usual. The other day he sang for the whole afternoon – a quiet recitative in a young boy's voice which sometimes became a young girl's. He is about seventy-five.

I have qualms about my selfishness, but I still believe it to be right.

We had another argument, this time about Baudelaire, lengthy and finally resolved. I can't help wishing it had never occurred. All roughness rankles. It's new for me to be honest enough to argue – after all, I used to be such an accomplished

listener, ready and willing to forgo remarking on anything I
disagreed with.

I am slightly tired, so slightly I hardly know why I wrote it.
In the afternoon I swam over the regions of darkness out into
the clear, clear blue, feeling nothing in particular. Just feeling
mortal, maybe.

July 1971
Hot, windblown, amorous afternoon – total pleasure is very
like madness, in that all control of one's own self is gone, one's
body feels like a lake from which something huge and
irresistible is rising – or in which something is lurking.

Swimming at night in the pitch dark, surrounded by little
pools of phosphorescence. Making love on the rock under an
enormously deep, starry sky. Next morning brilliant – lying in
the shadows eating figs, white and blue, watching a red caique
go past. The essence of perfect summer, of happiness, of the
Mediterranean, or even, dare I say it, of home.

I woke up tired – every little movement, dusting, washing,
dressing, gave me a sensation of being about to faint. Even
swimming began to tire me. The afternoon was hellish – I felt
like a cripple, unable to concentrate, even to think. At night in
the café we talked. But I can never properly convey to him my
horror of myself or my fear of losing him.

I always feel like smiling in the water.

Wading through the papers – John Osborne, the dollar
crisis, drugs. One's desire to be *au courant*, to keep oneself
informed, is constant. Perhaps only in extreme youth and
extreme old age is one wholly indifferent to the affairs of the
outside world.

September 1971
Meredith's contrivances in the English language are beginning
to irritate me. To experiment so pretentiously you need
Shakespearian accomplishment.

Am I getting wiser or more sentimental? Sometimes the
truth of something, or some sensual impression suggesting
truth, chokes me and mists my eyes. To know you are alive is
an insupportably strong sensation.

I am more totally at ease than ever before. I should like to drink the sea up. I count the days in a daze of realisation, as if this were all a memory already.

We are going, going. Sea and summer. I wouldn't mind drowning. I was too happy here. Standing above the foaming, tremendous sea, we see two dolphins leap.

* * *

Soon after arriving in Rome that autumn, with the mixture of good luck, lack of fuss, and sheer instinct that characterised their decision-making, they found, and immediately started negotiating for, a flat in one of their favourite parts of town. The Vicolo del Cinque is one of a maze of busy, low, narrow streets, not far from the Piazza Sta Maria in Trastevere. With its little tailor shops and garages specialising in the repair of clanking old scooters, the quarter has a rackety, metropolitan toughness. Diminutive layabouts whistle at girls at least a head taller than themselves on every street-corner. For all that, the neighbourhood has a kind of chic – there are patrician palazzi, a couple of famous and beautiful churches, and numerous restaurants catering for a clientele far more affluent than the indigenous Trasteverines.

The flat was on the third floor at the top of the building. Though on a small scale, it had good proportions – it was in fact just the right shape and size to contain with perfect snugness a couple so purposefully uncluttered as Justin and Ursula. There was a double living-room divided by an arch, a rather dark bedroom, whose door – whenever I went there at least – was firmly closed, and kitchen and bathroom, both a little too small for ideal convenience. The best feature of the place was the view from the living-room windows – a foreground of higgledy-piggledy pantile rooftops given relief by the graceful, baroque façades and cupolas which hung in the middle-distance, and above it all an expanse of luminous sky.

That winter was spent decorating and furnishing the rooms in their usual rather monastic style. The only signs to be seen of the twentieth century were the record-player and the light bulbs – though, unless either Justin or Ursula were actually reading or writing, candles were preferred to electricity. For the next ten years they never changed the appearance of the flat in any essential way. Occasionally some newly acquired statuette might be given pride of place over a predecessor, but the plain wooden table always stood in exactly the same position to the right of the arch, the divan with its Moroccan coverlet always in the far, left-hand corner.

ITALY

Rome. September 1971

We have found the very flat I've imagined every sleepless night since Malaya.

Last night we sat in the Piazza Navona watching the faces of all the other watchers – the cloaked man with the court of louts, crude Peruginos and Signorellis.

A plump, middle-aged spaniel trembling by the arch of the Via della Lungara, apparently unable to get up – shock? injury? master's orders? We offer it an unsuitably alcoholic cake (the only type available on a public holiday), and go away. Feeble responses of pity – fear of getting involved even with a dog.

November 1971

Spent a lot of time (too much) reading a biography of Bertrand Russell. For one who lays such emphasis on love, even ecstasy, he seems a stranger to both.

December 1971

Five minutes alone in the empty, wet Campidoglio. Full moon behind thin, racing clouds, the sky strangely blue, the flanks of Marcus Aurelius's horse striped with gold and patina and damp.

January 1972

J. read me two splendid stories by Gorki, 'First Love' and 'Creepy-Crawlies'. His honesty is his great quality – nothing like it for conveying emotion of any kind.

An appalling night with thumping, irregular heartbeats. Alcohol – I had one Bacardi, a quarter of a litre of wine, one grappa. One must remember everything or pay the price. The sound of thunder mixed in with the confusion of my dreams, already chaotic from the churning of the organs. It went on till morning – a rainy day. J. read *Lost Illusions* to me after lunch. The sun came out and warmed my back as I lay on the divan – I cheered up and forgot about myself.

Tristan and Isolde – enticing, terrifying undertow of the sea. Smooth, seductive, hypnotic singing of Isolde. Nothingness, annihilation, night-time, the ultimate in love. J. has become an expert bravoer – I, with my immutable reticence, find his shouts embarrassing. How tenacious one's foolishnesses are.

Watching people from the car when one's stuck in the traffic can be a tranquil exercise – one feels a removed kind of benevolence.

I must be religious by temperament. Without something absolute to believe in my life, by now, would surely be quite pointless. First there is the curiosity, the appetite, the obscure hope that one will get what one truly desires. But all that wears thin – the curiosity and the appetite are satisfied, hope turns out to be a mockery, so that in the end a sense of fate becomes as necessary as oxygen.

J. started reading me Gorki's *Childhood*. How well I understand those vodka hangovers, the irresistible despair, the self-destructive pleasure. I have begun to experience with great clarity the stages of falling asleep. The way the mind gets tired of logic and slips into the arbitrary – the approach of oblivion as if one had taken a drug.

The Amadeus Quartet playing Haydn, Mozart, Schubert – perfect flow, the timing of the complexities. Mozart's controlled pain, Schubert's marvellously 'modern' passion – I am thinking of the twangs of the cello. Tomorrow we start on our Venetian trip.

Ravenna
The tomb of Theodoric. I can't quite refrain from searching for the imprint of my own 17-year-old body in a sarcophagus 1,500 years old.

Venice

After much meandering through the corrupt and poisonous city in the rain – trivial shops and a strange lilt in the voices – we find a hotel which smells as pleasantly unhygienic as a Persian one. Airy, spacious, and providing a large bed (on which we make love to recover) it costs 3,500 lire a night. The rain is like the monsoon – the Piazzetta a haze of wetness lit by hovering lights. Shiny gondolas bob up and down with morbid gaiety. No light inside St Mark's, but one senses all the gold above one . . . The glittering, rounded corners of the arches continue, stage by stage, into invisible, velvet cupolas.

Titian's 'Pietà' – disquieting picture – perhaps it tells one more about death than one should know.

Italians have more features per face, more style per person than any other race.

It has become a little warmer – greyish, springlike air. We wandered along small canals. A fruit market on barges. Delightful absence of tourism in the little squares. A lovely night – little lights, flowers in windows, echoing, lilting talk, chugging motors in the distance, lapping water.

Four good-looking Japanese. Three men – one gentle, clean-shaven, one moustachioed and Samurai, one Westernised intelligentsia. One beautiful woman with a long nose and big eyes. Very self-possessed and sophisticated and interesting to watch. Lunch, feeling dangerously happy. We walked to the Palazzo Franchetti in the evening.

After a short and futile attempt to get into the countryside on small roads littered with scruffy factories, we are diverted back to the motorway, and arrive quite soon in Bologna.

Bologna

Walked about in the evening. Haunted, justifiably, by the continual worsening of the visible world.

Rome. March 1972

A bass-voiced, bourgeois party reminiscing about other fish at other lunches.

Reading Lowry's *Dark as the Grave Wherein my Friend is Laid*. It's impressive, but naive and self-indulgent.

Dinner in the little place with the cat, the waiter a maltreated, ever-grinning Pulcinello. A nice-looking, serious-seeming young man comes in and sings some simple songs – we feel agonies of embarrassment on his behalf. I thought I would 'grow out of' that kind of embarrassment – an altogether idiotic idea.

The gentle nostalgia, the longing, the sadness of Turgenev. What a sad man he was. Or what a sad world it is.

Haydn's 'Creation' at San Ignazio. Great, magnificent sounds echoing round the church. An excellent bass. An old woman coughs incessantly. J. says that since she has paid for her ticket she will die here if necessary. Absolutely infantile, uncontrollably shaking fit of the giggles.

The Barberini in the morning. I can feel amazingly bored by masterpieces. Nevertheless the brushwork of the Titian, the Tintoretto 'Adulteress' and the two Grecos flanking it did look very graceful, positively sublimely graceful to me this morning.

Annie Fischer at Santa Cecilia – Beethoven, Schubert, Chopin, Liszt, a typical Central-European concert in fact. Quite unexpectedly I was overwhelmed by all the sensations I had at thirteen in similar circumstances. It is at least a sort of achievement that I can listen to it again without a maniacal fit of depression. What attracts me to that kind of music is what attracted me to drink – an orgy of the feelings, undirected but no less powerful for that, which one suffers in adolescence, and in my case also afterwards, long afterwards.

I could never have become a musician because I have no talent for sublimation.

A late Beethoven quartet, the uncanniness of those unfinished and infinite notes. Afterwards the evening market was exhilarating – the flowers, the dirty fountain, the hoarse eloquence of the very virile strawberry-seller who turns out to be a woman after all.

April 1972
Pasolini's *Decameron*. Coarse, yet in perfect taste – nothing false or added on except the self-complimenting. His non-professionals are quite amazing. Not for nothing are Italians

the race of the *commedia dell'arte*. Are they also the last primitives of Europe?

Delicious music, red roses smelling strongly in the cool garden. The division of mind from body. After an anaesthetic you still groan as your body is lacerated. You know nothing of this, the doctor tells you afterwards. And while you are falling asleep there is that strong, physical sensation of slipping, of falling. After you have fallen, somebody else gets up. Sleeping and waking like being in a car on a hot, straight road.

GREECE
Koroni. May 1972
We have bought a boat. Doubts about its seaworthiness.

Driving in the dark, only smelling the landscape.

Our old friend, the molelike waiter, shows a warm interest in J.'s gun. He himself has five, and is clearly very fond of shooting. Apropos of shooting, our neighbour Irene saw a crane – ah, such a beautiful crane. She threw a stone and hit it on the head – brilliant shot. A truly wonderful crane, just back from Africa, you know. In two days it died – such a terrible pity. But, we ask, astounded, desperately struggling to get some logic into the conversation, why did you stone it? Well, they catch the chickens, you know. The fact of the matter is that Irene keeps her chickens in a cage.

I'm sitting under the eucalyptus with its delicious smell and listening to the sound of J.'s blow-torch in the distance. The boat is nearly all black now. Reading Machiavelli, Valéry, Kafka's *The Trial*.

All this housework – keeping guilt at bay, trying for more independence, more adaptability? Or is it simply that one is used to it? Nevertheless there's superstition somewhere in my insistence.

We finally went out in the boat. It is fast and not too small and good to look at. Something wrong with the engine, of course – patience is called for.

Being polite becomes a burden as soon as one feels one can't afford to be frank.

Marvellous afternoons drinking mint tea, lying in the hammock or sitting in the shade on our shingle beach listening to J. reading *The Brothers Karamazov*. Everything is saturated with well-being – my state of grace.

The boat has engine trouble – time-wasting, life slipping away. I flounder in the petty misery of the cheated.

July 1972

We left in the boat before dawn – heading towards the Mani. Past Kotronas, where we tried to buy a little house last year, is a bay, the most beautiful and perfect we have seen. Why not buy it and build on it?

There is wind on our way back along the west coast. We made one false move, launching out into mad, glistening, green waves, which rode towards us like mobile, slippery hills. Moonlight. The boat is comfortable when you get used to it. We want to buy that bay.

I feel more assured than last year, full of a dangerous confidence. Full moon, full of pleasure.

August 1972

Another boat journey to the Mani. We telephone the owner, who doesn't want to sell the bay.

The dwarf, Athanasios, was worried – we shouldn't swim so far, the dogfish would get us. Lamplight among the olives.

At night inside the house – letting down the mosquito net, stretching out on the bed. The sense of isolation in love.

Read the idiotic Mayan letters of Charles Olsen, alias Prophet of the Black Mountains. This morning I watched the dwarf fishing from the rock.

I feel vividly that the Germans belong to another species altogether. Today, after reading a memoir of the holocaust, the sound of pigs being slaughtered was doubly horrible.

Sometimes one perceives the depth and the vividness of things so acutely that it calls one to account. Respond. Such lucidity might be intolerable if one knew one's time had been limited to a year, a week.

Last night J. read his latest poem. I felt as privately pleased as if it had been my own. I certainly rely on instinct when it comes to verse – or anything else for that matter. I've got a peculiarly unanalytical sense of language – all guessing and feeling.

I got up from the sofa awkwardly this evening and felt that excruciating tremor in my back. It's so familiar now – the last time I had it was after falling from the hammock in Puerto Angel. The fragility of health – the miracle of possessing it.

We painted the ceiling. Expecting another year then?

September 1972
Swimming in a state of wild elation, chasing each other's fishy feet, clasping each other's solidity. I feel things so intensely, see things so sharply, I wonder if I am about to die.

Kotronas
Last night in the dusk we walked together towards the tower, ' and catching sight of the cypress hill and the bay we were seduced all over again. The hill, a peninsula really, is called Nysi. It belongs to a gipsy-looking man, who claims it is a 'gold-mine' of mosaic stone. He wants 250,000 drachmas for it. He has a café made of cement, for which he owes money to the bank. He also sells food, mainly fish.

It is raining on Nysi, and it smells like a spice garden. Rocks, shrubs all perfectly laid out by nature. Sea on three sides and a perfect natural landing-stage. Absolutely determined, we walk back for a short talk. We all sit under an olive in sight of the divine place, and settle for 200,000. Evidently elated, the owner gives us lunch in his frightful establishment. In Gytheion we send telegrams – and cross our fingers. Gytheion is lovely – gipsy girls dancing.

We walked to Nysi to convince ourselves yet again. All three brothers are present this time. Of the two we don't know, one is an ex-policeman with heavy eyebrows and a mournful expression, somewhat modified for bargaining, the other is a Petty Officer of the Merchant Marine with a weak, vain face, who alternates between transparent politeness and the sulks. They bargain shamelessly, incoherently, stupidly. Up to 250,000 again. In the presence of the notary, who suddenly materialises, the sailor lets the cat out of the bag, and leaves us holding the tax, so to speak. Deal and payment concluded.

Lunch and more money-counting, while the ex-policeman has a bilious attack. Exhausted, triumphant, we own a divine piece of Greek soil.

Packing without the usual sinkings of the heart – not so much the lure of Rome, I think, as an increase of love with which to ward off the world.

ITALY
Rome
The Signora had lost the key, and when we finally got in we found that the bedroom was flooded. We spent the day miserably cleaning up, and J. put a sheet of nylon into the roof. In the evening, exhausted, we went to the Piazza Navona for a drink.

Summons for tax. I wait apprehensively in the car as J. enters the lion's mouth. He returns with the problem solved – we have escaped with the minimum to pay – poor little foreigners, obviously confused and probably innocent. I am filled with admiration. To deal with these monsters in Italian immediately after wrestling with Greek notaries, and remain even-tempered, cheerful even, is heroism indeed. I myself am feebleness personified.

The roof is leaking, the neighbours are noisy – but Rome is looking exquisite.

October 1972
Concert of organ music at San Marcello. Bach – great crystal domes growing on top of one another, domes of icy power affecting me enormously. A small man holding a plastic bag turns up very late, and shuffles through the orderly ranks of the music-lovers.

Another roof-mending quest, walking over to the Via dei Riari. I felt that awful self-disgust, both physical and spiritual, which still assails me, albeit in shallower waves these days. My face becomes paralysed – I realise it gives me away, but there's nothing I can do about it. But by dint of keeping quiet and hanging on to J. like an anchor as we walked round the Corsini Gardens, it abated after a while, and the dampness, the deep, moist, smoky chrysanthemum smell of the evening brought

me back to my senses. I begin to believe that J. understands
what it's all about.

Now that the bed is under the window we spend more time
looking at our exotic, baroque skyline. We are going tomorrow.
I have decided not to take my new notebook, since London no
longer has any bearing on my life.

* * *

*In 1970 I moved from London to Tuscany with my family. I
had never really lived in the country before. My parents had
bought the Thames-side house about the time of Justin's birth,
and by then I was already at school. Before that we had lived
in London, and I never completely succeeded in transferring
my allegiance. The Tuscan house was in a fairly remote stretch
of vine-covered terrain about twenty kilometres from the
nearest town which, although undoubtedly beautiful as a place
to visit, provided absolutely nothing in the way of compensation
for a homesick city-dweller. After sweating it out for a year or
more, I had the idea of taking a room in a cheap hotel in Rome.
I would come home every other weekend, and my wife would
visit me periodically in Rome.*

*This experiment was one of those failures for which you are
grateful in retrospect. I learnt a lot about the more straightforward mechanics of loneliness and self-pity. I found myself
flirting with an American girl who lived in the same hotel, for
no better reason than that she was someone female to talk to.
In no time I was in the ridiculous position of locking myself
in my room to escape her attentions, which turned out to be
both time-consuming and voracious. Still I wasn't safe – on
one occasion I was stretched out on my bed, having omitted
to take into account the breadth of the view commanded
by the keyhole. After some knocking and rather impatient
knob-rattling, Maybelle's voice rang out, 'Hey, come on
now, open that door – I can see your foot, and it's jigger-
ing.'*

*Justin and Ursula were one of my reasons for coming to
Rome in the first place. My hotel was in a back-street off the
Campo dei Fiori, within easy walking distance of their flat in
Trastevere. Since I still didn't know to what extent they had
rejected the concept of friendship as most of us understand it, I*

used to try to see them at least once a week. We talked about what we'd all been doing since last meeting. After an exposition by Justin (who, it must be remembered, was still only twenty-three and had learnt everything he knew from Ursula) on the influence of African sculpture on Bramante – Ursula gently pointed out later that he meant Brancusi, which made it a bit easier to understand – I found I had nothing better to offer than my little Maybelle story. Either I still hadn't profited from the lesson of Justin's stern reaction to the fiasco with Marie-Thérèse in Egypt, or else I was stubbornly hoping to persuade him that such fiascos were not without a certain pathos. Either way I was wasting my time, because Justin was not amused. The fact that Ursula was only made it worse. The levity in her voice as she asked, 'Vhy did you not reply, "My foot always jiggers vhen I'm asleep"?' caused him to turn aside abruptly and start sorting a pile of photographs which he had recently printed.

While he was undoubtedly naive in supposing that my bad example could provoke any deeper response in Ursula than a mild diversion, he was right to be alive to the danger of her infidelity – a habit from which he had apparently converted her. He must have guessed that nobody is ever cured of the deepest-laid vices. In the event it was her regression in this respect that prefigured her death.

When my wife came to visit me I felt better immediately. Rome, whose splendour I failed to appreciate during my self-imposed isolation, came alive as soon as she was there. The winter sun, at least ten degrees warmer than usual, brought out sumptuous smells of coffee and fresh paint. One day, after a delicious lunch, we began walking down from the Piazza Farnese towards the Via Giulia, vaguely conscious of another couple at the far end of the street. They were moving very languorously. As we, rather more rapidly, approached, Harriet suddenly stopped and grabbed my arm – Justin and Ursula. They too stopped, exactly as if we had turned a switch. They turned to face one another without, however, noticing our presence fifty metres behind them. Justin cupped one hand round the back of her neck in its sheath of silky, yellow hair, while he tenderly stroked the curve of her jaw with the other.

They looked fixedly into each other's eyes. There was a feeling of slow motion – he was caressing her with an intimacy all the more erotic for being slightly distanced. No question of anything like a clinch, nor had they in any way ruffled their immaculate grooming. After a minute or two, when we didn't dare move for fear of being caught in an act of blatant, if inadvertent, voyeurism, they slipped an arm round one another's waist and resumed their leisurely progress towards the Tiber. We quickly retreated to the Piazza Farnese, where we burst out laughing – though both of us knew that what we had just seen was no laughing matter. It was the laughter of relief.

By this time – and strictly within the limits of the family circle – it must be admitted that Justin and Ursula had become a bit of a joke. It wasn't that we were unsusceptible to the grandeur of their style or the complementary impressiveness of their physiques, but more that, since they were inclined to treat us all de haut en bas, we had to get our own back as best we could in their absence. Why not to their faces? Well, though there was a distinct solemnity about them that invited teasing, as a couple they weren't really teasable. Singly perhaps, but then it was nearly impossible ever to see them singly. The defiant bastion that they had constructed against the rest of mankind wasn't defensible without constant surveillance by both of them together. Ursula later described herself as 'one of two heads on the neck of a single beast'. It would, for some reason, have seemed indecent to have pricked pins into this imposing, yet fragile, creature – and hence the probably shameful, but still irresistible, giggling we all indulged in behind their backs.

The laughter of relief, I called it. Harriet remembers it as having been more like the nervous titter of jealousy. 'I think I'd always admired and envied them – but although everything in their lives was so well-organised and so just right, it was still a bit unreal. When we saw them standing there at the end of the street, it was a tremendous shock to me, because they really were in love, you see, it was all true – and I suppose that made me more envious still.'

To check my memory against Harriet's, I recently asked her

*what pictures she retained in her mind of the times when Justin
and Ursula used to visit us in Tuscany, usually on their way
to or back from England in November. 'Well, there were
certain awkwardnesses, no doubt about that. I was always
embarrassed that the house was so scruffy – I mean they were
so grand, almost in a class way, and so fastidious. When Justin
stood with his back to the fire and his hands behind his back,
while Ursula sat on the sofa very upright with her hands in her
lap, I felt that they thought they were doing us a favour by
coming at all. I don't suppose that was really true, but it's
what I felt. And then the way they talked about their life, the
things they had seen – one of them would start off describing,
and the other would wait for a pause and then take over. It
made me nervous for some reason. But I remember us all
enjoying ourselves a lot as well.'*

*'Do you think Ursula liked you?' 'Oh yes. I found her
extremely sympathetic, not at all patronising. She seemed to be
very aware of me, of my situation, of how I felt. And we
amused each other. I remember us egging each other on about
silly little things – like the way Italians sprinkle the cheese on
to the pasta without looking – and managing to find them
terrifically funny. I was very fond of Ursula. I was miserable
when she died. I think those visits were much easier for me
than they were for you. Justin was jealous of you – you and
she were the same age, you knew about the same kind of
things, you enjoyed talking to each other. Also you did
flirt, you know, both of you did. Not serious flirting, but
noticeable.'*

*This last remark came as a shock. On reflection, however, I
had to acknowledge that there was probably something in it.
Although my fundamental emotion was the desire to get close to
my brother, to know him, to be on terms of equality with him,
I was thwarted by his consistent refusal to spend time with
me alone. It was exasperating, because Ursula was such a
challenging conversationalist that I found it almost impossible
to concentrate on anyone else if she was in the room.
Whenever Justin stuck his oar in, I found his appropriation of
her mannerisms undignified – I was always wanting him to
assert more autonomy, perhaps an earthier approach.*

This was unreasonable – it's difficult, even undesirable, to avoid influence at the age he still was then, and I had been just as heavily influenced myself. But, I felt, he was being unreasonable too in denying our caged relationship the chance of spreading its wings. One way and another I couldn't think of him without a lump in the throat. If Harriet's observation shocked me it was by making me realise that I had no one to blame but myself, with my eleven years' extra experience, for my failure to give shape to the amorphous, ungainly, unrequited sort of love I felt for him. That I should have attacked, in revenge, his weakest point, his insecurity over his hold on Ursula, is unforgivable. And yet, after every death, the mourners are assailed by guilt for the inadequacy of the love they gave when it mattered – and the commonest mistake they make is that of overestimating their own importance.

Harriet also reminded me of Justin's kindness to our children. He didn't make a display of this – I don't remember him giving any of them presents – but he treated them with the kind of courtesy that most people reserve for adults. When Soph was nine, he was very impressed by her poems, as indeed were many other of our friends. Justin went so far as to collect together about fifteen of the best ones, type them immaculately, and present them to her in a hard-backed, loose-leaf folder.

One day, years later, when Charlie was little, Harriet was taking him for a walk with Justin and Ursula. Justin was carrying Charlie and pointing things out to him in his observant, affectionate way, when Harriet intercepted Ursula's glance – her face was clouded with loneliness and misery. Trapped by her father's tyrannical ghost, she was apparently powerless to put into reverse the vow of childlessness that she had taken in adolescence. She also knew, though, that Justin loved children and deserved, like anyone else, at least a chance of being a father.

It was suggested to me by Betty Morris, in whose house Justin had stayed while studying at the crammer, that the intensity and near perfection of the marriage was the result of childlessness. It's very hard for a couple with children to sustain romantic love – the life-and-death importance of the business of upbringing tends to put it in the shade. But the

childless couple, by channelling their maternal and paternal
instincts into one another, reinforce their sexual passion with a
parental sense of responsibility. This was certainly true of
Justin and Ursula. At the beginning it obviously fell to Ursula
to play a motherly part – but gradually the pattern changed,
until Justin came to resemble a watchful protector of a brilliant
but dangerous daughter.

ENGLAND, FRANCE
November 1972
I think more and more often, though without any particular
deliberation, perhaps another year or two would do. What will
I remember from this month? Wishful trips and Freudian
lapses, subjects to avoid, subjects to belabour, animosity to
dodge. Brief reflections of the past through taxi windows, an
old friend bumped into on the doorstep of a hotel, genially
ready for gossip. Paris was pleasant and cold, but unremarkable
this time.

We sit in the Tuileries in pale sunlight by pale, splashing
water. A small, patient Spaniard asks the way, but we can't
help him – a vivid and painful sense of guilt as he trots off,
cold and small, to ask someone else a long way off, someone
who won't even be polite perhaps.

ITALY
Rome. December 1972
Fauré at the Gonfalone, unquiet music of moods, dissonances.

Concert after concert. At the Gonfalone Beethoven piano
music played by a frail American negro – desperate, passionate.
My response is hot, useless tears, the force of my admiration
tainted by envy. And at San Apollinare a long-nosed
Pulcinello playing Bach on the harpsichord, one of those rare
musicians whose face one can watch and gain from the
experience – utterly absorbed, gentle, ugly, humorous.

The day of our departure for Africa is getting closer. Visas
at consulates, lurching stomach. Will I be able to endure all
that pain and pleasure? Will we ever get back here? I dread
travel and I love it. And what about Rome itself? I will never

have enough of somewhere I'll never quite succeed in knowing – true of everything one loves.

Our new Land Rover has arrived, just in time.

TUNISIA
January 1973

A crouching man holds a dozen camels on reins – they radiate from his hand like stems from a branch. The head and neck of each one seems also to share the same nodding, masticating source of energy.

Some amazingly well-behaved children invite us into their troglodyte dwelling.

I'm interested in the absence of interest. The monotony of the landscape is like a mental achievement, I revel in the nothingness.

Thin, improbably brittle colours, creases of salt mud sparkling with silver, membranes of shallow water on the salt, a trembling sapphire blue, a faded aquamarine, a fluctuating purple. Mud of a deep, rich rust colour, the texture of velvet. Distant, shining layers of water changing into mountains. A superb disregard for optical probability. Are the mountains really there? A calligraphy of tyre-tracks on the flat sand.

ALGERIA

You see nothing, hear nothing – the eye pulsates in the emptiness. The curves, the pink other-worldliness are revealed in the after-image. One wants to stay here – a vague wish for self-annihilation.

Black shepherd children, wrapped up in white turbans and burnouses, bouncing about on the dunes. White cupolas in El Oued.

We are robbed in Algiers – I hate this seedy, malevolent town.

Ghardaia

Remarkably comfortable hotel, a garden oasis. Space, arched windows, central heating. J. has backache, and as soon as I start massaging the bed collapses. Dinner – venison pâté and a bottle of wine in luxurious seclusion.

First, a camel appears out of total nothingness – then a man, in short, black tunic and Touareg turban, and carrying an azure coat, comes running with huge strides. Marvellous bronze limbs and a fine hawklike face. Laughing, panting, he asks for water. His wife and their beautifully shaped infant, amulet round its neck, soon catch up. They put the baby down on the sand, and we sprinkle water over it. The woman is beautiful too, she wears a white, silky, loose garment, a black veil, and amulets. The most distinguished family I ever came across.

NIGER
Agadès
In the souk a black woman is in a trance. Wrapped in a blanket, she stands motionless on one leg. Her eyes are empty, lifeless.

We stopped at a watering place. Peuhl cattle have the longest white horns imaginable. The shepherds are tall, flamboyant, birdlike creatures – some wear nothing but striped, bright blankets bunched round their shoulders. Others have silver ornaments and swords, elaborate coiffures, inbred, delicate features and gestures like those of the Nubian princes in Egyptian frescos. Two arrogant youths stand back to back – short leather tunics, swords, and hats like shields slung on their backs. Their slim waists, fine, sneering faces, complex hair-styles, sculptured calves. The cows bellow their heads off, the goats screech – men jump up and down, arms and legs flying, trying to separate their animals. A princely man in white displays an Aztec profile, while a man with a very long sword and a short black tunic belted at the waist looks like a Pisanello dandy without the tights.

Niamey
One of those hotel limbo days, not quite certain where one is. The air is full of languor. J. has a fever and I have nightmares. In the morning the sky is misted with dust. We should probably pay more attention to our health.

Agadès
In the hotel there is a small, shrunken European, who appears

punctually for every meal and obviously lives here. One always speculates about such people. Intermittent drumming all night like irregular heartbeats.

After bush, scrub. After scrub, nothing. Nothing and more nothing. Sand, wind, sky. The horizon trembling, changing indefinably. Nothing to guide us – the compass is working erratically. At last a single, faded, but unmistakable sign. We follow it and it leads to the frontier.

* * *

The order of the entries makes the itinerary of this trip something of a mystery. From Agadès in Niger they drove to Niamey, near the frontier with Nigeria, and then apparently back up again to Agadès, as if intending to make a return journey the way they had come. However, the next entry is headed Taroudannt in Morocco, indicating that they veered sharply westward. Even as the crow flies, straight across the Sahara, the distance from Agadès to Taroudannt is well over 1,800 kilometres. There's a limit to how interestingly you can go on writing about nothingness, and it seems logical to assume that Ursula simply dried up in sympathy with the geological conditions.

MOROCCO
Taroudannt. February 25th, 1973
An old negress in mauve and a dark, round-skulled, Turkoman-looking woman in lemon-yellow. Soberly elegant old men. Burnouses in white, brown, rust, olive-green, always with matching turbans and babouches. Thin, ascetic faces with burning eyes and pointed beards, the marabouts of my imagination.

Via Tiznit, Marrakesh, Fez, to Tangier, where we take the ferry to Algeciras.

SPAIN
Seville
There is something violently sexual about Flamenco. Like all sexuality pushed to the limit it is ambiguous.

Among some undistinguished Roman fragments, a Leda

plaque even more explicit than the British Museum's. The woman standing with bowed head, the curve of her torso enveloped in the thrashing wings. Did Yeats know Seville? It captures exactly the paralysis of pleasure, though the execution as such is in no way exceptional.

The gardens of the Alcazar – golden sunlight, peace, the smell of grass, tinkling water. Wandering about, eating a lemon here, a grapefruit there – sitting on a wall, smelling box and jasmine. Quarrelling blackbirds in hedges, a man cutting fronds from a palm. After dinner we lost the way in the half-deserted streets – we looked into shop windows and laughed about nothing in particular.

Barcelona
As we book into the hotel two men hurry upstairs – one tall with débutante gestures, plucked eyebrows and hair dyed red-gold, the other sturdy, dark and furtive.

A pleasant, old-fashioned bar, where a correctly dressed and elderly gentleman reading *Le Monde* engages in playful conversation with a down-at-heel drunk.

ITALY
March 1973
Miles and miles of tubular tunnels. Lorries carrying tree-trunks looming into the headlights. Trembling, damp-stained walls – flickering, yellow lights. A storm – black sky, fork lightning, a glowing patch of gold on the horizon. Driving rain, sulphurous flames from oil refineries.

Rome
The end of another journey – we are alive. The flat, this time, is unharmed. Relief. The ease of Italy, the pleasantness, even something very like security.

Last night a tramp slept in the car. He crumpled the map of Rome, took a pair of sunglasses and a packet of throat pastilles. With pillow and rug provided, I imagine he must have had a very passable night.

Our neighbour has recently discovered Piaf. We, on the other hand, have discovered, or very nearly, the secret of detachment – today in the depths of the traffic I almost felt as though I were at a café table.

A night in the flat – the view through the window with us and our objects reflected in the same glass.

* * *

Justin and Ursula decided to go to Greece in April that year, a month earlier than usual. This was because they had very little idea how long their house at Nysi was going to take to build, and wanted time in reserve in case of any serious setback. They had bought a few acres of steeply terraced land, planted with olives and cypresses, but uncultivated for years and run wild. Their property formed a little promontory, shaped like the prow of a ship on whose forward deck was a conveniently flat area on which to build. Justin drew up a design for a small, simple house which was firmly based on the traditions of local domestic architecture. This he succeeded in getting passed without trouble in the Town Hall – for a foreigner to build in the Peloponnese, particularly on such a humble scale, was a rarity, and local bureaucracy hadn't yet devised ways of making it difficult.

Justin assembled a team of four or five workmen, some of whom were already friends from previous years. One of his qualities was an officer-like sense of responsibility when it came to getting things done. He was impatient with time-wasting and silliness, while at the same time commanding and retaining the respect of anyone who found himself temporarily in a subordinate position. To continue the military analogy, he also 'led from the front', humping the heaviest blocks of stone and mixing the smoothest buckets of plaster to such effect that the house was ready to sleep in by the end of May. If this sounds extraordinarily fast work, it must be remembered not only that the workmen were familiar from childhood with the techniques required, but also that it was approaching the season of maximum daylight.

The materials used were the grey-blond, irregular-sized blocks of local stone that you see in walls all over the Mediterranean. Inside, the stone was plastered and white-washed. The two main rooms, living-room and bedroom, had wooden floor-boards and a shallow-beamed, wooden ceiling.

*Two french windows led from the living-room on to the terrace,
which ended with a low wall, flush with the cliff-face, about
fifteen feet above the sea. You had the feeling of living as
nearly as possible outdoors, and also the security suggested by
a commanding position.*

*Ursula's need for privacy was becoming obsessive. Of all
Nysi's obvious advantages as a site to build on – the beauty of
the vegetation, the views – the chief for her was its isolation.
There was no kind of road to it at all, it could be reached only
by sea. They would stock up in Gytheion with abundant
supplies of non-perishables, load them on to the boat, and
return to conditions of voluntary siege. They then lived for long
stretches on fish and fruit and vegetables. It might be weeks
before they saw another human being.*

*After Ursula's death Justin sold Nysi to Christopher and Riri
Howse, who were friends he had made in Sudan. Riri told me
that the locals were astonished at Justin's non-stop industry
during the building of the place. 'He never ever rested, not
even for a minute. Nobody who hasn't seen Nysi could possibly
appreciate the work he did there, a real labour of Hercules. He
terraced all the slopes, carried tons of white pebbles to pave the
front and back of the garden. And over the years Ursula
apparently cleared the whole area of the tough thorn-bushes
that plague the neighbourhood.'*

GREECE
Koroni. April 1973
Waiting for the launching of the boat, I succeed in getting
gloomy. It's impatience – waiting for anything reminds me of
the existence of a future, which exasperates me. One must
simply enjoy today, the moment, without worrying what is
going to happen next.

We get up in the dark on a still, warm, moist night – setting
off for Nysi. Only a fisherman or two stirring. The thud of the
engine in the dark, clear stars, phosphorescent water. A strong
current slows us down. The sea rises up against us, glittering
malevolently. We make very slow progress – is there enough
fuel? Finally in the café at Yerolimeni, stiffened and deafened
by the sea, fishermen tell us that the wind will drop. It does.

But at Kotronas it's still too rough to anchor – we shout across the roaring water for someone to send a rowing boat.

May 4th, 1973

We have dug the foundations at Nysi. There is enough clearing of scrub and weeds to keep me busy for a year. Strange to be so occupied with physical work. Sitting by the marble slab preparing lunch for our team of workers, looking out on to the olive-covered hills, the sea, the island, the monastery up on the spine of the mountain, one sees how hard the place is – it extracts everything from one with its beauty, its finality, its reminders of death.

June 1973

We went to Koroni for the last time, and left without regret. Nysi belongs to a much more ancient Greece. On our first night in the house the jackals howled nearby. White gravel, the new yellow ceiling, the new yellow floor, the assorted striped rugs.

This morning we got similarly and enjoyably dirty, J. constructing the steps and I cleaning the ink-fish. But here I am, completely at leisure, and it's just after six.

Lying on the wall, the sea sighing underneath, the stars glinting up above, and the village lights in between haloing the hillside, I think of change and of the strangeness of all this.

July 1973

We went to the rock-pool in the boat. I lay on the Lilo bobbing about, while J. climbed up to investigate three little facets of quartz on a cliff – he looked like the first brown man on the rocks.

August 1973

One must learn to be worthy of all this perfection. The light in the mornings, the inevitable quality of every view through every door and window.

Reading Carr's *Romantic Exiles*. And Cavafy's 'Afternoon Sun' again and again – a perfect poem.

An owl on the cistern last night. A lizard comes for grapes

at lunchtime. And a pair of martens come and visit every morning and evening.

The first thing I saw on waking was the face I never dare try to describe. A brown face, innocent, with square-cut lips – hair which stands on end in the morning, its tips white with sun and salt. The terrible feeling of helpless tenderness. I would like to be omnipotent, to ward off all danger, all pain, all sadness. But I'm not, alas.

One gives oneself up, naked, to the warm darkness, the gathering night, to death.

Rowing over the leaping sea. Swimming in silvery darkness. Making love while the sea sounds softly in its infinitely centrifugal motion.

ITALY

Rome. October 1973

Went out shopping and despaired mildly at the futility of it. In certain moods I find it quite paralysing. Self-adornment, objects one doesn't really need. But it also amuses me, and why should I come to Rome, of all places, if not to be amused?

Went out shopping again, and this time I bought, with amazing ease, some trousers, a shirt, and a coat. A delight when it's so simple, but a negative delight, delightful for not being tiresome.

Feeling very conscious of everything – every trivial detail I see pleases me.

* * *

Considering that Justin and Ursula had no ties – no job or career, no children, who would have necessitated an organisa-tion of time dependent on delivery and collection, term and holiday – they adhered to a timetable of astonishing regularity: spring and summer at Nysi, October in Rome, November in England, with a week in Paris (to catch up with the theatre) interposed before or after, then back to Rome in December for the concerts. Their journeys of exploration began around New Year and lasted until March, but they took place only two years out of three – on the third they spent the equivalent time in Rome, with occasional trips inside Italy, or perhaps to Austria or Spain.

The days were mapped out with the same attention to balance, and the same regularity once the balance had been found. In Rome, for instance, Justin got up at half-past eight, and went downstairs to get rolls from the corner baker. Then he made the coffee, always bought at the Tazza d'Oro, and took Ursula her breakfast in bed. At ten they would set out to look at the Caravaggios, say, at the Villa Borghese, or visit one of the lesser-known Borromini churches. This would be followed by shopping for the evening meal, often in the Campo dei Fiori market. Lunch was at one of their two or three currently favourite restaurants. I particularly remember one in the Piazza della Quercia, perhaps because it was so typical of their style – they required of restaurants absolute authenticity, both gastronomic and sociological, combined with the moderate prices that ought to, and still sometimes do, go with it. The habitués of this one were working-class, with a smattering of students. Justin and Ursula, with their measured dignity and impeccable, interchangeable clothes – perhaps soft leather waistcoats over silk shirts and linen trousers in colours that rarely overstepped the narrow arc of the spectrum between cream and ochre – were immediately noticeable. For one thing, they were the only people there who behaved undemonstratively – they discussed quietly and seriously whatever it was that they had been looking at that morning.

They ate rather little, but devoted a lot of time to the choice. They drank half a litre of Frascati between them – never more, though occasionally they would finish up with a caffè corretto con grappa at a neighbouring bar. Ater lunch back home for a short siesta. Between four and seven was the time for reading or developing photographs or working on the writing either of them had in hand at the moment. Supper, perhaps a sea-bass just the right size for two with a light green salad, would be cooked by one or the other, or both, and washed down with a bottle of white Chianti. The last partition of the day was devoted to music or the cinema – it might be the new Pasolini film, it might be late Beethoven quartets at the Gonfalone. By twelve-thirty they were usually asleep.

If I've given rather a lot of space to this average day, it's to indicate that it contained an unusual amount of pleasure, *treated not only with the discipline most people are disinclined to waste on anything but work, but also with a sensual moderation designed to reap the maximum rewards.*

ENGLAND
London. November 1973
Nureyev's *Nutcracker* is Tolstoian. Every possible subconscious motive is cleverly exploited. Very impressive the way he hobbles, the way his face moves and is transformed by movement.

Bergman's *Cries and Whispers*. Solitude, rigidity – the agonised, involuntary hatred of anything facile. The only possibility of escaping self-hatred lies in the love of another person. A good film, cruel, but not gratuitously.

FRANCE
December 1973
We made a tour of the châteaux of the Loire – Chambord, Chaumont, Amboise.

ITALY
Lucca
Woke and packed early in the winter morning dark. Someone prays in a whisper – the sacristan scrapes up the fallen wax. Driving through the garden hills of Tuscany I thought of love – an impractical condition, a gift or an affliction according to your nature. The absence of civilised values in it, of affection, of compromise. It consumes, destroys the taste for everything else.

Rome. January 1974
One coffee too many after lunch and I am palpitating. What a frail carcase – everlasting precision is called for. My ears ring, I feel like going away. But where, and why? Does it mean that I should get rid of the burden of my body once and for all? No, because one has a duty to accept oneself before the end. It is extraordinary how one puts up with routine, any routine, as long as it stops one thinking. Perhaps this applies to women more than men.

Rome is a marvellous town – a constant feast for the eye, a constant *memento mori*. But even at this time of the year I am full of parched dreams of running, plunging, floating in deep water, green shadows.

Venice. *February 1974*

J. is drawing me as I look out of the hotel room window – I see the garden, the Grand Canal, the Accademia. I am happy as only an egoist can be. Simply being with him, here or anywhere.

A large and respectable mouse on a pedestal in the Accademia reminds us of a Beatrix Potter ogre, until the hitherto lethargic guardian leaps up crying, 'Topo, topo', and grabbing a feather duster. The animal disappears instantly into the forest of uncongenial marble. 'Eh, era un bel topolino,' (All the same it was a nice mouse) says the guardian, sounding rather regretful.

Prato

Lippi's 'Salome' in the cathedral. The adolescent boy with the small cat face, who looks at us instead of the picture, unselfconsciously, curiously even. Lunch in a workmen's trattoria. Hard-worked, expert waiters, peasants gobbling with their hats on – we share a table with two of them. They inquire if the *minestra* is any good. Then, discovering by discreet eavesdropping that we are English, they begin to talk about cousins in England and a 27-year-old whisky one of them tasted recently.

Rome

I dreamed of losing him in some way or other. I was left with the memory of a great and vital love, and complete incomprehension at the loss of it. Where is he, it? What am I? How did it happen? Amnesia would be like this for someone who had been happy – a faint echo of the happiness would remain and with it an immense and inexplicable sense of loss.

A woman drawing a fountain in the Corsini gardens. Her spaniel stands beside her, quivering with fanatical attention and benevolence.

March 1974
In the doorway of Santa Maria del Popolo a middle-aged, swollen-faced woman asks us to say an Ave Maria for her son, who died two days ago. How impotent one is in this cruel world.

An insane quarrel over a triviality leaves me weak with self-contempt and a sincere inability to understand the purpose of living. My taste for life depends so totally on love, that if you remove this element it evaporates altogether.

GREECE
Nysi. April 1974
They greet us as if we had left yesterday, and indeed that is how it feels – the shrinkage, the unreality of time.

I exhausted myself straight away with weeding. The sinful idiocy of not feeling well here. Fuddled with beauty and brightness.

At dinner we talked about how a simple misunderstanding can destroy the hair's breadth balance of our harmony. Attention to detail.

We slept on the floor, which I really prefer to the bed for a variety of reasons. Fell asleep in the firelight, exhausted with love and fresh air. On waking we reconstructed the bed with planks and shortened the legs.

I sat down to finish that short story I care so little about now. My journals are the only thing I have ever written that hasn't produced this after-effect. The stories seem so much less interesting than the reality they come from.

We went on a shopping expedition in the boat. It is good to go away, and it is good to come back. But will one ever be anything else but a wanderer on this ugly, beautiful earth?

June 1974
How happy I am, how solid is happiness when you can grasp it, like that old dream of mine about holding something in my hand that was 'the shape and size of rightness'.

My desire for affection is boundless, but because I am conscious of it my defence mechanism is overdeveloped.

Before you go away you regret what you are leaving behind

– that is to say, you think you will regret it. When you have gone, you have gone and you forget what was there before. I never yet wanted to relive any part of my life. A good or a bad sign?

The saints are those who never forget.

J. wrote a story which was a mixture of how things were with how they might have been. It had the same effect on me as my nightmare about the loss of love.

July 1974

To put it vulgarly, any fool can be unhappy.

Writing the journal adds concreteness to my day, to my life – or does it add stability?

One should leave life, according to Montaigne, as one leaves the dinner-table – the appetite not quite sated. That, of course, implies a choice of the moment of leaving.

J. is translating a Cavafy poem into English, the one about those who rose from the mattress and dressed without speaking. I once found it very poignant – now I have to make an effort to remember why it affected me. But I remember lines of J.'s own poems as if they were my own. Our lives are mixed like wine and water.

Am I getting idler, was I ever anything but idle? Hay-fever doesn't help one's energy. But I swim and swim without noticing how far I'm going.

August 1974

Talking about Machiavelli, the stylist, the man of sense.

September 1974

Life would always be possible in the certainty of love – a temperamental peculiarity. Some need it, others don't.

ITALY

Rome. October 1974

Divine peace and warmth in the flat. J. develops photographs while I read.

The garage man dropped a tool into the engine of the car, which necessitated taking it apart again at our expense. I sat down and watched the multitude walk past, hideous and quite unselfconscious.

We lost the keys to the flat and my purse on the same morning. Then I lost my composure as well – and bitterly regretted it. This is my one and only life, and what is left of it I am wasting. Such pettiness is inexcusable.

After a fruitless visit to the British Embassy for residency papers, we got lost in the latest one-way system, which ensures that you cover the shortest possible distance in the longest possible time.

A monkey with transparent eyes is eating an apple in the front seat of a delivery van. Monkey's eyes always make me feel foolish.

ENGLAND
November 1974
I lived here too long. My dislike of it is similar in kind, if not equal in intensity, to what I feel about Central Europe. Now for Africa.

* * *

They planned their second Saharan journey from another angle. This time, perhaps because of Ursula's dislike of Algiers, they landed at Bizerte in Tunisia. They drove directly south-west into Algeria through Guelma, Bou Saada, Ain Sefra, Colomb Béchar near the Moroccan frontier, Tindouf, into Mauritania through Chinguetta, and reached the Atlantic coast at Nouakshott. Then down the coast to St Louis in Senegal. At Dakar they cut sharply back into Mauritania through Kiffa, then south again to Kayes in Mali. On to Bamako, then eastward into Upper Volta through Bobo Djoulasso and Ouagadougou. At Niamey in Niger they were on familiar ground, and from there until Agadès they followed their 1973 itinerary in reverse. This time, however, they continued eastward to Bilma near the Chad border before heading north towards Algeria. At Touggourt they branched east into Tunisia, and took a ferry from Tunis to Sicily.

This expedition, which was even more ambitious than the previous one, took a little under two months to complete. If you read Ursula's jottings together with those of the earlier trip, it becomes evident that she is now more affected by Africans than by Africa. Before, whenever she mentioned the Saharan landscape, it was with a kind of awed astonishment. What impressed her so much was the grandeur of all that nothingness. This time she hardly has a word to say about the desert as such – she concentrates on the magnificence, the incomprehensibility, the capacity for self-abandonment of the people. You are left with the impression that she thinks them slightly superhuman. This admiration of a section of mankind contrasts with her accounts of other journeys, and particularly with the entries on Nysi and Rome, where Justin and herself are always centre-stage.

ALGERIA
December 1974
Stopped in the desert to tighten the everlastingly leaky oil-filter. Our life is an unending series of preparations for departure.

SENEGAL
St Louis. January 1975
Two white remittance men – one very old, with wisps of long white hair escaping from under a knotted handkerchief, the other younger, but with a ludicrously exaggerated air of seediness and fraudulence.

The potted palms in the hotel garden awaken pungent memories of Campeche, Cambodia, Goa, in one sense confusing the moment, in another making it headier still.

Dakar
Hotel Provençal. A marvellous room – like the one in Vientiane, except that this one is marginally more respectable. Wooden ceiling, shutters but no windows, so that the air circulates languorously. A big bed, brown wooden furniture, tiles on the floor.

Two faded nineteenth-century cafés in the docks. We talked idly of two alternatives – we could take a cargo ship to South

America or we could spend a couple of months at our hotel here. Both tempting, both quite easily rejected.

We woke up in the middle of the night to the sound of wild and resonant drumbeats. There was a big group of men and boys outside in the street. Threatening, pleasurable, or both?

MALI

The forest road, which is abandoned, approximately follows the course of the river and the railway to Bamako. An exotic journey via Bafoulabé.

UPPER VOLTA
Fada N'Gourma

The Peuhl women are magnificent. Indigo robes are worn with great silver necklaces, bracelets, and crescent-shaped earrings – some have six in each ear. Their hair is worked into a great crest decorated with silver coins, inserted and suspended. Others have cornelian necklaces, pointed with silver. Indolent, graceful, gipsyish carriage. There is much hand-shaking, and everybody is extremely polite.

NIGER

Just across the border there is a market, a miracle of exoticism. The men very dominant.

Niamey

J. went to the garage at dawn – oil leak as usual. I read about the Sahara in the subterranean darkness of our big old room. We supplied ourselves with wine for the cold Saharan nights.

Tahoua

We left Niamey in the dark with J. feeling sick. A mistake – one should always insist on enough rest. But no harm done this time. A market – butchered meat, heaps of spice, the dust of which seeps into the brain through the nostrils. Racking coughs abound. The Touaregs, tall, black-draped, idle past like camels, ready to beg and to despise. Catching glimpses of strange, beautiful shadows one can't quite believe in. The whole thing is like a dream, a black dream, a bad dream, a

hauntingly beautiful dream. We are having a long siesta before
going to bed early and getting up late.

The Peuhls are like figures in Egyptian reliefs from the
Valley of the Queens, both men and women – the princes of
darkness and strangeness, who live in emptiness and delirious
light. I am coming to a complete understanding with Karen
Blixen's infatuation with the Masai.

An evening at the races. A great crowd – huge numbers of
people on horseback, but also spectators on foot, who hop up
and down with excitement as the finish approaches. Everything
a total shambles – horses drop in and out at random at the
whim of the child-jockey. Clouds of sun-separated dust, flying
arms and legs. Camels pass, cattle and goats cross the race-
course. All the time a drummer sings a truly marvellous chant,
rising high, then falling to a deep velvet growl – beside him
another man gives responses in a speaking voice. Squealing
little boys' voices, the occasional falsetto laugh. Where we sit,
the sun casts its last, low, golden glow on the sand.

In Gall
At 3 p.m. it is uncannily bright. In the open space in the
middle of the village is a dark, chanting mass, a crowd of
fantasy, dark as dreams at noon. Peuhls in a circle, arms
around one another, swaying. A four-note chant with repeating
cadence. The close, black mass of fantastically made-up faces,
bodies, feathers, lances, swords. There is a pause, some
talking, then J. is dragged inside the circle – they try to pull
me in too, but I resist and stay where I am behind the women,
who form an outer, immobile circle. I am quite overwhelmed
by it all. J. takes photographs as long as he can stand the
feeling of interfering with the ritual. We present my Jordanian
bracelet to the *Maîtresse de Cérémonies* – a great success.
Allah's blessing is called upon us – and we are dragged back
into the whirlpool. Faces of unnerving intensity and decadent,
androgynous ambiguity sway and chant in the burning sun. It
makes one's head swim.

Later I had hay-fever, and slept badly, dreaming of the
Peuhls.

February 1975
We dined in our lamplit hotel room, sitting on the floor on the mats we bought in Mopti. Afterwards we listened to faraway chanting from a starlit courtyard.

We decide to travel to Bilma in a convoy of lorries. But at the first deep sand they get stuck. We wait in the shade of a tree, and watch other, Libyan, lorries pass by at speed, a hundred huddled figures festooned with water-skins, jerry-cans and bundles on each of their roofs – the height of the whole thing is staggering. J. tries to tell our people the correct way to get out of the sand, but nobody will listen. I sit and read French poetry – Vigny, Baudelaire – occasionally exchanging greetings with a Touareg woman who is selling cheese. Just after five the Libyan lorries return. We want them to guide us to Bilma. Their Toubou boss, with a small, strongly articulated face, very deep-set eyes, a moustache, and wearing a white turban and burnous, accepts at last my flat, gold, Spanish, circular earrings as payment. Arabs gather round to enjoy the bargaining, rub and appraise the jewellery. We set off, and later stop among some trees, where great fires are lit. We slept outside on our Mopti mats.

In the morning we took the guides in the car ahead of the convoy to avoid the dust.

We are lost. We wait in burning silence, listening to imaginary sounds, seeing imaginary vestiges of water. Shapes to make Brancusi weep, colours defying description. The guide proceeds by instinct – finally we arrive at Bilma.

Bilma
Suddenly we are stopped by the military police – they begin searching the car extremely thoroughly. The pistol is illegal, so I slip it into my pants – a soldier, despite J.'s attempts at distraction, notices me fidding around. 'What you put there?' he says. I, indignantly, 'A woman . . . surely you know . . . intimate affairs.' While J. finally succeeds in distracting him, I get the little gun into one espadrille and the ammunition into the other. I then put the face-flannel into the front of my trousers. We are led up the dune to headquarters, me hobbling painfully. We are told I will be searched by a female guard.

Burning with shame, I produce a corner of the face-flannel. They collapse – apologies, offers of gifts, buckets of water will be delivered to the rest-house.

ALGERIA
Djanet
We fell asleep to a chant, a kind of ululation accompanied by frenetic drumming. A dusty wind and the end of the journey in sight.

TUNISIA
Kairouan
Hôtel Splendide. Brown and white striped rugs, bedside lamp, blue painted table. Warm water in a capacious old basin. 1900 mirror, black and white tiled floor. Out with the books and dressing gowns. J. is at the garage, and I am waiting for him here with an easy heart.

ITALY
Rome. March 1975
After a bath we start reading *Women in Love*, but find it too hilarious to continue.

Diminish unnecessary contacts, eliminate what you can – in the end, sterile though it may be, you have more idea of your own identity.

Reading Aldous Huxley. The melancholy, the lovelessness of his England, of my England, of England.

These last days in Rome are spent putting possessions into trunks and suitcases, marvelling at how many of them we have accumulated and at how little they really mean.

GREECE
Nysi. April 1975
Interlocking dreams. I dreamed I had a bad dream, from which I woke up with relief but the relief didn't last, and I'm still not really awake. All this in some seedy African hotel near the Atlantic.

On the way back to Nysi in the boat there was a rainstorm. While J. struggled against the elements, I wrapped myself in a blanket and crawled into the hull, feeling as irresponsible as an embryo.

May 1975
The first swims. Divine, astringent, heaving sea. Love-making with brine-soaked skin in luminous timelessness.

We fired off one little shot each with the pistol – a derisive, reassuring sound.

It takes one a lifetime to grasp a simple principle like moderation.

Perhaps fiction, 'literature', is only worth reading when it is 'great'. Otherwise history, memoirs, even journalism are more enjoyable.

Gasping for air while making love – the pleasure takes the breath away like icy water.

J. is painting this and that with amazing facility and amazing results.

I long to hear again the chant of the drummer in Tahoua.

June 1975
What a season for fish. The cat is ecstatic. I couldn't sleep last night – thinking about how unnecessary people have become for me. Animals are another matter – we found a small hedgehog with very large feet on the gravel. He refused a slice of cucumber. I am happy and dependent – my dependence is so single, so concentrated, that it contains all the benefits I ever imagined would derive from freedom.

We heard of the possibility of 'development' in the Mani. But I am not attached to this place, for all its beauty. He is my only anchor, all the rest, including myself, an illusion.

July 1975
My pain for the big fish killed and dragged alongside the boat. And an obscure and threatening memory: my smoke-blackened cheek, my wounded hip, my awful, alien cry.

We slept in the boat, and woke in its swaying womb clinging to one another like unborn twins, indivisible.

August 1975
I lay uneasily listening to the sea, embracing J.'s sleeping body, which I had just been dreaming of as cold and shivering, ready to be submerged – that urgent, impotent desire to ward off all harm, all pain. I got up to look at the boat in the moonlight – in another part of the dream I had been climbing into it out of the icy water. There was a horse too, a beautifully trained chestnut – I was talking to it as we galloped through forest and neat little villages, perhaps in Austria, hearing the hostile murmurs behind me: 'It's that Russian woman.' But I could rely on the horse, it understood me. It was a good dream really, and at last I slept again.

September 1975
Walking in the mountains with the gun. Cleaning in all the obscure corners, because we are leaving.

ITALY
Rome
Feeling a little sick makes you more receptive.

We have developed one of those regimes which we quickly devise and just as quickly abandon. J. gets up at eight or before. I sleep another hour – when I waken in the dark, I see that the light is on in the other room and that he is at the window writing. There is the little picture of the Moghul notable on the wall. Silence. I only have to make a sound or a movement and we will be touching again.

Como. October 1975
Hotel Terminus, room no. 33. An old favourite. As if a moment or a lifetime had passed since we were last here. Lake, mist, bare trees, scentless chrysanthemums, polenta. Great contentment at being here, which is to say nowhere in particular, in each other's company.

ENGLAND
Dover
On our way back at last. Do I absolutely dislike this country then? Not when conditions are perfect, but then they never

are. The past looks ugly when you go back on to its stage.
People you never really liked, you like a little less each year –
the advance of intolerance. One's *mépris* gains in permanence
what it loses in virulence.

FRANCE
Paris. November 1975
This afternoon I heard a howl which I understood at first as
'J'ai horreur des Arts'. With some disappointment I realise it
must have been 'des Arabes'. We plan to spend Christmas in
Madrid.

SPAIN
Navarra
A carved wooden crucifix in a dim, empty church inspires me
to pray, to concentrate my will on contacting some power
hidden in that agonised body, that bony, remote face. I pray
that I may die worthy – but worthy of what precisely? We turn
on to the Madrid road in a spirit of desolation.

Madrid
Drinks in the bullfighters' bar, shrimps and green olives in
another. Manzanilla, crowds, drums, singing, dancing, clap-
ping, drinking. Low life with a lot of spirit.
    Goya's ominous brilliance. Velázquez – the eye detached,
concerned with the intellectual mysteries of the visible.
Mirrors, reflections, components of an insubstantial reality.
    Christmas. Crowds, drums, masks. Faces like masks.
    We went into a cheerless bar for a coffee. Down the street
came three youths with a gasping drum, a bottle and a stick.
One of them sang a sad, defiant song in a clear, harsh voice.
They came into the bar to have a quick drink before going on.
The town looked different after that.

FRANCE
Narbonne
Sitting in the cathedral – outside the wind beat uselessly
against the stone – I was suddenly overcome with fatigue and a

sense of pointlessness. Life can lose its meaning as suddenly as one loses a hairbrush.

ITALY
Florence
The Uffizi from end to end with just one break for an espresso.

Why do I take such pleasure in orderly, provincial well-being, which is so alien to my nature? Like the villas of Rose Hill in Budapest.

In the Museo del Duomo I ask for the lavatory – I am shown a photograph of an Arnolfo del Cambio statue by the expressionless guardian. It emerges that the lavatory is concealed behind the original.

Rome. January 1976
The Quartetto Italiano played the Beethoven Quartets at Santa Cecilia – magnificent. Unhinged, dangerous sort of music.

These days I find myself disapproving of the amount of time I spend polishing and anointing in the bathroom. It was a habit based on the need to escape – bathrooms were asylum in Budapest, Paris, London. Now, like everything else, they are shared. How unnatural privacy can seem.

February 1976
A Corelli concert – very eloquent. The violinist was a virtuoso, an anxious, undergrown child of twenty-eight. He was trained in Warsaw. A worried, unsteady smile, hand held to his heart in thanks for applause.

Moravia's *Amore Coniugale* – limpid writing, a most impressive grasp of emotional complexities. The period of fullness before the onset of desolation.

In the Corsini gardens I catch sight of J. on the far side of a fountain, a handsome young man in a pair of pale trousers. We live so close together, and in such a literal sense, that I am always startled when I see him at a distance.

I should like to die somewhere far away, in a place I have never spent much time in – Bamako, Rio possibly. Someone who has never felt at home anywhere should die in a place that isn't even familiar. This is important.

GREECE
Nysi. April 1976
It pours all the time. J. is outside in his oilskin, cutting and bringing in wood. I am inside, arranging this and that. A couple.

A silence greater than that of the summer – coolness lurking behind it, perhaps disquiet – heat anaesthetises thought. This fog is the second natural phenomenon of the year.

A partial eclipse of the moon. What a year for wonders.

One must impress the impermanence of things on one's mind, otherwise all this could make one feel immortal.

May 1976
Jhabvala's *Heat and Dust* – the best contemporary English work I have read for ages.

The blood loud in my ears with contained excitement. At times I like being entirely passive, which doesn't mean less passionate. I'd like to be eaten in one great gulp.

June 1976
Dostoievski's endless fascination with the abnormal. Everything is abnormal. I am abnormal, decadent, even naive. I am always surprised, and simultaneously relieved, to discover how well J. knows me.

We fished off Vatha. Fish after fish was brought to the boat by my fisherman in a dreamlike sequence. Then I swam along the turquoise base of the mountain. In the evening the biggest fish yet – a 15-kilo rufo, shot stone dead in the head.

July 1976
Couldn't sleep last night after the cat woke me – this year he only appears at night. I listened to J.'s breathing and thought that it's the only thing that keeps me afloat on the sea of nothingness. Shivers and ambiguities. The inexhaustible appetite for heat, simple, reassuring, dominant heat.

Happiness is helplessness.

Everything temporal seems to have ceased absolutely – one's heart aches at the beauty of this, and I can't sleep for knowing that: it is now, this is it, I am dying.

Descending the hill in the half-dark, laden with tamarind, blue figs and cyclamen. Later J. transfixes two great silver fish together on his lance. Grant us such a double death, O God.

One looks in the mirror and remembers how little one knows oneself.

August 1976

A compelling, ugly dream. A resort in a steamy place – Malaysia? De luxe living on a dubious footing – spongers perhaps. Odd drinks very late in a deserted bar. Recognition – the risk of being 'exposed'. Time running out. A walk down a shabby causeway, the cheap, popular end. Cement, open staircases. People in bathing suits lounging in lukewarm shadows, violent, brash music from juke-boxes, gambling. A couple go up the cement steps to a cabin for obvious purposes. A stiff brassière of leather or plastic obscene on a full, fresh body – the man's ugly, over-muscular arm. Then a meeting with an old friend, who has gone utterly to pieces, but still has the power, the intention of suggesting *the end*. He convinces me that I owe it to him for having failed him, betrayed him once. Anyway it is too late. We arrive at an agreement without words. I recognise that this, after all, is what I have been waiting for. The empty cement corridor, the fear that he might have gone. Besotted smiles over a magazine, ash on the lapels. Utter incomprehension and horror. Escape.

September 1976

This afternoon, the last afternoon, we lay half-asleep in each other's arms – the blazing fire, the sound of the leaping sea.

A cabin of our own. Calm sea, flying fish. Sunset over Lucania.

ITALY
Rome. October 1976

Bach at the Gonfalone – thoughtful, searching, of itself, of me. Planning the South American trip.

My photograph – I dislike my face because I dislike myself *tout court*. But if I had dark hair I would look even more like my father. The combination of my mother's nervous delicacy, the mobile, delicate nostrils, the corners of the mouth, the transparency, with my father's animality, not to say aggression. What a terrible mixture.

Max died of a stroke on 52nd Street in New York. We had nothing more to say to one another. For him I was no longer an individual, I had become one of two heads on the neck of a single beast. One can't converse with Siamese twins. But anyway he had forgotten the meaning of the word conversation. He made nothing of his real generosity. I came closer to him than I was with anyone in the world with whom I had nothing physically to do. But afterwards I met my miracle, which obliged me to make one final bid for seriousness. He had no such luck. Perhaps it's for the best that he doesn't have to pretend any more.

My nature is secretive, then, Oriental. My frankness is obsessive, exaggerated. My idea of inferno is to be a public personality, my constant ambition to disappear.

Anything that is real has its shadow-reverse. Ignore this at your peril.

ENGLAND
London. November 1976
Dinner at Chez Victor. Strangely, I seemed to be pleased with London this time. Or I should say with being in London together. We were talking about art being a defence against the inevitable, every man's monument.

As we leave I feel inexplicably light-hearted. The time we save by our detachment from all that idiocy.

The subdued sound of passing taxis from our unremarkable hotel room. The scratching of two pens, the warmth of two bodies. Tomorrow we shall be in the air.

* * *

One of the fascinations of Ursula's journal is that her extreme sensitivity to place obliges her to use, if not a different style, at least a different tone of voice for each of the countries she deals with. This obligation is both involuntary and consistent – you

can take a random entry written in Nysi, and be unable to
date it specifically to any one of the seven years they lived
there. Read end to end, the Greek sections sound like one long
nature poem, full of flora and fauna, peace and love, sea and
weather.

In Rome, on the other hand, the irritations caused by the
traffic or by red tape call for philosophic control – she's always
having to calm herself down, remember what life's all about.
None the less, music, paintings, architecture stimulate her
intensely – in Rome, more than anywhere else, she records her
responses, a habit left over from her training in art-history.

Her brief, dismissive entries on England leave you in no
doubt how much she loathes it. India encourages her melancholy,
her sense of mortality, while the Sahara concentrates her mind
on infinities of time and space, and the possibilities for
grandeur in the human race.

In South America, though, she comes down to earth. I find
this a relief, being reminded more vividly of the woman I knew,
admired and feared. Up till now we have had a sadly meagre
ration of Ursula's malicious humour. Though it has compensatory qualities, none of the journal represents the bite of her
conversation – not only because it necessarily lacks her
comical facial expressions and vocal modulations (the down-
turned mouth, the exaggerated drawl for extra absurdity),
but also because she was sharper in spoken English than
written. So the frequent mischievousness in these pages is a
bonus.

Ursula, in life, was curious about people, from the glamorous
to the drab, from close acquaintances to strangers glimpsed
through car windows – and none of them could escape her
satire.

There seem to be two reasons for this change of tone – one
circumstantial, the other temperamental. They had decided
that the trip to South America should be made by public
transport, one of the main attractions being the prospect of
travelling down the Amazon by riverboat. Travelling by car
has enormous, obvious advantages – you are free to stop and
start whenever you choose, you can carry with you a
substantial amount of luggage, and, even more important, you

are insulated by this mobile machine that becomes almost as much part of you as a carapace. But for the real traveller this security can be counter-effective. On the one hand, it's only too easy to be lulled by the drone of the over-familiar motor into a kind of introspective apathy – hours and miles swim by without your noticing anything but your increasing hunger or niggling stomach-ache. On the other, like all security, it fosters anxiety – what's that curious rattle, why on earth didn't I stop at that last filling-station? Going by public transport, you're at the mercy of its vagaries, and this promotes lightness, alertness. Everything is strange, not least your fellow-passengers. Your powers of observation are heightened, your sense of responsibility diminished. And there's nothing like keeping up to date with your journal for killing the time which would otherwise be spent passively hanging about some dingy bus-station.

Temperamentally too Ursula appears to have been liberated by South America. Her journal, as usual, mirrors in atmosphere the surroundings in which she wrote it. The welcome lack of either rapture or respect reflects the cynicism she found there, the resignation to corruption and violence. The downgrading of the importance of life and death suited her fatalism, and even before she went to Brazil she had once or twice cited it as a place where she'd like to die. The flavour of South America was a cocktail whose ingredients corresponded with several facets of her nature, whereas most of the other places she liked satisfied only one at a time. Nowhere else could she have been within reach of terra incognita – *some of the most inaccessible mountains and unexplored jungle, populated by some of the most primitive people in the world – and yet still be surrounded by the architecture of a Mediterranean culture and speak a familiar European language.*

VENEZUELA
Valencia. December 1976
By bus from Caracas. A decent old hotel in a dark-green plaza in the old town. Another bus in the morning – multi-racial love-play on board. Indian women dressed either as whores or as drudges. Flamboyant hair-dos and transparent, *décolleté* bodices even on the frankly elderly and toothless. One young

but deranged creature, entirely disfigured by burning, hops on
and off. A mobile bordello?

COLOMBIA
Cucuta
It is hot. The broad, calm faces of the Indians in the hectic
main square, where all the buses forgather. I'm afraid of not
being equal to this trip. Bought insect-repellent – must attend
to one's wretched surface.

The Indians walk drunkenly when not burdened with
bundles – strange, light, delicate steps. The secretive,
farouche demeanour of an old woman eating alone.

Dawn over the Andes. We zigzag down by taxi on to a sleazy
river plane, running over a mange-eaten dog. A madman with
a matted beard, lurid pink, melting ice-creams dispensed from
a filthy bucket. We share the taxi with a ranchero, complete
with whip, and a provincial lawyer and his young son. The
lawyer is on his way to sort out a murder. He says, 'En
Colombia se encuentran de las cosas singulares. Dan la paz los
militares y los civiles la guerra.' (You find some funny things
in Colombia. Soldiers bring peace and civilians war.) There is
an incident in a village street, the crowd are grabbing hold of a
man. 'Lo matarán,' (They'll kill him) says our driver, after
having a careful look. He mimes some slashes to the face. The
lawyer shrugs.

We wait for a boat on the banks of the Rio Magdalena.
Eating-places in the undergrowth – rice with fish or fried
meat, boiled sides of meat for soup. A woman making herself
up next to a fish stall consults a male fish-eater about the best
colour for her eyelids – he shrugs. At last we embark on a tin
tub with a massive engine attached to its tail. Soon the river
sights and smells are rushing by at high speed.

El Banco
We change boats. The confusion and heat of the cafés, the
market. An old man with a creased, round, European face has
no idea what Europe is or what are its components. But he
does know that 'there are rich Italians in Mompos'.

Mompos
No electricity, just candlelight and moonlight. The town an
entrancing stage for quiet groups of talkers. They stand on
steps, leaning against the white mouldings of the street-
corners and dark lamp-standards. An old woman, barefoot, in
a neglected white shift with silver rings in her ears. Her
greying black hair is twisted into a chignon. One hand is on
her hip, the other holds a fat cigar at an angle from the elbow
away from the waist. She spits accurately to one side, and casts
a genuinely contemptuous look at the world. As she examines
the rubbish dump she has all the allure of an aged marchioness.
Our dinner was pork, beans, rice, beef, bananas, and potatoes,
all dumped in together and rather good.

No one pays the slightest attention to us – we are more
at our ease in public than anywhere we've been so far. From
the street we hear the children's whining voices: ' . . . su
misericordia . . . la vida eterna . . . propongo vivir sin pecado
. . . amen.'

Wooden ceilings reminding one of Moorish Granada – the
criss-crossing of the world. We are going, but how easily I
could sink into such a place, traceless.

Pamplona
The heaviest heat in the world in our room, and the fan no use
at all. On our way to eat, we follow a trail of blood along
the street till it ends in a great pool at the restaurant door. A
silent circle of gazers. One dead, they say, the other escaped.
We decide it would be preferable to eat somewhere else.

An amazing sculpture, a Calvary, in the church. Beyond the
high-pitched and morbid reality of the effects, the work is
astonishingly good, even great – and that by any standards. I
never expected to see such things in South America.

Popayan
We met an old American woman at the bus-stop – of Russian-
Polish ancestry with a Slavic face and bizarre clothes. She's
been on the road for seven years and yet she seems quite at
home. Travelled in India, Russia too, she always goes by bus,
stays at youth-hostels, etc. She is on her way to Rio, which she

thinks, for reasons that remain obscure, might be the end of the road.

ECUADOR
Ibarra

This altitude doesn't suit either of us – one is roasted, then chilled. A night of generalised unwellness.

We went to look for a cock-fight and nearly found a bull-fight. The pleasant little hacienda road ended by a white farmhouse, all fenced round, where a bull was refusing to follow the herd inside – a woman was trying to shoo it in with a red handkerchief. J. 'helped' – he had it by the horns when it got unpleasant. A nasty moment. On the other hand, we saw a long-tailed humming-bird exploring some Japanese lilac.

On the back of a lorry to San Lorenzo. A hopper plane along the coast, then a bus up to Quevedo, an ugly town. One weak bulb in our squalid room – all the electric cables are occupied by swallows like African stump beads. A study in tropical hopelessness.

Indians play strident march music as we hurtle over the highlands towards Latacunga – recorders and trombones played in an angular, urgent, pentatonic rhythm. Perfect blend of music and barren landscape – one might be in the Atlas.

Latacunga

Pensión Imperial. The verandah of our room is a tailor's workshop.

Riobamba. January 1977

Could be any room, past, present, or future. A limbo of privacy from the white-hatted Indians outside. There is a market full of little people in grimy felt bonnets, stunted from digging, from lifting, and from the eternal upward climb. Some of this place is so strange as to produce an almost total sense of *dépaysement*. A shuttered, quiet town, even on market day, as if life had at some point departed from it and the remaining Indians were strangers. Little barbarians run to and fro with great, nude pigs strapped to their backs.

The bus – dust and jolting on an exceptional scale. The unfortunate proximity of unchanged nappies and sockless feet in wellingtons. We are in the clouds, with nothing to look at but mist. Highland phobia.

PERU
Tumbes
A confused and sinister frontier. We were searched by male and female customs guards, and caught with undeclared money. Never take risks except when necessary. But here there is soft air at last, and a wooden café with a verandah. An old dog is on the roof, guarding the lavatory.

Piura
The dry air of Africa. The river Chamaya is like the Bamako – broad, beautiful, shabby, and overhung with a haze of rubbish smoke.

Paita
A legless, grinning beggar playing court jester to a pair of fat, coarse, Japanese fishermen.

Lima
A city between grey zenith and grey nadir, the dry and the wet inferno. Suction and repulsion. And yet, even here, we find a sanctuary – the Hotel Pacifico near the old station. We fill the little room with our odds and ends, and wake to familiar Chinese noises, lung clearance, etc.

Tingo María
The Huallaga, one of the origins of the Amazon. A blue room, violent rain. Waiting for a boat. Making love to the drumming of the rain – a sense of heatwave indolence.

On the boat. The river turns paler and paler blue with the evening – dolphins roll indolently on the surface, sometimes leaping a little. An amazing creature appears – pink, about three or four metres long, with a long beak, which it keeps out of the water, along with about four centimetres of its back.

A member of the crew, on being jocularly asked whether any of his mates have died of the 'filtered' water, laconically replies, 'Uno muere cuando es hora.' (A man dies when the time has come.) And the cook, asked when the meal will be served, 'Cuando está preparado.' (When it's cooked.)

We have entered the Amazon proper. We lie on a large straw mattress – fireflies at night. A magnificent thunderstorm. Exhilarated, we go happily to sleep.

Fish soup lunch with a gold-chained, well-starched, hairy-whiskered old trader. Forty years in these parts. A habit of blowing kisses like a belle-époque maestro of the *café-chantant*, and another of lifting his forkful of food and tenderly inspecting it. Solidarity arose between us with the arrival of a troop of boiling, under-dressed, barbarically noisy Americans, bawling for cold beer like an invading army. We all three raised eyebrows, shook hands warmly, and departed.

BRAZIL
Manaus
The sad confusion that overtakes one when, after a while in the back of beyond, one returns to the conditions that most of the civilised world lives in all the time. Yet what a relief to be in a room in an old house with a large bed, to have an unhurried shower and then lie sprawled in the cool under a mosquito-net.

Santarem
We get on another boat, low, ample, galleylike, and painted parrot-green. We have a small cabin, thanks to J.'s great talent as a grabber of accommodation. Gambling – for dollar stakes. Faces of every possible nuance of Portuguese, Indian, and negro admixture. They play all night, and then continue through the day with quick and functional stops for food, and few superfluous movements of face or body. At present, since the table has been taken over for the passengers' lunch, they are carrying on downstairs on packing cases.

A negro with a sun-dial face, all features concentrated in the middle – small, full lips, negligible nose, little, solemn eyes, permanently half-closed. The rays of this black sun are a massive halo of hair. He wears a black T-shirt, with a diamond-studded, black crucifix in the hollow of his powerful neck. From time to time he covers one eye with his hand for a better squint at his cards.

A tall, emaciated Portuguese with an ugly but sympathetic, stylised face – long, sharp nose, deep parallel lines, hollow cheeks, long, thick neck. Piercing blue eyes, thick eyelashes, dark hair *en brosse*. His arms and legs are very long. He has a natural flamboyance in the way he uses his wrists and hands, which are long-fingered, long-nailed. He wins sixty dollars.

Belém. *February 1977*
Sitting in a handsome square of huge, dense trees while J. searches for lodgings. Some children are playing a war game in the thick, long grass, and then refusing to obey the rules they have just made up. An infectious air of ease, of pleasure – a quiet night in an unknown town.

Went to an exhibition of stuffed animals. A black humanoid monkey, called Satan something or other, is Solzhenitsyn to the life.

São Luís
Linguistic nausea. The mélange of languages – Portuguese, Spanish, French, Italian, Greek – that mill about in this strange, exotic, exhausting place on its river or lagoon or sea or whatever it calls itself. The real whores seem to wear hats to distinguish themselves from amateurs. The humidity enhances all the smells of corruption.

Teresinha
Whores in the bleak waterfront bars. Fat women in all stages of undress. How right the Muslims are – most females need covering up.

Bahia
The famous market is incomparably filthy – an amalgamation of excrement, rotting fish and meat, bones and windpipes, sunk into the mud. A woman sits on the pavement, nursing her knee and moaning loudly – I know exactly how she feels.

Sex and evil always equated in this Afro-Catholic consciousness
– little ithyphallic devils for sale. Deliberate degradation.

A huge and elderly blonde in black trousers, tight gilet, and
white shirt stares menacingly at a group of arts-and-craftsmen.

Maragogype
Beautiful country straight off the lid of an old cigar-box.
Behind a crumbling Franciscan convent is one of those secret,
miraculous gardens for which I feel such an atavistic nostalgia.

A long bus ride over rolling, infinite country – blue hills and
scrub and river-beds, glinting with illusion.

Diamantina
I sat under a tree and saw a spectacular worm wriggling
around on the trunk. I poked at it with my pen, but it struck
back formidably. I resumed my scribbling.

Our pension has a solid, *fin-de-siècle* charm – a huge bed,
excellent linen, marble-topped side-tables, and mirrored
wardrobes. The building is surrounded by a vine-shaded
verandah affording classical views.

Pure peace in a milky light. The little green meadow where
the horse grazes, and the charming old town floating behind us
into the evening. A breathing-space suspended in one's mind
as if it were already a memory.

Congonhas do Campo
We stumbled out of the bus and picked our way across an
expanse of mire to the waiting room, but a negro, dead drunk,
soaking, and partially covered in sawdust, was blocking the
entrance. No one took any notice, until a brutish father with
howling brat in his arms thought that the scene could have
distraction value – he poked the body with his foot, then lifted
the head a little by one ear, and let it drop again with a painful-
sounding knock. The infant was, moderately, amused.

São João del Rei
A delightful town with a natural-looking blend of architectural
styles. Pleasant smells and colours, ornate 1890s' kiosks,
ornamental trees, an old arched bridge, wrought-iron benches,

and bird-cages inhabited by friendly miniature monkeys, one of which tugs at my ring. A little street of brothels.

On the bus to Rio, which is too well-sprung – sick-making as it swings round the curves. We had a last, naked lunch in the room before departure. You can't eat out in this country.

Rio

Tiradentes. Sitting on a suitcase as usual while J. searches for a room, this time at night, and what's more in the middle of Rio. Ample opportunity to observe. The most blatant whore-market I ever found myself in the middle of. A fragile, dark-gold creature is sitting on the ground and painting her nails. She is profoundly absorbed, oblivious of the impatience of two ugly, whitish men, who are waiting for her to finish. She has dyed red hair and carmine lips and the very frail body of the 13-year-old that she probably is. She spatters her long, loose dress with nail-varnish, but the effect entrances her none the less – she wiggles her long thin fingers to display the scarlet decoration at their ends. One of the men hands her some money – she balances it briefly in her palm with fingers rigidly outstretched, then abruptly flicks the note to a woman sitting beside her with her back against a lamp-post. This woman is thin too, but wrinkled and battered and toothless and dressed in greasy rags. She might be sixty-five, but there is a baby at her withered breast, attempting to suck – it raises its head breathlessly from the dug, and, exhausted, stares up, its face all puckered, into the blinding neon light.

On the beach. There is an immense attraction in this simple, selfish, mobile life. We've got a white cubicle facing the sea to live in. As the sun goes down we savour the pleasure of exhaustion from heat and movement. Then the beach empties of athletes and fills with fornicators, probably devil-worshippers. If we lived here I would grow nostalgic for shadow – and anyway it is too far away, and the language is impossible, and the people are nothing special. But isn't this just the kind of anonymity one seeks? A sunny, anonymous death.

* * *

I always wanted to know more about Justin's attitude to art, or more precisely his relationship to the artist inside himself. When he was alive the ambivalence of our dealings with one another seemed to preclude any direct questioning on my part – and one way or another I never had the conversation with him that might have illuminated the subject. After he died I searched Ursula's journals for guidance, making a long list of her references to any activities of his connected with the creative act. These ranged from entries such as 'J. has built up the wall beneath the upper cistern' to 'J. is painting this and that with amazing facility and amazing results.'

In itself the experiment wasn't very helpful, and merely confirmed what I already knew – that Justin had a resistance to specialisation. Although he described himself as 'writer' on his passport, he devoted more man-hours to photography than to writing, and didn't appear to begrudge (unlike Ursula on his behalf) the days, even weeks, on his back repairing the car or up ladders retiling the roof. But my list did lead me to a more interesting line of conjecture – that it may have suited Ursula to suppress the artist in him.

Having found out through her pitiless self-awareness that a career as a committed writer was unsuitable to her, she developed a compensatory conviction that it was anyway more honourable to 'live' than to 'create' – 'creation' implying a bourgeois garnering of experience for an ulterior motive, an undignified insurance policy against an old age she didn't intend to endure. She can't be blamed for infecting Justin with this strictly personal idea – after all, he was only too ready to hear her every utterance as the word of God. But she might perhaps have discouraged him from treating the care and protection of herself as his major opus.

That Justin had the makings of a very good writer is proved, I think, by the story quoted earlier in this book, which was written a few weeks before his first meeting with Ursula. If he didn't fulfil its promise it was because, though he had talent, passion and tenacity, all attributes vital to the making of art, he lacked the most vital of all, which is the desire. He was compelled more by love than by art. If he'd fallen in love with a woman who stood to gain by keeping it in focus, his talent might after all have borne fruit. Ursula, though, did little to correct his insistence that his life's work was nothing more or less than herself.

As it was, the work that Justin left apart from Style – *a volume of poetry, numerous sketchbooks of drawings and a huge mass of photographs – is mostly inhibited, almost apologetic. The day I spent looking through his 3,000 or so enlarged photographic prints left me puzzled and oddly depressed. Roughly speaking they fell into three categories: studies of the indigenous people of the places he had visited, 'art photos' (a lemon and a glass, or the glare of the sun on the sea), and portraits and nudes of Ursula. All three categories shared a feeling of lassitude or inertia quite at odds with Justin's vigorous, industrious nature. It was partly a matter of technique. Whether in black and white or in weird and monochromatic colour, they were usually underdeveloped, which gave them a bloodless quality as if they'd been strained through a sheet. I wondered why on earth, in seventeen years of nearly continuous photography, he should have persisted in producing this pale and timid effect. Could it have been nothing more serious than a lack of confidence?*

Once, feeling that confrontation with an audience might be beneficial to Justin, I tried to persuade him to contribute to poetry magazines. He seemed interested, even flattered. Next time I saw him I asked if he had taken my advice. He told me he had sent some poems to the London Magazine, *which had rejected them. 'Oh, I know,' I said, 'that always happens. You have to be prepared to be quite persistent. Why not try some of the others?' 'Oh, I'm not going to do it again. It was worth doing once if only to confirm my belief in the trashiness of the London literary scene. London is appallingly provincial of course. Anyway I'm not the slightest bit interested in publication.'*

Whether or not Ursula held Justin back deliberately – and I really don't think she did – there was plenty about her to nurture the lack of confidence revealed by this transparent piece of bravado. Few people knew more about either visual or literary art than Ursula. She had seen everything, read everything, and as far as it's possible understood everything.

How could he hope to produce work that would come up to her standards, particularly living as he did under her incessant scrutiny? Her praise would have sounded condescending, her silence dismissive. It must have seemed more rewarding to him to treat the whole thing as a game, to write and photograph as he fished, repaired the engine of the boat, built the garden wall – occupations that were superficially useful but really ways of doing what seemed appropriate at the moment, of passing time, of avoiding boredom . . . even of returning to childhood.

I had a vision of two precocious adolescents, siblings perhaps, incestuously playing through a succession of burning summers, alone with each other in defiance of the rest of the world. Les Enfants Terribles *in the territory of* Le Grand Meaulnes. *Not a sign of adulthood – no forms to be filled in, no money worries, no jobs, no responsibilities. But the children are cast in opposite moulds. The boy is active, inventive, dynamic, the girl passive, reflective, watchful. One of their games is called Art – it's a device for proving their superiority over adults, whose arteries have hardened to a point where they're incapable of remembering the experience of beauty. The girl is the instigator, the general. She names the form that the game will take that day, then supervises its development from a distance. As the boy plays strenuously in the sun she reclines in the shade, recording everything in her exercise book.*

FRANCE
Paris. March 1977
We landed at London airport, collected the car, and here we are – a freezing morning in Versailles, not a single chestnut bud yet open. When it began to snow, the agony turned to hilarity, and we ran about in the falling flakes. A fountain with white, cascading icicles – white statues, a frozen lion. Great tall trees creaking in the wind. We rushed back to Paris to put our fur coats on, and then straight out to the little glass cage of a café in the Luxembourg, the snow still falling, to drink Calvados and coffee laced with our Brazilian rum, marvelling all the time at the extravagance of our life.

ITALY
Rome
In the garden of the Pincio the chestnuts are in flower. I sit in
the translucent shade on one of those very low benches half-
sunk into the deep gravel, gazing at that headless statue with
the upraised hand. Now that the head is gone, the gesture is
musical rather than commanding – an unfinished musical gesture which suits the place and the odd, intense, disconnected
hours that I have spent here in all seasons.

New books, a new red dressing gown.

GREECE
Nysi. April 1977
Lambis is dead. I only became aware of his existence last year,
and now his face is still vivid. He knew he was going to die,
and perhaps it was that which gave him a certain style, the
style of a man determined to enjoy himself without taking
anything seriously for a minute. We are told that he choked on
an orange and his heart stopped there and then.

Panayoti has had a stroke – he lies immobile, his lopsided
face resting on gaily coloured pillows – four round loaves are
airing on a rafter – he contemplates them, and listens to the
wind. When visitors come, he tells them stories of his youth.
But sometimes, without apparent reason, he weeps. His
overweight, good-natured wife wipes his face and tells him to
keep quiet. The children have inherited her beautiful, rather
slanting eyes – Ilias, the son, massages his father's legs.
Panayoti was, is, a handsome, virile man – last year he was
sixty.

I am stitching a new mosquito-net, hoping it will get dirty
in many an African doss-house before it disintegrates.

May 1977
We watched some boys dancing – one of them had a gauche
but genuine dignity. It was that rather grim, casual kind of
dignity which the French so lack, which is what makes
Montherlant, for example, so passionately overestimate it.

June 1977

Becalmed in the phosphorescence. The cool dark water lights up as if from the energy of one's own body – sparks fly off one's toes, deep down and clearly visible.

J. has reached that stage in a fisherman's progress when he will not consider anything above or below a certain size.

Valéry's idea of the 'accidental' suicide. The idea is so interesting and the act so easy to accomplish – the finger on the trigger is independent of the mind – that it comes about, as it were, by itself.

July 1977

A heavy heart. How very precise that expression is. A weight where weight should not be. How much poison can one absorb without dying? A little poison might not be such a bad thing, it could immunise you to the larger dose. But the essential point is: do I want immunity?

The marten comes and calmly drinks from the trough while we are dining. He takes the figs that we lay out for him. Some of these he puts into empty birds' nests, some on to the sawn stump of a grafted tree. Others, presumably, he takes away and eats in comfort.

I am alone on the boat. J. is fishing, already down in the depths. I say to myself, as if I'd thought it out long ago: Everything has been paid for. But for a long time I can't see him. Have I been taken at my word? An awful, lurching impatience.

J. has built up the wall beneath the upper cistern, and I washed garments I may never wear again. To stay on here is a great temptation. The moon, the clouds, the ever-changing sea.

Last night the sea began to thud. We made love in the dark with that great unfurling in our ears. That's when I know I am alive.

September 1977

The pointless elation I get from liberating the wild bushes I like from the wild creepers I disapprove of.

I have certainly never imagined I could stay permanently anywhere but here.

ITALY
October 1977
The ribbon of road slips away under us in the dark. Late, empty bars, drinking coffee that acts on one like a real drug, a stimulant, a poison.

Rome
As soon as we get to the flat, we don't feel tired at all. Dusting till one in the morning – we get to bed at three. The yellow moon, which we last saw misted over Campania, sits low and improbable on the Fontana Paolina. The time to live is now, only now.

I am dazed by fever, artificially held in check by antibiotics. Eyes dry and oversensitive, arms dry and burning. The condition always makes me extra perceptive – the top of a stone bollard in the palm of my hand is heavy with an inexpressible significance, as in a dream. One must always be ready, always practise for the last performance.

* * *

Early experience had taught Ursula to be wary of the family unit. Indeed, until she met Justin she had little experience of families. Kenelm was an only child whose father died soon after Ursula met him. This meant that marriage brought with it only one adjunct personality, Maureen – and Maureen was a heaven-sent asset, typical of Ursula's luck. We were another matter, and the idea of being part *of us (or of any family) was repugnant to her, whatever she may have thought of us individually.*

The close relation of Justin's she preferred was outside the immediate family circle and, significantly, another woman of her mother's generation. This was my father's sister who was married to the historian E. H. Carr, best known as the author of the huge History of Soviet Russia *and* The Romantic Exiles. *My aunt, C. B. A. Behrens, also a respected historian, was until recently a professor at Cambridge. She and Ursula were immediately attracted to one another, since they shared a taste for educated ideas exchanged with wit and laughter. When I wrote to my aunt asking for her impressions of Ursula, she replied, '. . . I always think of her wearing a large hat. I was impressed by her elegance and dignity. I could talk to her about things that I couldn't talk about to any English person.' An entry in Ursula's journal of November 1978 casts an oblique but intimate light on the intellectual ground they shared: 'I: "You are a believer in the doctrine of Original Sin?" She: "Yes." Her shrill, high, delighted laugh.'*

Justin and Ursula always spent some time with the Carrs on their yearly visits to England, and the Cambridge house was one of their favourite ports of call. Although my aunt admired and loved them both, particularly perhaps Ursula, she was conscious of missing out on the emotional recognition that is usually the basis of friendship. She wrote of Ursula:

I never felt I understood what made her tick. I am . . . rational . . . Every now and again Ursula, who always seemed to me to be on her guard, would say things that made me realise that the rational way in which she liked to discuss books and problems was, as it were, just the icing on the cake. What were the ingredients of the cake? This I never discovered. Of course I know what Justin said [afterwards], and out of it I could construct a sociological study . . .

Of Justin and Ursula as a couple my aunt had this to say:

What seems to me the most remarkable thing about them . . . was the emotion . . . that bound them to each other. To be able to feel for another human being what Justin felt for Ursula, and to sustain the feeling over a lifetime, and die for it, must surely be something of which only one in several million is capable. I look on it as a gift which is beyond the power of reason to explain. 'Cogito, ergo sum' seems foolish by comparison.

It was my aunt who, referring to the difficulties she had had in 'understanding' Ursula, made the observation that she came 'straight out of Lermontov'. Because at the time I was feeling the need to redress the balance disturbed by the popular misconception of Ursula as a glittering prima donna with Justin as her stolid factotum, I guessed this to be a red herring, and wrote back saying so, albeit in deferential language. But something about the tone of my reply, its complacency perhaps, must have irritated my aunt, who immediately rushed off another letter, insisting on the relevance of her original claim and including the query, 'How long is it since you read A Hero of Our Time?' *A long time, undoubtedly. Still, I felt a resistance to exploring that line of approach – probably an instinctive, generalised unwillingness to define people by means of relating them to an inherited cultural background.*

Finally I pulled myself together and began reading my copy of the book, which had been glaring at me from my shelf from the start of the correspondence. After a few pages I realised that it was completely new to me – I had somehow succeeded in confusing it with And Quiet Flows the Don.

My aunt was right, of course. The similarities between Ursula and Pechorin, 'the hero of our time', are many and striking – the dandyism, the painful honesty, the streak of puritanism, the arrogant consciousness of being one step ahead of everybody else, the frankest self-interest combined with the yearning for self-forgetfulness, the cynical coolness and the passionate quest for love, and particularly the dicing with death equated with the search for the ultimate sensation. Ursula, even without the prescience of tragedy prerequisite for the role of romantic 'heroine', would have seemed heroic anyway, by virtue of her beauty, her courage, her independence, and her out-and-out rejection of anything second-rate.

It's the word 'Time' which suggests an anomaly. Lermontov's novel was written in the late 1830s, Ursula's journal in the 1970s, yet Pechorin, being a prototype, still sounds brand new, whereas Ursula often gives you the feeling that she's a throwback. She knew it, of course, and even, with Pechorin-like determination to make strengths out of weaknesses, embraced it as part of her stance in relation to the rest of the world.

No reference to A Hero of Our Time *comes into the 500-odd unedited pages of Ursula's journal. I certainly never heard her mention it, nor can anyone I've asked so remember that she did. And yet, not only in the poignant similarities of attitude, but also even in several significantly repeated usages (the rhetorical question, for example) and words ('pleasant') in Nabokov's standard translation – Ursula didn't speak Russian – there is enough to make you suspect a direct influence. However, Ursula wasn't one to conceal a literary preference, and I gradually came to the conclusion that she might simply never have read the book. If this is the case, it's made even stranger by the knowledge that at one stage of her life she thoroughly immersed herself in the Romantic movement, reading Goethe, Pushkin, Byron and other key figures in their entirety.*

I used to have a close friend who reminded me constantly of Proust. In conversation he could weave his way in and out of a subject, embracing a mass of fascinating detail and cross-reference, without getting lost and without losing touch with the originality of the insight he had set out to expound. Nocturnal by nature, he interspersed hours of hard work with sorties to night-clubs or taxi-drivers' tea-stalls. He was intrigued equally by the aristocracy and the criminal sector of the working class, and those of his more intimate friends who weren't fellow-artists were usually part of one or other of these social groups. Although he himself was too influential a figure for the idea of his having personally been influenced to be easy to accept, I had always vaguely assumed that the emulation of Proust had occupied most of his adolescence. When, after having known him for some years, I made some casual reference to Madame Verdurin, he replied rather humbly that he was afraid he had never read Proust. I remember that a silence followed – I was too astounded to think of anything to say. Later it seemed clear to me that some instinct had warned him not to waste months ploughing through all that stuff, since he knew it by heart already. You can't read everything, so you must have a rapidly functioning, inbuilt mechanism telling you what to leave out. Ursula, omnivorous reader though she was, had one too – the likelihood is that Lermontov got neglected for the same reasons that Proust did by my friend.

ENGLAND
London. November 1977
Tea at Brown's before the theatre. As we read the papers we listen with one ear to the Pinteresque conversations around us. Two old and immobile country persons: 'It is 6.15.' Two minutes' silence. 'I make it 6.10.' Two minutes' silence. 'The clock says 6.17.' Two minutes' silence. 'What do you make it now?' Two minutes' silence. '6.20.' Silence. All I can see is a heavy hand on the armrest of an upholstered chair and the top of a bald head.

Ritual closeting with Eve for twenty minutes in her study – a place of unread books, breathless telephone calls and a lot of charm.

ITALY
Rome. December 1977
When one can't sleep and one's heart beats irregularly, one wonders what on earth keeps it beating anyway. Africa is again shimmering vaguely but promisingly on the horizon. Will it mean the end?

The cold evils of melancholy, ennui, accidie, aimlessness, self-dissatisfaction, all melt in the fire of self-annihilation and resurrection. If I am religious by temperament, this potential has its perfect realisation in the act of love. Complete trust and self-abandonment are *only possible with him*. Any attempt at analysis would be both silly and impious, because reason, while it is essential for everything else in life, won't work for the things that are really important. The real fusion, the real grasp of essentials takes place at the moment when reason abdicates control. We have decided, without either of us knowing why, to go to Vienna.

GERMANY
Munich. February 1978
I feel something like embarrassment at the idea that the

German language lurks within me. Impossible that I should have spoken it. But English pushed it out, thank God.

Würzburg

We have the inspiration of lunching on the banks of a river, complete with ducks. I invade the *Konditorei*, full of fur coats and whipped cream, to answer what is known as a call of nature. One should not desecrate the snow.

Is it time to change a little? More conscious hedonism, perhaps? After all, the years are passing.

At a curve we started skidding in the snow, and ended up with a cracking sound in a ditch lined with cement – at a very odd angle. J. climbed out, stopped a car, and went off to get help. I stayed with my legs braced against the door. *Memento mori*. Death would be all right, but fate is so often petty. One feels calm on these occasions, several steps away from oneself. It was still snowing. A red-faced peasant assured me that the *Polizei* were on their way. A stout, open-faced constable arrived in a Volkswagen and took us to the station. Very *gemütlich*. A casserole of water bubbled on the stove, while a man in shirt-sleeves sorted out the ledgers and another whistled. Scrubbed boards, the crackle of the fire. Outside, a pleasant village street with low, old houses, and lined enchantingly with snow-covered trees. A rococo pavilion, a circular Romanesque chapel. I waited there while they went to pull the car out, my arm and elbow getting steadily stiffer. Suddenly there it was outside the window, somewhat bent and with both doors inoperable on the passenger side, but, as they say, in working order.

AUSTRIA
Vienna

A return to Vienna – twenty-two years later. Then too it was snowing, and my leg ached rather more than my shoulder does now. J. has a fever, and I have also developed disc pains, an empty trembling in the small of the back. We lie in this room full of echoes, the occasional car splashing by in the melting snow, and hope for a swift recovery. All the rooms I associate with fever – Mérida, Peshawar, Penang, Niamey, Tahoua,

Pamplona. Did I come back to look at the distance then? But this time I do not have to depend on myself alone – I have already cast the dice that were then only rattling in my pocket.

A sad town, on the whole. A café – cakes, magazines, regulars. After a bit one would hate it.

ITALY
Rome
Wild wind and rain at night. The luxury of a roof over one's head, a bed.

To write is to slow down, to remember, to attempt the impossible.

GREECE
Nysi. March 1978
Physical work is a powerful mental stimulus.

A week of rain and enforced leisure. This marvellous room, with wet views all around and a crackling fire. The new books to arrange in the bookcase.

I spend the day savagely pulling dark, entangled growths out of bushes of thyme. The performance of a necessary ritual also serving to sublimate aggression?

As soon as the sun comes out one forgets all uncertainty.

In a certain type of elderly couple the man always seems to go further into negligence of health, of money, out of bravado, contemptuous of the shrewd self-preservation of the woman.

The moon began to wane and my sanity with it. One of those prolonged blackouts – twelve hours this time. Fear and desperation and self-disgust add up to the knowledge that I am no good, worse than no good, a disaster. But finally he drags me out of it, and the reprieve is like a rebirth – discovering simple laughter, simple pleasure, knowing where I belong. *Les vrais paradis sont les paradis perdus?* I am unconvinced – the present is always best.

June 1978
I see something white in the distance and swim out after it, with a strange feeling that I am making a mistake – it will beckon me on, but the current will always keep it out of my

range. It is already outside the confines of the bay, but I swim on. As I get beyond the point I feel something smooth nudging my stomach – gurgles can be heard and bubbles rise. In the choppy water, glittering in the last rays of the sun, nothing can be seen – not that I would dream of looking. Quaking with horror, heart thumping, empty-headed, and swallowing mouthfuls of water, I thrash back towards the shore. I can see the boat now – I yell ineffectually. Then again the soft explosions, the gurgling, the bubbles. A hideous feeling.

July 1978

I lay in bed watching the lightning and waiting for the crash of thunder, and remembered a certain summer storm by the lake. People in armchairs looking out through the open french windows into the dark. A party – clinking glasses, low laughter, my father's deep, over-pleasant voice. I could see the haystack burning, the huge flames were momentarily *real*.

August 1978

From a certain simple and perfectly valid point of view it is madness to leave this place. But would one really be so moved by it if one never left it? Practise for the end. Readiness is all.

From time to time I have an eerie sensation of being back in the spiritual climate of my adolescence.

Soon, God willing, we shall be in Africa – the dark continent, heart-shaped, armed with spears and arrows. I long for it as I long for darkness, for sleep.

I, in my way, have become a nomad, though without a nomad's easy benevolence towards the world – one must be born for that, it seems.

ITALY
Rome. September 1978

The voices of bakers and cats. The trees across the river still in full leaf. A nightmare – I was flying heavily, like a damaged heron, the villains at my heels.

Slowly unpacking everything – the colours of the carpets unfolding, the objects finding their places. We go out, tremulous with excitement. I am still alive, and life is so uncertain.

Sudan ahead, perhaps more life ahead.

October 1978
Deep, bronze bells are tolling all over Rome. St Peter's is floating, bombarded with light. A new Pope has been elected – a Pole, it appears.

The anachronistic obsession of the backward part of Central Europe, from which I came, with weapons, horses, and futile grand gestures.

ENGLAND
London. November 1978
A dream. Windblown, nude, marshy country – salt flats, sand dunes. An empty house with rattling shutters. J. is making up a thornwood fire in the hearth. It is smoking. I am both there and not there, yet we manage to communicate. There is something we have to burn, but there is too much wind and the fireplace is too small. The long passage is wrapped in dusty cloth, strapped to the wall with leather belts. As the fire finally catches, I recognise what I've really known all along – it is my body he is, we are, burning. I am detached, pleased. I peer down, thinking: Now it is all done with, and so much the better.

EGYPT
Cairo. December 1978
The filthy, enticing, menacing real world again.

* * *

The section that follows is a record of the first of three trips to the province of Darfur in the west of Sudan that Justin and Ursula undertook in successive years. Each of these trips had a different purpose and a different character. It would be as well to summarise these briefly, in order to avoid the complete bewilderment I felt myself at first and even second reading.

The first journey began as simple exploration. They had no very definite plans, since they didn't know what to expect. They knew only that they still felt the pull of the African magnet. The Sahara, being uninhabitable, hadn't been what they wanted – they were after somewhere just a little more like Greece.

They landed in Khartoum and took an internal plane to El Fasher. From there they used public transport, which in Darfur usually means a lorry whose probable destination and timetable is broadcast by word of mouth. They were thus at the mercy of circumstances, and while this involved a lot of hanging about and discomfort, it's clear from Ursula's often amused tone of voice that she enjoyed the lack of responsibility. After travelling through Kass to Zalingei, they reached the frontier with Chad at Foro Burungha. Here she left a clue for the future: 'We've found it after all, the impossible, perfect place in Africa – big trees, horses, houses, semi-desert climate, semi-benevolent authorities, absence of other Europeans.' It was to Zalingei that they returned next year.

On that first trip, however, they travelled on towards the south-east of Sudan. From Nyala they went by train via Babanusa and Aweil to Wau. They took a lorry to Azande, near the frontier with the Congo, where they had been invited to stay by a friendly Greek. Finally they travelled by riverboat up the White Nile to Kosti, and from there by bus to Khartoum.

One of the most surprising elements of the trip, or at least of the record of it provided by Ursula's journal, is the way in which they abdicated control into the hands of random strangers. There is something hippyish in the way they proceed from place to place with complete disregard for comfort and a lack of planning that at times almost puts them in the position of spongers.

Ursula would have disliked the comparison – some of her best satire was at the expense of hippies, whom she referred to as 'the vow [wow] generation'. But during these two months certain standpoints – resignation to whatever fate has to offer, trust in the willingness of other people to help them out, combined with the knowledge that, if the worst comes to the worst, there are always the traveller's cheques to fall back on – undeniably give her an affinity with the targets of her humour. There's a slackening of tension – one entry hints that she'd prefer to be drunk for a better appreciation of the

*drumming. It's significant that drunkenness, which had been
inconceivable to her for the last fourteen years, opened the
door to the dissolution of spirit which was necessary for her
suicide.*

*Previously, even in South America (where she was unusually
ready to observe and record the oddities of the people around
her) it seems as though she and Justin lived together inside some
membrane that insulated them from the outside world. Now
the spiritual communion, the 'interdependence' she used to
refer to so often and with such gratitude, is beginning to
weaken, with the result that other people are allowed to touch
her emotions.*

A glossary of Arabic terms is included on page 257.

SUDAN
January 1979
Expectation. Waiting for a lorry. It was there, it was not there,
it had changed its route. Then it was there again. We got on.
False start as far as a petrol-station. Finally it got going, only
to come to a sudden halt in a sandy street. We were invited
into a freshly painted house with mango trees in the courtyard,
for the celebration party of a recently returned *hadj*. J. was led
into a formal reception room, with goatskin rugs and sofas
occupied by robed gentlemen, while I, alas, was swept into the
less formal women's quarters.

A stop for prayer. Bowed and turbaned heads by a row of
huts. Infinitely refreshing tea with lime. Too tired to hold on
to any idea for long – but then that is one of the fatal
attractions of tiredness.

On in the lorry by moonlight to Kass, where we are dropped
outside the police-station. An oil-lamp illuminates two men
reclining on mats, half-asleep beside their rifles. One of them
takes J. off into the darkness of the big trees. J. returns alone.
We sit and wait for the man among the roots of a huge *haraz*
tree, eating our last grapefruit and gazing up into the delicate
foliage of the very wide-spreading branches, which filters a
pallid light. Birds hoot. At last the white-robed *haris* comes
back with the keys. We have two beds with sheets, candles and

water-pills. In the morning we discover that our soap and
shoes have been half-gnawed through by rats.

As we are getting up, the *haris* arives with two glasses of tea.
The *m'hafiz* offers us a ride in his new Range Rover (of all
things) to Nyala and Galole. Rolling, open country with the
same giant *haraz*. Passing horsemen have sheaves of small
hunting spears and long, broad-bladed lances. No doubt it's
splendid riding country.

Galole

Fur country. J. acquires a hen with great difficulty – it is
cooked by the official savagess. J. also finds a guide, a Forest
Ranger, who is shy and pleasant, and actually likes and knows
about trees. His verandah looks on to a sort of jungle Eden,
but for all that it is much in demand from stranded officials.
The peace is broken late at night by a pandemonium of
drumming.

After days of indecision, the moon-faced Forest Ranger gets
into a sudden fever to be off. He leaves without warning us.
To howls of encouragement from the official savagess, who
naturally wants to be left alone in her sylvan paradise, and
from the furiously impatient lorry crew, we fling things into
suitcases, and rush through the forest to the stream, where the
lorry, smoking, roaring, hooting, has paused.

Nyerteti

The road is unbelievably rough. The village is in a ferment –
the Minister of Agriculture is expected at any moment. We
wander up to a triumphal arch, and are greeted very formally
by an elderly *Forawa* in very dirty European clothes. In fluent
Oxford English he suggests that we join the reception party.
Range Rovers, dust, and important personages. Orange juice
and fresh strawberries materialise, of which we partake –
breakfast. To sidelong, puzzled glances from the Minister we
take our leave with the person detailed to guide us to the souk.

We are invited to stay with Haroun, a relic of the Emirate.
His verandah is neglected by local standards. He appears in a
grimy *jellabah* and produces deckchairs whose leather seats
will still just withstand the weight of a human form. 'This

bloody world is going to the bad,' he says, as a blaze of strip-lighting suddenly reveals the full extent of the neglect. A meal is produced, although we have already eaten. Afterwards, in the last of the daylight, we are shown his model fruit farm, obviously his greatest pride. Then we go to the farm-manager's house, where a circle of officials is sitting on the lawn in the light of the rising moon. One of these instantly suggests that we proceed with them to Zalingei, where they will take care of our accommodation. Oddly, we are reluctant to accept – perhaps the invitation was uncomfortably precipi-tate – but otherwise we would have to wait for a lorry. We are given beds in a pleasant, though long unswept, hut. Then dinner, the third meal of the afternoon. Camels are taken care of. One of our new hosts was educated in Russia, where he acquired a satisfactory wife and a fund of very amusing anecdotes. He is looking for minerals in the bush, and hoping for a spot of riding and shooting on the side.

In the morning J. meets a certain Monsieur Vanderelst, the Belgian EEC representative, who becomes petulant on hearing that we too are travelling to Zalingei – it smacks of British interference. He is last seen, still looking petulant, breakfasting with his spouse on the chicken-legs left over from our dinner.

Beautiful desert savannah with occasional great thorn trees – camel- and cattle-dealing nomads on foot or mounted. Good little horses, mountains in the distance.

Zalingei

Clean and comfortable rest house in a sandy place under vast acacias. Our room has a big netted window. We are barricaded in while the Common Market discussion takes place just outside our door: 'The scheme's unsatisfactory – production is low and organisation poor, to put it mildly.' A dressing-down pure and simple from this Common Market man. His high-pitched voice and blue denim shorts impel an uncomfortable silence. We can't stay, since a representative of the World Bank is expected. J. is out looking for somewhere else to stay. He comes back saying that a child has been leading him all over the village. He found various abandoned rest houses and eventually the wife of the Assistant Commissioner. Off we go.

I get covered in scent, though J. resists. We are offered freshly squeezed lime-juice. Then we are whisked off to a picnic on the wadi.

A dry hillside with a tobacco company and a disused but luxurious rest house. A stone pyramid, with an inscription that reads: *Under this plot lies Edmund M-B, died 1931, aged 34.*

J. has learned the *Forawa* greetings. All the old women are highly amused.

Umm Balla

Drumming all night, mostly dull but some excellent. One really can't participate sober, though one would like to. One is both close and distant, that is one of the joys of Africa.

Foro Burunga

Our acquaintances all sit inside a very small *ghautiyya* – though not at all rowdy, they appear to be in a condition of alcoholic elation. *Arak* is in evidence. Some manage to fit on to a very small bed, while the rest are huddled on the floor on the mat. Food – raw gut marinaded in lime-juice, roast meat, salad, and *kisra*. Orgiastic gobbling.

We've found it after all, the impossible, perfect place in Africa – big trees, horses, houses, semi-desert climate, semi-benevolent authorities, absence of other Europeans.

When one starts writing in these exposed positions, the effect is like that of a witchdoctor laying out his equipment in the foyer of Brown's Hotel.

Driving through semi-cultivated bush in a lorry. The landowner is with us, but neither he nor the driver seems to have the faintest idea of where we are going. We have been driving for ten hours, though the journey is supposed to take only six. No sign of any wheeled vehicle ever having passed before. Groundnuts have been loaded so high that it's difficult to imagine where the other passengers have got to.

We have our own hut in the middle of the compound. We are given food, water, bedding. Between the thatched roof and the circular wall we get a clear view of life in the compound.

The races. The *hakaama* sings the praises of the riders for a

fee, failing which she sings about things they would prefer
kept quiet. Drunks.

Our unique position as the only, and relatively minor,
foreign intrusion in the celebrations. In spite of being rather
too boisterously mobbed by the over-excited little *Forawa*
children, we got back feeling elated.

El Fasher

Once again on the road, with yet another departure in view.
Green parrots squabbling in the grey-green foliage of the
haraz trees. *Dépaysement* – belonging, yet not belonging.
Some of the happiest moments of my life have been spent in
situations of limbo. The odd feeling that one has found the
original of the sensation one has always looked for, after a long
series of approximations.

An excruciating stomach cramp on a crowded bus – seeing
everything through a sort of mist, unable to think straight. I
hobble back to stretch out in the hotel. Appendicitis? But an
hour later it has passed, and I feel reborn.

Refuge in the old-fashioned dining-car of the train from
Nyala to Babanusa. Through the thorn-scratched, bullet-
holed window our own reflections and the evening savannah
slipping slowly past.

Babanusa

Dinkas. One man has a miniscule straw hat held in place by a
strap encircling his massive, bushy coiffure and fastened
above his eyebrows. He wears a white gown, stud earrings,
bracelets, black plastic walking shoes, and a formidable
throwing stick, yellow and shiny with use. He is unaware of
the fortuitous success of his outfit. By goods train to Wau.

Hassan, the *m'hafiz*, took us again to the *stiraha*. An elderly
haris was in a subdued rage because of the non-appearance of a
prison-governor – everything, including clean, white sheets,
had been prepared for days. So we get the sheets.

The railway building. The prevailing feeling, which we
share, is that there is little hope of ever getting away.

We hire a cart – two wheels, an axle, and a wooden platform
– to the *zariba*. Another Babanusa appears, with clean, sandy

streets, solid, whitewashed, walled compounds – the blue-washed houses are surrounded with trees and have netted verandahs, green shutters. A long conversation of little import with a sympathetic family. I am dressed in my usual trouser-suit and hat – from time to time they reassure one another that I am a man.

Drumming at night synchronises with my abnormally fast pulse – I checked it against J.'s which, thank God, was normal.

A trainload of *Dinkas* from Wau transforms the station.

Our train arrives at last – a filthy cattle-waggon to ourselves. J. makes a masterly speech in Arabic to the station-master. As a result a sulky old man, escorted briskly by a young policeman, comes with a small rag and cleans up some of the mess. J. does the rest. Grateful for the privacy, I attend to my toilette. We lie down on the single bench, which is hard, but, for the time being, tolerable. Just outside of Babanusa, and tantalisingly within sight of the *stiraha*, we stop. Someone says that the dynamo has packed up, and there we wait till daybreak. We have tea and snacks in the guard's van. The guard, Abdullah, tells us his life story.

Aweil
We get off the train, assured that it will stop for several hours. While we argue with the police, having been arrested for photography, the train leaves, two hours before schedule, with all our stuff aboard. After a ponderous negotiation with the dignified *m'hafiz* and the payment of a fine, we chase it in a Toyota.

After four days and three nights on the train we have covered perhaps 250 kilometres.

Wau
Dinkas in the market have long, brass-bound pipes. One of these smokers wears a T-shirt with the words 'ever ready'. He looks less ready than anyone I've ever seen – he slouches elegantly about, wearing tiny earrings in his beautiful little ears, in a veritable limbo of unreadiness.

As we emerge from our room in the evening, we see the

smooth river disturbed only by the huge bulk of a hippo yawning in the middle. The town has something faintly Portuguese about it – a hint of Goa, Maragogype, Malacca. Full moon over blazing stubble on the other bank of the river. *Dinka* songs sound, hollow and demented, over the water.

A merry *Dinka* police officer, who promised to take us to Gogrial, left, unexpectedly, for Khartoum.

Silvas, an old Greek with a *Dinka* wife, is obsessed with Dionysus and Odysseus. From fourteen to twenty he worked as a clerk in his uncle's shop in Alexandria. He worked in the mines as a prisoner-of-war in Silesia. After that Africa was a relative paradise. He invites us to stay with him in Nzara.

In the evening we strolled up towards the bridge. An old, stone-walled garden with a big frangipani, then open country along the shallow river. Heaps of oysterlike shells the size of plates among the red, porous stones of the bank. Blue-black bodies soaping vigorously in the pale water. Later, wearing only a dressing gown, I recline luxuriously in a long-armed chair, drinking lukewarm lime tea.

Next morning the usual delay – no bus, no lorry. J. is out on a bicycle scouting for transport. I read Noh plays to calm myself.

Anzande

A lane, at the end of which is the frontier with the Congo. We wander down it, attracted by the distant sound of a xylophone. Delicate, haunting music, played, it turns out, by two boys in a yard behind a grass fence. We leave and return in the dark to record them. They play the same piece again, and then produce a lute and begin singing. They are very good-natured and completely natural with us. I sleep in the curtained cab of the lorry, J. on the ground outside.

Nzara

Silvas, the Greek, is a man of his word indeed. Utterly exhausted, we staggered out of the lorry to find him at the gate of his neat house, built out of pale stone in a colonial-English style. Furniture, including easy chairs, in mahogany, reading-lamps. Tolstoi and Dostoievski, as well as Maurois's *Histoire d'Angleterre* in Greek. Silent, well-trained servants and three grey parrots in a cage. A real bathroom and a spare room for us. A good lunch, cold beer, and Greek coffee, freshly roasted and ground. As if all this were not enough, he confesses to a love of solitude – the man is a paragon. In the evening we go for a drive in his windscreenless jeep through thickly-wooded, undulating country, the soft, blue luminosity tinged with green. Silvas drives like an absent-minded English gentleman. A village of neat bungalows, with its own lake, in a clearing – ex-British residences for the cotton-factory functionaries. A lavishness of flavours, a feeling of irresponsibility. We are guests. We go to bed. In the morning there is home-made, fresh bread and butter with exotic wild honey – fresh coffee or tea.

Days of complete well-being, the kind of thing we dream of during our arduous travels. Every morning tea is brought us in bed by a servant whose particular task it is. Green shutters and faded pink sheets in the moist, cool morning. The blunt, rust-coloured stone of the wall merges with the other muted colours of the view – dead banana leaves, mango flowers, grass roofs, jungle. An excursion into the bush to Silvas's shop, to collect a barrel of honey. The young man who runs the shop already owns half of it, and will inherit the rest. That is the only way to do it, Silvas says. A solitary man. Long talks into the night. Silvas's real past slowly emerges – intensely felt and vivid memories of childhood. He is from Florina. Wine-pressing with bare feet, apple trees, snake-hunts. The sharing of these memories of simple attachments is a specially Greek phenomenon, and in this sense we are treated as Greeks.

Odd screaming from the souk – rage, joy, madness? I remain detached. When the mad refugee woman in the souk at Wau howled at each of us in turn, I remained detached as well – from close up the actress was unmistakable.

When we say goodbye to our host, his eyes shift uneasily behind his lenses. He snaps at a beggar-woman with unnecessary violence. His eyes are on everything – what would life be like without attention to detail? Living on his own he has become an Argos – with the inevitable eye-strain. Clearly he cannot leave his post – and for all his hospitality, he clearly looks forward to returning to his routine. Disturbances, however pleasant, should be brief.

Yambio
Lorries which may or may not come. J. manages to persuade the military commander to take us to Maridi some time in the late afternoon. He drives with maniacal speed and seems to lack even the faintest understanding of mortality. At one of his lurches J., who is in the back of the car, hits the roof very smartly, and this causes considerable mirth – as if it were an intentional repayment for our shameless asking for favours.

Maridi
In a cupboard of our room we find a few personal possessions – fine cotton shirts made to measure, socks, white ducks, a piece of yellowing satin. Under the shirts are a wristwatch which doesn't work, some bone dice, and the cartridge of an elephant gun. I throw the dice by torchlight – if they fall on an even number, it's a good sign. Sixteen. Do I deserve it?

Juba
Silvas entrusted us with an unaddressed envelope, which, he told us, contained letters for his family in Greece. We opened it, and found, as well as the letters, another envelope addressed to 'my dearest friends' with our names touchingly misspelt – inside were fifty Sudanese pounds. So one was right about the depth of feeling. What an awkward, moving, Greek gesture – to give to those who do not need it and whom you will never see again. The impulsive shyness of it reminds me of my godfather.

Riverboat on the Aswa. Fierce and beautiful people on the bank. A black Achilles, naked except for his brass arm- and leg-bands, armed with some very long spears. One man who got off the boat to buy sugar-cane got left behind – he ran miles along the bank, howling and clutching his purchases, to shrieks of laughter from the passengers.

In response to a polite request for food, no matter how little, a boathand brandishes an onion-knife at J.'s throat –

however it fails to intimidate him, and in the end some bread and jam are produced.

Kosti. February 1979
Our perfect little room is totally luxurious after our so-called first-class cabin. Round the corner is the jewellers' street. Gold snakes, hollow bracelets, half-moon earrings – at last all the things we have looked for in vain elsewhere.

Khartoum
Plastic dawn at the airport after a night of mosquitoes and insomnia.

AUSTRIA
Vienna
We landed briefly in Athens and thought of Nysi. Overnight stop here. Back by bus to the airport to catch the London plane. Glades between smooth, busy roads, duck flying heavily up from the canal. An accident – a crumpled figure in a white coat lies on the back seat of a crushed Volkswagen. Someone hurries along the road with a blanket. The bus radio plays a tinkling polka at a discreet volume.

FRANCE
Paris
Ten days of England behind us. We were met by Manuel at London airport, fur coats on his arm – suddenly we were members of the pampered classes, as the chauffeur drove us to the country house. Am I living my life or am I having it led for me? More likely that we are both being led by similar or identical powers beyond our control. Anyway the feeling was pleasant, as if we were impostors, as yet unsuspected. But then we drove away in our own car.

A still, cold morning in the Palais Royal – the piled-up chairs suggest conversations recently ended. The pigeons are too plump to feel the cold.

We walked to St-Sulpice in a lurid evening light, and then up to the Luxembourg with its blue-black, denuded trees.

ITALY
Lodi
The last day of a very crowded month, beginning on the Nile.
Greece, Austria, England, France. Here I am in our hotel
room wondering what can have happened to J., since he went,
without the car keys, to collect something from the car. A
pleasant *albergo* with ample bath towels, polished tiles, and
polite old waiters. And a nice town too, including the station.
The hoot of departing trains in the snowy night – fog and
steam.

Will we get back to Sudan? An idle question expecting no
answer – it should *never* have been asked.

Rome. March 1979
All the bits and pieces that we have here – how important are
they? Armed with one's memory one really ought to be able to
do without all these photographs and notebooks.

In the afternoon I had a peculiar feeling of disorientation, as
if the world had suddenly stopped making sense. But, of
course, what is so much more surprising is that most of the
time it does make sense.

GREECE
Nysi. April 1979
I recognise certain bushes which I pruned and weeded last
year – they certainly do look better. I acknowledge the point in
retrospect, never anticipate it. I do what I do because I like
doing it now or because it is necessary now.

We bought our year's supply of cheese in the foothills of
Taygetos.

A few last, strenuous efforts, and I have stopped weeding.
This headland has never received, will never receive again,
such a thoroughly aesthetic going-over.

May 1979
We have begun our Arabic lessons. I listen admiringly to J.'s
deep, hoarse gurgles, feeling a mixture of nostalgia and
misgiving. Africa *again*? Death must have his chance – what I

really have doubts about is the dust in the eyes, the mortified flesh. But such considerations are petty, and refer, besides, to the distant future.

A round, heavy badger, which we disturbed raiding the pears, went charging up the hill exactly like something from *Alice in Wonderland*.

July 1979

We might survive this year, of course, but my cycle, the one I have in my mind's eye, slightly compressed as we pass from light into shadow across the continents, seems just now so complete.

It's strange to be driving the boat, following that barely visible indication, J.'s black snorkel pipe, as it wanders at random over an unimaginable landscape – to me, above a chaos of bright and shifting water; to him, below, a familiar place of rocks and hillocks, sands and caves.

September 1979

While J. was looking for some ghost castle on the horizon, we ran into the back of another car, crushing our bonnet. How close it always is, not even waiting for us, merely there.

ITALY
Rome. October 1979

No desire to do anything in particular – it is enough merely to be here, now that the sun slants through the bamboo slats. The yellow embroidered silk gleams, so does the smooth, gold head of the little Buddhist monk.

Italian art is the consummate realisation of certain aspects of existence. The delightful lack of intellectualism. That's what we like about Italy itself, and why we live here in preference to anywhere else except Nysi. The innate Italian ability to make life pleasant, worthwhile, sometimes even irresistible. It is all done so simply, so cynically, so intelligently.

We wake up warm in bed, while the rain pelts down outside, knowing there is nowhere we need go, nothing we need do. We lie there for a while in the half-dark, the carpets glowing deeply. A day ahead – breakfast of the best chocolate,

Brancati, Dante, the library, the Corsini gardens, clothes to wear, food to prepare.

Near the back gate of the Villa Medici there is a strange stirring of invisible birds. An owl calls sonorously and J. answers it. It comes nearer, and so does a cat, a young, neat, compact tabby, which sits down every time it wants to listen to something. Then it rushes off in sheer frustration, incomprehension.

FRANCE
Lunéville
The perfect room, Hôtel du Cheval Blanc. We have finally perfected our European travelling too. Pity about England.

ENGLAND
Slough. November 1979
At Eve's one gets to bed at one or two in the morning and up at nine. The mornings are delightful – the damp, green light filtering through the foliage, the solitude and luxuriance of the garden, the smell of strong coffee and toast.

* * *

I mentioned before that each of the successive Sudanese trips had a different purpose, a different character. The second, which had been planned in advance during the summer at Nysi, was for house-hunting. It seems more likely that they meant to acquire a house in Sudan for regular late-winter living, forgoing their voyages of exploration to other parts of the world, than that they wanted it as a substitute for either Nysi or Rome. On the other hand, Ursula always craved the unknown, and anywhere that you can call your own quickly becomes familiar. Perhaps they never reached the point of deciding. What they had already decided was that the vicinity of Zalingei was an ideal hunting-ground. This was because of its climate, the attractiveness of the people, and, not least, the suitability of the country for riding and the availability of horses.

This year they set about investigating the possibilities in detail. Three new themes are immediately noticeable. One is Ursula's sociability. Yiza, the Mawlana, *the Emir, Jaffr – these people are referred to in the easy, teasing, but respectful language you reserve for friends. Admittedly, they are all in some way seen as potential landlords or house-vendors, but still the impression of genuine affection remains. The second new theme is riding and the concomitant worsening of Ursula's health.*

Ursula had already come to the conclusion that her life was lacking an element – strenuous physical risk, of a kind that she and Justin could run together. Perhaps she was envious of his moments of violence underwater at Nysi, where he faced enormous fish with no more protection for his nakedness than a harpoon. They had ridden together once or twice in India in 1970, but apart from that riding was merely an exciting childhood memory. Throughout the journals Ursula is alert to the idea that dangerous living shortens the odds on accidental death. She writes about such death with sang-froid, with resignation, with longing, but most often with the caressing familiarity you lavish on some childhood secret. She never seems more than academically interested in suicide in its more straightforward form. It's the bolt from the blue she's after, the precipice, or the neck broken in a fall from a galloping horse.

In March 1976 another sister-in-law of mine, my brother Jonna's first wife Janey, was killed in just this way at the age of twenty-five. Justin and Ursula were between Rome and Greece at the time, and the news arrived too late for them to be able to go to England for the funeral. I next saw them in November that year. Ursula questioned me at length on the details of the accident. At the time her interest didn't strike me as morbid. Although she had scarcely known poor Janey, and although she didn't easily admit that Justin's family had any special right to be considered as relations of hers (she never used the terms 'brother-in-law', 'mother-in-law', 'father-in-law' with reference to us), I thought her concern natural enough – after all, I knew nothing of her preoccupation with death.

Since then I've found out that suicide is infectious. If you have suicidal instincts and somebody in your immediate circle kills himself, it's hard not to think, whether consciously or not:

He had the courage to do it – why shouldn't I? Too many of my friends have committed this 'imitative' suicide for me to be able to ignore its threat. Although there was no question of Janey's death being anything but a tragic accident, I'm now convinced that it suggested to Ursula that riding, which was, by the way, an exercise 'heroic' enough to appeal to her Pechorin side, was also dangerous enough, given a nudge or two in the right direction, to provide an ideal opportunity of 'giving death his chance'.

As it turned out, the only harm riding did her was back trouble, a legacy of her accident in 1961. This would normally have been the last thing Ursula wanted, since she attributed any passing physical malfunction to the gradual decay of the body, the descent into the unthinkable trough of old age. There was a certain weakness of logic in her attitude. While she had always accepted that her beauty required constant maintenance, which argues the expectation of a future, she didn't feel the same about her health – she expected it to take care of itself. She thought it more important to do exactly what she wanted at any given time than to hold back for fear of aggravating a complaint. And now that she was getting impatient, she even welcomed the pain in her back – anything to precipitate things, to break the stalemate. *'My back is in agony – I can feel every muscle as if I were nothing but an anatomical drawing. But there is nothing I can do to stop the jolts.'* 'Of course there is,' you want to remonstrate, 'you can lie on your back for a couple of days, and wait till it's better.'

Ursula's third new theme, though only given the space of one entry, introduces a note of spiky warning. Justin goes for a walk, leaving Ursula alone by the wadi. *'I consider his move tactless. Tactlessness is often taken for sincerity, and sincerity in turn is often taken for a compliment. Let no one ever be sincere with me – it is a failure of respect, and respect is a thing one can never get enough of.'* This is the only occasion, in ten years of journal-writing, when Ursula ventures even the slightest criticism of Justin. That the criticism seems unreasonable increases your sense of shock. She wouldn't have been human if she never felt critical of him in all those years – the

*point is that she never before said so in her journal, which
Justin was in the habit of reading. In other words, she is herself
indulging in a sincerity far more tactless than his, which she so
deplores.*

*Justin was Ursula's counterbalance. They both understood
that he had the weight to correct her leanings towards oblivion,
but only, as Justin later explains, when he could interpret her
death-wish as a periodic aberration. When, next year, he
realised that it had taken her over completely, there was
nothing more he could do – loving her in her entirety, he
wanted whatever she wanted, including, if necessary, her
death and with it his own. This attitude must have been
exasperating to Ursula. A suicide pact is only a tolerable
solution if both parties want death equally. To be the murder-
weapon of the only man she had loved, who had given her the
greatest happiness of her life, just because she knew that
she, and only she, had to die, seemed an unjustly harsh
responsibility. She could think of only two possible ways out of
the dilemma – to carry on living or to jettison her love – and in
the end she chose the second. The chill so noticeable in the
remark 'I consider his move tactless' is merely the first written
indication of her switch of emotion. Justin himself was
certainly already aware of it.*

*If any single quality can be said to have directed my
brother's life, it's the kind of moral and physical courage often
to be found in the characters of men of action. That the quality
was innate is clear from this story of his childhood told me by
my mother: "Justin was ten – I can date it because 1958 was
the year we took that house in Villefranche. One day some
people came over bringing their children, so it happened that
there were four or five little boys of about his age milling
around – Jonna wasn't there for some reason. The others all
wanted to dive off a high rock that overhung a fairly narrow
stretch of water. It really was awfully high, maybe fifteen foot
or more, but we could see that there was no danger because of
the depth of the water. They went up there one by one and
dithered around at the top, making all the appropriate gestures
without one of them managing to screw himself up to take the
plunge. Justin had been playing somewhere else on his own,*

*but when he saw what was going on he calmly climbed up and
dived off without hesitation. After that of course the others had
to do it, and in the end most of them managed.' 'Rather bad
manners to show up his guests on his home ground, don't you
think?' 'Good God, he was only* ten. *I think you've always been
a bit jealous of him yourself.'*

This had already crossed my mind as I progressed with the
researching of the book. *Justin was inaccessible to me. In spite
of the emphasis he and Ursula put on their close encirclement
of one another, I was always aware of his aloneness. Uneasy
with other men in general (and particularly wary of me), he
could even be seen as a solitary knight engaged on a highly
anachronistic mission – a quest, involving feats of daring
for the benefit of one woman, which was irrelevant to my way
of thinking. The analogy of the knight isn't wholly fanciful
either – there was something archaic about him, discernible in
his identification with primitive culture, his immaculate
clothes, even the occasionally eyebrow-raising stiltedness of his
language. He really did resist the twentieth century. I'm not
entirely at ease with it myself, but like most people I inevitably
feel obliged to give it the benefit of the doubt. But Justin was
both a hero and my brother. Heroes are by their nature
uncomfortable with ordinary contact, and for Jonna and
me, his brothers and therefore his most obvious rivals, he
was doubly difficult to approach. My frustration with the
distance he kept from me hardened slowly but surely into an
unadmitted jealousy of his heroism.*

SUDAN
El Fasher. January 1980
The heads of camels bobbing along, seen above the yellow
wall. The desert air, the air of nothingness.

The bank manager says, as he hands us our money with a
glass of tea, 'Your speech is delicious.'

Zalingei
We are staying in Yiza the *Fellata's* house. We have two grey
horses – and all this only a fortnight since leaving London. J.

is outside talking to our host in what sounds like fluent Arabic. I am in the pleasantly disjointed state of not knowing quite who or what I am.

We got here by bus and lorry via Geneina and Saraf Umra. In Geneina a party with the young *m'hafiz* with food, sherry, and some rather gauche shuffle-dancing. Then another at the house of Moustafa, the merchant, which is next to the Emir's above the village. A marvellous verandah. Good carpets, good food, good whisky, though we didn't really want it. Moustafa's anecdotes, in broken French about disastrous money speculations in the West, were amusing. The lorry broke down on the way to Saraf Umra. The driver disappeared into the distance with the steering column on his shoulder. We were picked up at last by a much superior lorry. Saraf Umra is beside the wadi among the vast trees. Nowhere for us to stay, so we were taken to ask the police if we could have their disused rest house. A saturnine Arab major with flashing eyes was in control – he told us that the rest house was occupied. Off we went again and finally met up with Yiza.

On our first morning out with the horses J. is thrown. While I am negotiating a gritty wadi, a youth comes running up to tell me that J.'s arm and hand are badly skinned and the saddle split. I quickly ride back alone in order to avoid a public demonstration of feminine distress. As I am unsaddling, there is a bang on the corrugated-iron door of the shed. J. stands there looking very grave. He was apparently dragged along on his back with his foot caught in the stirrup. We go to Doctor Hassan, who treats the wounds with alcohol and penicillin, and wraps his arm in gauze. They ride off again to the wadi, while the sun sinks and my heart with it, coming back in the dark with another horse, which has proved lame on the way.

Next morning, full of Westerners' resolution, we march to the *mawlana*'s house. A large carpet is set out, on which we sit, instantly reassured by the charm of the setting. We drink tea and try as best we can to understand the ancestral tales.

We ride together without incident, having exchanged J.'s horse for a grey Sudanese beauty with a curving nose, taller and darker than mine. They look splendid together – let's only hope they get on.

When a stirrup-leather broke my horse bolted, dislodging something in my spine. But this wonderful landscape compensates for the aches and pains.

My horse trots lightly and well, but is capricious. J., who has ridden it, agrees. It does not gallop regularly, nor does it like stopping, if not in the mood.

Up to Jebel Conya. The horses are upset by a pack of baboons, and we are obliged to depart in blazing heat, just as we were stopping to rest in the shade. We make for the *haraz* forest, which fringes the distant wadi, but once there, we cannot dismount, because every square metre of the forest is planted with tomatoes.

Disgust with my body and all its aches, pains and imperfections. How long do I propose to put up with this? J. massages my trembling back, and I, in return, dress his wounds. One's carcase interferes with the simple resolve to enjoy oneself.

Another pack of baboons kept at bay by the *mawlana*'s dog. Beautiful country around the banks of the wadi Azum – *haraz* woods, distant mountains, mango-fringed ponds. Blue and yellow-green fields of onions. We had a superb picnic with the *mawlana*, sitting on a Libyan rug.

My horse gets maddened, first by two fighting dogs, then by a mare on heat. J. rides up to help, which only makes matters worse. But the *mawlana*'s stallion, being only eighteen months old, is another matter, and finally he calms mine down. I am taking Brufen for my back.

A caravan – the camels are tied neck to tail with leather thongs. Three beautiful young women – thin, intricate, greased plaits trail delicately on to their gleaming, black shoulders. They are people who have come over from Chad and who can hardly speak Arabic.

Another bout of bucking causes a rapid, red-hot reeling in my back, which I can do nothing to control. J. rides my horse furiously until he calms it down a little.

My back is in agony. In the morning we left the village by the Garsila road, made a detour behind the hills to the south, and finally settled in a sandy cove in a shaded tributary of the wadi Kadengaro – rocks overhung with deep foliage. The horse sounds as if he has pneumonia.

I can feel every muscle of my back, as if I were nothing but an anatomical drawing. But there is nothing I can do to stop the jolts. The lorry is carrying, besides ourselves, seven passengers and a sheep, which groans and struggles because two men are sitting on it. The *mawlana* laughs with that gentle laugh of his, like a woman's cough. He has a beautiful face, the face of a dreamer, though sometimes it can look almost mad.

We got back home at 3 a.m., shaken but triumphant. All the same, when we were driving along with the moonlight shining on the barrel of one of the passengers' guns, I thought: Why not? I thought it again and again.

This morning J. gave a sound whack to my horse, which distressed me. But as a result, and perhaps because of our short-rein policy as well, he behaved perfectly from then on.

The *mawlana* proposes a visit to a grove he owns beside the wadi – he suggests that we might build there. We find it at the edge of the village, with big mangoes providing dense shade. I certainly like it, but there are nomads squatting here at present, though the *mawlana* claims they have no rights at all.

The conviction that all is right with the world and with one's own place in it is a feeling so rare and strange that to experience it at all is a kind of self-justification.

There is great pleasure to be had in jogging along on horseback down the dusty road, exchanging Arabic and *Fur* greetings with all and sundry, native and nomad.

An obscure longing to return into the dark, to communicate with a self that ceased to be my own when I was riding. Afterwards we go for a walk in the dusty darkness, lit up here and there by little fires. The *mawlana* is sitting by one of them, wrapped up in white, with his eldest son. We talk about the house – the plan is as nebulous as a dream. He lays his fine, black hand on J.'s and gently refuses our offer of money for his orchard. He would build the house for us, and would only allow us to pay for the zinc and cement. 'By next year it will be ready, insh'Allah.'

At night, as the horses cough and wheeze, J. quietly exposes a shadow side of this exotic and possible deal with the *mawlana*. But I am absolutely determined not to get worked up about being swindled on what would be an essentially minor scale – a certain respect for elegance must be brought to bear on our dealings with people here. All right, says, J., as long as I know what kind of thing to expect.

The flavour of fever, with its intensifying, distancing effect – a reminder that dying is an art, like anything else. How much longer do I intend to live? My body creaks – even my eyelids grate against my eyes. Only an effort of will can hold the structure together. And will, which is composed of obstinacy and abstention, ebb and flow, to be replaced by indifference, the free fall.

They kill the sheep. The blood drips from the small, brown, soft, astonished face into the bowl. Nothing in the way of flesh is wasted. No false delicacy, no ambiguity in this celebration of the survival urge – one must be eater or eaten. But, all the same, we did travel with the blameless creature, wait about for lorries with it.

A picnic in the grove – J., perhaps feeling claustrophobic, says he is going for a walk, and I am left to be haunted for an hour without ghosts. I consider his move tactless. Tactlessness is often taken for sincerity, and sincerity is in turn often taken for a compliment. Let no one ever be sincere with me – it is a failure of respect, and respect is a thing one can never get enough of. And the only kind of respect worth having is the insincere kind.

The plan for that simple little house by the edge of the wadi is running into predictably baroque convolutions. Trying to do things with other people, explain to them one's purposes, one's tastes, is often too much for one's powers of communication. But we eat a mango – cool, firm, yellow, luscious flesh – and recover our spirits a little.

I awake alone at dawn to an alarming sound of whinnying. I open the door of the shed, and there is J. struggling to separate the two stallions, who are fighting in a cloud of dust – mine with its pole in tow, J.'s still tied up.

We met an old *Baggara* in the long grass beyond the crane-infested pool. 'Are you the *mawlana* 's Englishman?' he asked, admiring J.'s horse.

Time is slipping away – one morning's cooing doves are indistinguishable from those of the next. One must grasp hold of time.

The other night we met the local hero, a self-made millionaire and a native of Kargulla, on his way to Nyerteti. He spoke of Wordsworth, and the difficulty, in a life like his, of profiting from a classical education. His London house is a stone's throw from J.'s parents'.

Just before we reach the veterinary Eden, my horse first scents, then sights the old white mare on the grass where she is always tethered. He breaks into a gallop. There is nothing to do but jump as he pulls up and tries to mount. The mare falls, so he mounts another, brown one, who is standing nearby. As I fly through the air I think: Well, perhaps this is it – not a bad way to go. J. and some peasants between them catch him. J. races him furiously up and down, breaking a crop in the process. I mount again, and hold his madly tossing head on a very short rein until we get to the house.

Back to the *mawlana* 's orchard. What a temptation, though the problems are immense.

Riding in the morning I had the sensation that my heart was actually enlarging, as if to make room for all that it had to take in – a sensation I have only rarely experienced before. Most enjoyable – all my shortcomings and my major and minor heartaches disappeared into thin air.

One must be certain what type of fulfilment one is after – and that requires an effort.

Riding in the dark behind Yiza and J., whose shapes are invisible and whose voices I hear only as a vague murmur, I think: This night is ideal – I should like to ride on and on into the warm, odorous dark, where unfamiliarity encourages self-forgetfulness. But J., whose girth is slipping, stops unexpectedly. When I pull up beside him, there is trouble with the horses, which suddenly turns into a violent kicking incident with J. on the ground amongst the hooves. J. is furious, I am mortified.

A new house idea. Yiza has offered to build and then rent to us. It is a question of finding a plot. Afterwards we went on to the mango grove and squabbled. Our abnormal sensitivity to one another's opinion sometimes has this effect. Love is not a very peaceful condition.

Goodness, if the *mawlana* is to be considered good, appears to consist in ignoring differences between good and bad, true and false, straight and crooked.

How often and impulsively the poor give money away. When one is destitute one feels the need for gestures.

All the beautiful places one would like to build on are outside the town, but not far enough outside to get clear of the need for planning permission.

Riding with an easy movement, being rather than thinking, gazing around with selfless elation. Yiza is supremely incompetent, both as a guide and as a hunter. But his mistakes, for instance the time when he fell off his feeble old donkey, amuse him as much as they do us.

While J. is shooting at some guinea-fowl, an ape comes out to see what is going on. My stallion, who knows all the tricks of a wild horse, is neurotically afraid of wild creatures.

A camel runs amok, and is chased for miles by two small men. We watch for a while, imagining what their bare feet must feel like in the thorns and grit and burning sand. Then J. gallops off to help, and his horse turns out to be an intrepid camel-rounder, blocking the bolter's way until he can be caught and hobbled.

We were shown the Emir's grazing land near Zalingei. A perfect place for a house except for the road. Jaffr, the Emir's heir, is at present the leading building contractor in the region. He approves of our plans – J. by now has quite a collection of drawings – and seems to think the whole deal would be very simple. In the Emir's house we meet again the handsome police chief, an Arab from the south of the province, who is interested in the history of his race.

The stuff one drinks, including, today, the brown water of the Gellul. In some way I must be rather robust.

The elation has worn off. The Emir's plot is really much too close to the road, where lorries arrive and depart morning and evening in accelerating cavalcades.

Perhaps we'll never ride here again, or smell the earth of the wadi after the burning uplands, or drink the smoky Arab tea, or lie in the shade of the mango grove. Time to be going – having composed the fugue of one's life on that theme, the final departure should be easy.

J. is picking mangoes for an ancient little *Forawa* woman of the *Dimengawi* family – to everything one says she answers, 'Semi semi'. This morning we went to the police to announce our departure.

February 1980

The Emir has another plot, which suits us perfectly. We agree on everything, including, improbably, the terms of ownership. And we are to be escorted to Saraf Umra on a *mughliz* truck, with a smiling little retainer of the Emir's as guide. The Emir lays his hand on the goblin's head with the words, 'He is our man, but he is also like a child.'

On our last ride – towards Dodo along the wadi – my horse missed his footing, falling flat on his side. I fell on my head, but managed to get hold of the reins before he galloped off. Trotted back in some pain, specially in my neck, but cheerful. My last chance of that kind for the time being.

At the Emir's house, an old, bedraggled personage came and sat next to Jaffr and J., who were peering at drawings and figures – he clicked his tongue in wonder, and eventually wandered off. Then the police chief joined in the negotiations. We establish that the land will remain theirs – we will live in it, but it will revert to them on our deaths. Jaffr agrees to put some of his own money in. J. proposes that we all 'sleep on it', and the deal is all but done.

The *mawlana* quietly suggests to J. that he has the power to make couples fertile should we be in need of a child. He embraces J. at length, rather as Eve does.

J.'s stallion has been sold back – a dead pigeon lies in his empty manger. Mine whinnies now that his old enemy has gone.

Yiza has presented us with an ostrich egg bound in leather, like the one in the Brera 'Madonna'. Most respectable people hang one in their principal *ghautiyya* to ward off evil.

Abakr, the Emir's goblin factotum, puts back the *arak* as if quenching an enormous thirst. He talks all the way to Saraf Umra – like a child, yes, but a child who knows a lot more than you expect him to.

Saraf Umra

The smell of fires, the taste of smoky milk. We had a gazelle zigzagging in our headlights – eventually it escaped into the outer darkness. We meet a lorry crew bound, immediately, for El Fasher, the two front seats empty.

Approaching mountains – blue, significant shapes breaking out of white sand into a crystalline sky. A huge herd of white camels. We stop, in fading light, in a level thorny place, rimmed by luminous mountains. The *arak* is finished, and Abakr has developed an appetite. As we eat, he tells us about Jaffr's family and their domains. He himself was a slave of the family by inheritance.

El Fasher

We say goodbye to Abakr. He stands there with the pockets of his clean *jellabah* bulging and a huge dagger in his plastic holdall.

Khartoum

The airline office. Twinges of familiar panic as the trap door is about to snap shut. World of security-conscious citizens, who sip their whisky to the sound of the piped music with apparent complacency.

FRANCE
Paris. February 1980

Something about London this time made me physically sick. Not exactly the ugliness of the place itself – the ugliness of myself when I lived there perhaps, which is the ugliness of myself *tout court*. One must learn more and more, what else can one's wits be for?

We bought books. Nowadays I hardly ever pick up a book in the hope of being amused – which is foolish perhaps.

ITALY
Rome. March 1980
J. has got one of his fevers, sudden, violent, incapacitating. I feel disoriented, as if I were alone. Aloneness, after all these years, would seem completely unnatural.

Irresponsible elation the last few days. The animation of city life. How can I possibly be so happy? One last exquisite coffee at the Tazza d'Oro, and back to the packing.

One wonders irresistibly why one is on the road again, and not in one's own delightful bed, within reach of one's books and objects, overlooking the beautiful, decadent city which is, after all, so well suited to one.

GREECE
Nysi. April 1980
Frantic weeding. Afterwards we sat in the briny radiance after lunch, drinking one last glass of wine. The young goats were clambering down to the edge of the sea. Then we read *Hamlet* together – lines of it have been ringing in my head like music lately, particularly on rainy Roman mornings.

Gytheion
J. is at work on the boat. I am sitting in the grass, full of wild flowers, facing the sublime view of Taygetos. A sudden nostalgia for African doves and the stamping of horses.

Nysi. May 1980
We still don't know *Hamlet* by heart, but we know if a word is missing.

Mortality. We have heard that Jaffr is dead. He did look moribund, but one isn't used to things being so straight-forwardly consecutive. Well, I suppose that little house would have been a bit too easy. Now, if we go back, we'll have to live on horseback.

I can detect traces of the 'walled garden' spirit creeping into my selective weeding. I used to prefer the enclosed confusion of the Franciscans' garden in Budapest to the sweeping view over the Danube – and I was already self-analytical then.

Mitsos offers us his Ionic capital, which, for twenty years, has been serving as a step into his chicken-yard. Next time we go, J. takes it away on his shoulder. Mitsos is a little crestfallen, but we are made ruthless by the self-righteousness of the visually aware – even though he hauled it forty miles, he doesn't really deserve it. J. cleans it one cold, purple, windy evening, and now it sits, appropriate and handsome, on the stump of the old olive outside the door.

June 1980

Poulikos's father could never be persuaded that the earth was round. His brother, G., owns the 'air' above Poulikos's shop – he proposes to build on it. They know all about Icarus, but think that Galileo was a Greek.

The little dinghy was mysteriously burnt to ashes. Are we getting accident-prone?

Here we are – this is the present, the earthly paradise. We fall asleep in one another's arms, just aware of the lapping of the afternoon sea. The top of the year – I have finally learned from J. the value of this moment of the season. Afterwards everything is a slow descent.

The fishing season has opened with two vast skate. I am as dazed by luck as by misfortune. We found a dinghy identical to the one that was burned for only 13,000 drachmas.

Androyallo

Montherlant is right – there is hardly enough time for the great masters, so how can you afford the time to read the Goncourts?

Nysi. July 1980

A cat jumped in through the bedroom window last night. Afterwards I couldn't sleep though I had not seen the cat, and I was not thinking of anything in particular. I could see, as if from a great distance, myself, the bed, the house, the mountains. The morning was like a luminous hallucination.

I am reluctant to accept that it is necessary for machines to go wrong, so am irritated when they do. But are horses more reliable than Land Rovers? In the end one's preferences are illogical.

A terrible and interesting dream. We are being stoned in a grim, dark, African town – running the gauntlet as lances are thrown from bamboo scaffolding. We are refugees from some nameless catastrophe in a Chinese hotel, which being neutral is a sort of island in the sea of hatred for the infidel. Yet there is hostility there too, and a note of hideous complicity. The other Europeans are all oddities, wanderers.

We talked, at a length that was inappropriate to the beauty of the day, about whether one can accept what one does not understand, like death, for example. And whether one can accept the defeat of one's understanding.

August 1980
We went to Sparta to get a spare part for the boat, which now turns out to be the wrong one. J. spends whole days toiling with the engine. At last, success – and we go out fishing.

We mention Africa more frequently these days. We live in unreality like fish in water. We come from it and return to it, and our grasp of what happens in between is not reliable. We ponder gravely the question of whether or not to go, in view of the death of the Emir. A surprising lot of philosophising has been going on. J. is doubtful on account of my health. But Yiza's house is there. We will go, we will always go.

Incapable of reading, I watched J. read – his face a little hollow from tiredness, serious, handsome, with a tinge of unfamiliarity, as if infected with the aura of things about to be left behind. We have thought, worked, eaten, bled, travelled, exulted, despaired together – yet we do not really know one another. In January, in thick moonlight somewhere in Africa, I thought: This is perhaps your last good winter. Remember – it is up to you.

A letter from Yiza – the ceiling, the verandah are all in order, he says. Perhaps one doesn't always know exactly when one is lucky.

September 1980
I cast the daturas and cyclamen over the cliff into the silent

sea, I empty the watering can. Perhaps we shall come back, perhaps not. Remember – it's up to you.

ITALY
Rome. October 1980
The Russian cellist Geringer plays the two Brahms sonatas. Torrents of straining melancholy and technical bravura, neither of which is allowed to overwhelm the other. His wife is at the piano. The *cancelleria* is lit by torches in dishes.

From J.'s dark room emerge some wonderful nudes on rocks. Africa looms from the prints like an ambiguous dream.

Our perfect flat – objects to rest our eyes on, books to read, a desk to write at. Every taste is gratified. Why risk it all? What nonsense – the risk is here, there, everywhere, as long as there is life, and let's not forget it.

J. is muttering Arabic next door.

Where would we be without that much-maligned virtue, vanity?

8

Ursula

The last two months of Ursula's life were packed with living and writing – the consciousness of time running out, always lurking in her mind but now precipitately to its forefront, evidently endowed her with a phenomenal energy.

The previous year she recorded several meetings with a 'handsome police chief'. This man, Ali, was a member of the ruling clan of the Bani Hashim, a tribe of black-skinned but Arab-featured nomads. On arriving in Sudan in December 1980 they met again. Justin and Ursula quickly established a friendship with Ali and his family – he was married to the daughter of a Sheikh who presided with feudal authority over the activities of the tribe. Ali and his brothers-in-law were distinguished-looking, leisured local aristocrats who liked a drink and who spoke a little English. This must have eased communications – though Justin's Arabic was pretty service-able, Ursula's was less so.

The Sudanese journal of the year before shows that Ursula was changing. The openness to friendship, the obsession with riding, and the beginnings of a distancing of herself from Justin were all new. The many pages and years of Ursula's absorption with herself, her love and her culture are little preparation for what follows – the new elements coincide and Ursula becomes infatuated with Ali.

Ursula recorded the pain of this infatuation, whose progression led inexorably to her death, in two forms. She continued to write her journal – in fact she wrote it at greater length and more continuously than ever before – but her language became so obscure, so convoluted, so vague and secretive, that the reader has enormous difficulty in deciphering it. This was partly owing to a need she felt, both to protect Justin from unnecessary pain and to protect herself from his possible disapproval – since they weren't in the habit of keeping secrets from one another, he had always felt free to read her journal, and vice versa. It was also owing to the reticence, embarrassment almost, that overcame her whenever her emotions got out of control. Over the years she recorded her occasional, though crippling, depressions with a degree of shame that seems exaggerated, absurd, so that the reader would be justified in thinking: Oh, come off it, you're only human – but if a few hours of periodic misery really jeopardise all these months of total fulfilment, please won't you tell me *why*.

If the journal of her final crisis was all there was to go on, this would still be a natural reaction to its agonised circumlocution. Luckily it isn't, and I have decided that to include it *in toto* would do nothing but obscure the issue.

Ursula also wrote a long story called 'The Monument' – Justin's book *Style* includes it and I borrow its title – which, being ostensibly fictional, gave her leeway to chart the course of the catastrophe with greater frankness. The events described in the story and in the journal are largely the same – the difference is that in 'The Monument' they are filled out with a minute attention to the emotional agonies of the narrator, which are quite acute enough to account for his final suicide. As you read the story the conviction grows that Ursula intended it as a testament, an apologia.

The narrator is a male, though distinctly feminine, European who has come across a box of papers belonging to E.F.-F., a young English official in Sudan who died fifty years earlier. Among these papers is a journal concerned exclusively with E.F.-F.'s passion for Abdullahi, a Beni Hashim tribesman. The narrator becomes obsessed with this touching and unrequited love story for reasons that he doesn't at first understand. He decides to go to Sudan with the initial purpose of finding E.F.-F.'s gravestone, the monument of the title, a small pyramid in the desert outside Zalingei. His researches lead him directly to the local police chief, Ibrahim, a carbon copy of Abdullahi (whose photograph he has seen among E.F.-F.'s papers). He himself falls in love with Ibrahim, and the development of their eventual affair follows, even imitates, that of E.F.-F.'s with Abdullahi, allowing for the difference in the mores of their two epochs. The narrative technique is a consistent interweave of the two strands.

Ibrahim, and Abdullahi too if it comes to that, are undisguised likenesses of Ali. Ursula indicates the narrator's gender only once – he has forgotten his shaving gear and borrows Ibrahim's – and it comes as a shock, because in every other respect he is her mouthpiece. There is, however, no counterpart for Justin in 'The Monument' – both E.F.-F. and the narrator are alone and apparently without ties. Art has no duty to mirror the reality from which it takes off, but Ursula was a reluctant artist. She remarked in the journal that her stories always bored her. She found their source material much more interesting, and it was for this reason that she preferred writing the journals. 'The Monument' has a double purpose, interior and exterior – she wanted first to enlighten for herself the shadowy confines in which she seemed to be imprisoned, and second to deliver a justification to the world which would at the same time be a thing of beauty. It's odd that she should have dispensed with a Justin character on either count.

One theory is that Ursula was genuinely in love with Ali. The speed and ruthlessness with which some people can transfer a complicated set of emotions from one lover to another is an awesome force. She may have failed to give Justin a fictional supporting role simply because her passion for Ali made his presence in reality an encumbrance. But the disillusionment with Ibrahim expressed by the narrator at the end of the story (and Ursula's parallel disillusionment with Ali in the journal) contradicts the hypothesis.

Ursula used Ali, she didn't love him. He was the instrument of her death, and therefore symbolised death. In her lifelong communion with death Justin had taken on the role of priest. Now that the ceremony was coming to an end he was already superfluous – she excluded her priest from her confession because she knew she was already past the point where he could save her.

I would like to have included 'The Monument' in this book, but for two considerations – the first is its length, nearly that of a novella, and the second that its fictional form couldn't help but undermine confidence in the historical accuracy of the subject-matter. In the end I decided to outline the gist of what happened in my own words, but to illustrate it with passages from 'The Monument', the journal, and Justin's text whenever possible, hoping that this approach would gain in comprehensibility what it lost in directness.

Justin and Ursula landed in Khartoum in December 1980. On the way from El Fasher to Zalingei the lorry in which they were travelling rolled into a gully and stopped two inches short of toppling over a precipice. When they arrived they went straight to Yiza's house, only to find that it hadn't been put in order, as promised. Yiza wasn't embarrassed by this, in fact he was pleased to see them – his excuse was that he had misunderstood the date of their arrival. They were undismayed and proceeded to move in.

In the morning Justin insisted on going to register with the police – but Ursula thought it an unnecessary formality. If they had followed her inclinations they might never have renewed contact with Ali. As it was, they immediately established a relationship. Flatly and with no strings attached, Ali offered them the loan of a mare each for as long as they wanted to stay in Sudan. When they tried to insist on some kind of payment, he refused on the grounds that it was a reward for coming back. Next day they called at his house and Justin tried the horses one by one. His own was rather frisky, Ursula's docile but not as smooth-running as the stallion she had had the year before. Ali acknowledged their thanks with a sombre dignity that they came to recognise as his usual manner. Later some friends appeared to play cards. It was a first view of the frantic gambling that was to be the background of Ursula's final despair.

They were invited to go with Ali and his friend Majid, a jolly, plump prison governor whom they had first met two years before, on a trip to the Chad frontier. They travelled in the back of Ali's Land Rover truck, wedged among the luggage. The jolting was hard on Ursula's back, and by the time they reached the village of Umm Balla, where they were to stay the night, she was in pain. She also experienced and recorded in her journal 'a great wave of despair such as I have not known for God knows how many years now, beginning in the pit of my stomach and making my whole body tremble'. She despaired because she knew that she was already enslaved to Ali and simultaneously that, since her body was plainly no longer up to the demands that she refused to stop making on it, it was time for her to die. 'The Monument' makes it clear that the two things were linked in her mind.

There's a terrible pathos in Justin's acknowledgment in *Style* of his possible culpability for, or at least complicity in, the circumstances of her death:

> No doubt the reader will have wondered how I could have allowed myself to subject her to such foreseeable hardship, when the previous year had so taxed her reserves . . . Either I was possessed by an unreasonable enthusiasm for our journey to the point of neglecting her health, or I was involved with her in search of a wild, a fantastic conclusion . . . I shall try to explain . . . Between us we had invented an improvisatory style of living, rooted in an aesthetic which downgraded reason. We respected reason, common sense too . . . but only as aids to the smooth running of our day-to-day lives. Neither of us wanted security in the sense that most people understand it – on the contrary, we needed its absence in all aspects of life except the reciprocation of our devotion. But we were under no illusion that our love was inviolable, which is why we sustained it with a continuous mental and physical tension . . . Swept along with controlled precipitation by the power of her death-wish, we gradually began to feel in league with each other – as we merged we relinquished control. In the circumstances I was incapable of being anything but her ever-present aide and protector against eventualities I trusted myself to deal with as they arose.

When we received the news of the Emir's death I concluded that our involvement with Sudan was at an end . . . I put this to Ursula and she answered, 'Yes, perhaps.' But even before the offer of the Emir's house, she had decided that she was prepared to return to Yiza's house if certain improvements were made, and even to put up with the same horse, difficult though it was. Somehow, at some time, a house would turn up that was worthy of our corner of Sudan, the place that was so in tune with our way of life. By now we had enough experience of Africa to avoid the more obvious mistakes. That summer in Greece we talked little either of the difficulties or of the seductiveness of life in Sudan . . . We lived in the present as usual, except that she imagined, anticipated, while I did not . . .

If she was irresistibly drawn towards death, either in Africa or anywhere else, I was by now disinclined to oppose her. I sensed in her diminishing patience the prescience of doom. I understood it . . . I knew that we could never again settle to a European existence that was geared to ignoring that doom. Our love was *willingly* doomed, an enchantment contrived for each other against an abyss. I knew that sooner or later she would propose the great leap, in the certainty that I would stay by her when the time came. Whenever she reaffirmed her determination [to die], I insisted that we were committed to die, as we had lived, together.

Once the events at Umm Balla had gathered momentum, I could do nothing to mitigate her suffering. I couldn't even redress the balance at night for want of privacy . . . I settled into a gradual, watchful withdrawal. I accepted the impatience and dissatisfaction that she expressed in private as calmly as possible. I didn't bother to anticipate . . .

Ali was an extraordinarily handsome man. I'd go so far as to say that his beauty was appropriate to Ursula's death. A powerful, half-Semitic black – tall, reserved and dignified, with no superfluous gestures. His expression was guarded, but his laugh was sudden and disconcertingly childish . . . His comportment towards both of us was as good as impeccable. [But] I suspected her infatuation, and told her so without preamble on two occasions . . . She said I was being absurd . . . What is certain is that she cast herself into the affair, rather than let herself be drawn into it. Ali was not to blame.

Justin and Ursula became part of Ali's circle. This involved them in something they had never known together before – a voluntary social life. It was an indolent round of hours-long picnics and expeditions to the sometimes distant houses of Ali's friends and relations. They attended these functions as privileged onlookers. Ursula wrote in her journal, 'Watching people pray, wash their feet or talk, I'm saddened that we are excluded – even though it's perfectly clear that we wouldn't seriously want to participate.' After dark, though, there were card-playing sessions, accompanied by heavy drinking, in which they did participate, thereby throwing overboard their system of calculated moderation. Temporarily this had a stimulating effect on Ursula. Her depression lifted, and hangovers made her extra-receptive: 'What a country. There is an abnormally high incidence of people with sympathetic, self-confident manners.' And, 'As a matter of fact I have *never* in my whole varied career met as many people I liked in one place at one time as here.' A little later she remarks, 'I can honestly say that *from one point of view* I have never lived more interestingly.'

This 'one point of view', though underlined, is unexplained. In Ursula's language living 'interestingly' meant living within spitting distance of dying – and by now she knew that her death was very near. Here are two passages from 'The Monument':

If indifference is dehydrating to the soul, then so is desperation – neither can be endured for long without some process of crystallisation overtaking the soul itself. Mine is about to crumble into dry shreds, leaving some organism that is horribly alive exposed to a sandy and devastating wind. No hope, no shadow of illusion – I shall have to take momentary pleasures as they come. Some may be of a dangerous intensity, and those will have to be paid for.

Perhaps I still have the cash. But what has to happen may as well be given a nudge – there can be no sense in allowing the agony to wear thin, become ignoble, almost bearable, that is. No sense in swallowing despair in assimilable doses, in watching an inflammable edifice mould to mildew.

My time is up, and the bureaucratic complications of renewing a visa require a long journey to El Fasher, which I am not prepared to make. So it has been settled for me by circumstances. My time is up. Very little has happened, but quite enough to necessitate my demise. Dignified or undignified, worthy or unworthy – all that is immaterial. It is only a matter of postponement otherwise. It was here that I held my hand up one hot afternoon three years ago, and saw that my blood was ebbing away. Time slipped between my fingers – the last white, dry grains of sand in the glass. My hand is too limp to be lifted any more. The heat is very great.

In fact Ursula allowed none of these feelings to show, indeed tried to hide them even from Justin. Their new friends had no idea that anything was wrong. Ali invited them to go with him and his brother-in-law Adem to Adem's father's house in Ed Daein. This meant a long journey by train and lorry. They arrived, exhausted, late at night at a huge compound. They woke up a servant, who showed them into a kind of dormitory reserved for the junior members of the Sheikh's family. Ursula described the set-up in the journal:

In the morning the courtyard looks splendid – pale sunlight on the swept sand, the shivering shadows of the *mimms*. It is surprisingly cool. Ali's father-in-law [is] an extremely handsome old man, beautifully dressed and very much the tribal chieftain. He receives us on the verandah. We are introduced, given tea, milk, and *gabbana*, and informed that his private bathroom and WC . . . are at our disposal. Here is a gentleman of the old school. He has a Bokkara prayer rug, English teacups, the finest of turbans. His own room is neat and minimal – the London safe, the revolver, the small, mahogany bed. Clearly he's a domestic tyrant – his eldest son is ordered about like a schoolboy. Ali gets the same treatment, though he is not expected to serve. Everyone sits neatly in rows on the verandah, except for the Sheikh, who reclines. Notables come and go after a display of fealty. I don't think relations between old and young are all that they might be. Ali's wife [the Sheikh's daughter] curtsies, and gets only a nod in return. So much for daughters.

The Sheikh's patriarchal authority imposed a good deal of restraint on the younger generation. But in the evening they withdrew to their own quarters, and the familiar, dissolute behaviour was resumed:

Serious gambling and drinking began – also *bhang* and more *bhang*. The dealer sings in a high, female-sounding falsetto. Ali is drunk, though he has only had sherry. He is prevented with some difficulty from going on to *arak*, but alas he participates in a joint. A fight develops between him and a plump brother-in-law with an irascible nature – there's a suggestion of class and racial friction between these two junior sons-in-law. Venomous blasphemies, attempts to get at each other's throat. They are held back, but then the uproar becomes general – chairs and tables are brandished. Ali is pinioned to the bed, while his brother-in-law is turned out of the room. Ali begins trembling violently, as if he were having a fit. The other man forces his way in again. Since I am sitting on the bed, which is being used as a couch alongside the card table, I find myself sitting next to Ali and holding his arm. What a very strange feeling, a mixture of detachment and something very different. Now Ali and his faction repair to the dormitory. Once inside someone has the brilliant idea of handing Ali a bottle of brandy, which he downs like water. That puts an end to the calm – the true African emerges. He stampedes around in a tribal dance, embracing everyone. He calls J. his brother and me his friend. He stomps and yells and strips off his *jellabah*. Then he collapses. J. tries to take him to bed, but he bangs his head against the wall in passing. The prince in his cups – still the prince, but what a melancholy affair. In the morning Ali is conspicuously absent. J. and Adem go visiting the sick. It's the real thing, he can't even move. J. provides Panadol. I must say I do have an iron constitution.

This account comes from the journal, so Ursula's feelings are censored in favour of an ironic tone of voice. In the more detailed version provided in 'The Monument' a special emphasis is given to the effect of Ibrahim's personality on the narrator:

. . . The other man, of course, was Ibrahim's brother-in-law, so everyone had an interest in keeping them apart. Ibrahim lay back on the bed, his chest heaving with sobs of rage and frustration. By then four men were holding him – by the arms, shoulders and knees. I too was still gripping one of his arms, and as he struggled to get free I kept repeating, 'Please, Ibrahim, please.' My legs were pressing against his thighs. Was he too drunk to notice? His unfathomable face was distorted with sobs like a child's, his eyelashes tear-tangled. I felt sad, sober and distant, as though everything were already over, as though the Ibrahim I knew had died of his own obliviousness. They dragged the other man outside the gate, which they locked against him. He pounded on it ceaselessly, while Ibrahim hove about like a diver desperate for air. At this point one of the drunker nephews produced half a bottle of brandy. He handed it to Ibrahim, who downed it in three or four gulps. Then, since no one was holding him any more, he rose to his feet. The pounding on the gate had ceased. Ibrahim stood unsteadily in a circle of men, who watched apprehensively as he stripped off his *jellabah*. Wearing only his white drawers, he stamped once or twice on the sand, embracing everybody in turn and calling each 'brother'. It was a ritual of African drunkenness, African brotherhood, enacted between men who lived together on easy, familiar terms – whereas I, the

European, was sober, incapable of dancing, and besides had never had the slightest idea of how to exteriorise emotion. After a while Ibrahim collapsed. Throwing a sheet over him, they left him where he had fallen on the warm sand. The party broke up, and the lantern was taken down by Hashim, who as usual was singing one of his quiet little songs. I lay on the camp bed that Ibrahim had wept on, and listened to his noisy breathing as he lay there on the sand. In all my life I have never felt sadder.

On the crowded train to Nyala on their way back to Zalingei Justin and Ursula reminded Ali that their visas were due to expire in a fortnight's time. Ali insisted that they must come to a last gazelle hunt. It took place near Garsila two days later. The journal states, almost parenthetically:

> [I am] in the grip of passivity – yet it is time for the execution. Ali has just shot at – and missed – a buck. J. is chasing it through the long grass, the driver follows. Ali and I are standing alone . . . 'Take it or leave it' is what I say.

'The Monument', as usual, is more specific:

> We stood side by side in the long and golden grass, while the driver slit the throat of my gazelle some distance away. When Ibrahim offered me a cigarette, I was sure that he deliberately touched my hand. I lit the cigarette, and said, 'I love you. You must consider it as a hand in a game of cards – take it or leave it. I am going to rent a house in Nyala – I'll wait for you there.' He said, 'I'll come.' His face was set, and his eyes were very hard. Next morning I left.

As soon as he was alone with Ursula, Justin provoked a show-down. They established that a crisis had been reached. Ursula asked for some time alone to sort out her feelings about Ali, and Justin agreed, because trust in her was the only solid ground that remained to him. For the last six weeks she had been increasingly preoccupied and distant. What made it far worse was that she had also refused to make love with him, thereby removing an opportunity for the renewal of warmth. The account that follows has been pieced together from Ursula's journal, Justin's notes, and from the conversations he had with me after his return to England.

On the night of February 19th they arrived at the rest house in Nyala after a particularly exhausting journey in the back of a police truck. Ursula's back was in agony, she had excruciating stomach cramps and was bleeding. As soon as they had settled in, Ursula said that she couldn't come back to Europe with him as planned because she loved Ali. Justin, whose pain was tempered with a kind of relief that something of the sort had finally been said, objected that 'love' couldn't really be quite the word to describe her feelings. Although he was aware as he was saying it that their own love had had its roots in a lunacy at least equal to this new one, and so that to devalue it was hardly rational, he was intuitively sure that he had grasped the truth. This was confirmed when Ursula, surprised, agreed. Grateful for the encouragement, he began to talk. This is a shortened version of what he remembered telling her.

'What concerns me is not what you feel about Ali, but what is real between the two of us. Everything has changed, as we knew it would before we came back to Africa. Your betrayal has put us into a new phase, which I was already anticipating – you have only made it all more clear-cut . . . There are two important things. The first is that you are not ready for death. You are beautiful. I admire you totally, more than ever. If I was becoming irrelevant to you, it's because you know that I help you to live. The second is that I will never leave you. You have taught me that life and death are interwoven, that the beauty of one is inconceivable without the beauty of the other. You taught me so well that I'm as involved in your death as I am in your life. I said you must not die yet, and I meant what I said . . . but if you are irrevocably determined, I shall die too. This is only what we have both always said. If you want me to go away, I've said that I will. I'll wait for you in Khartoum. We'll find a house for you here. But I want you to promise in return that you will come to me, *whether it's for life or for death*. I'll stay away for three weeks. I'll make reservations on four different flights for London, and I'll be at the airport in time for each flight.'

Ursula promised, and the next two days were comparatively serene. They quickly found a house for her to stay in, which is faithfully described at the end of 'The Monument'. Although she still refused to make love with him, she promised again and again, apparently in good faith, that she would do nothing drastic in his absence. On February 22nd they said goodbye. They kissed twice on the doorstep of the new house. They never saw one another again.

Justin found a place on a lorry to El Fasher, and from there took a plane to Khartoum. He went to a travel agency, and made reservations on London-bound flights for February 28th, and March 4th, 11th, and 15th. Then he took a room in Hassan's hotel.

On February 28th Ursula wrote to Justin. The letter, the only one that she sent, took seventeen days to reach him:

> I can only say that I admire the style in which you treat my regression into darkness . . . That I didn't expect it . . . shows that we still do not know all about each other . . . I am living in limbo, in prison. I talk to myself and write . . . [This place] reminds me of that old Chinese hotel on the sluggish warm China sea just over the Malay border . . . There is no foolishness left in me. I know that the last plane is on the 15th. If I can come before I will try and let you know . . .

When Justin got this letter the last plane had already left, and he had waited for her at the airport on each occasion. The evening after writing it Ursula made love with Ali.

Justin managed to locate a British firm of agricultural consultants that had a radio telephone in daily contact with Nyala. He sent a message asking her to ring him at his hotel from the next-door house to hers, which belonged to the landlord, a Copt. Ursula succeeded in dragging herself out. The landlord's family were sitting down to a meal in the room where the telephone was. As she explained to Justin, in an

attempt to account for the weak and nervous sound of her
voice, this was inhibiting. All the same, it seems extraordinary
that the landlord himself noticed nothing unusual about her
manner. She excused her failure to arrive in time for the flight
by saying that the doctor had forbidden her to fly on account
of her palpitations. She added, with what Justin thought he
recognised as a note of menace, 'Non ti immischiare' ('Don't
get mixed up in this.' They had been speaking Italian so as
not to be understood.) It was a fearsome kind of deception –
by banking on his respect for the privacy she required to
conduct a love affair which couldn't fail to threaten him, she
was covering up for a determination to exclude him from her
death. In reply, Justin simply said that he had already booked
places on yet another flight – for March 22nd. He said
goodbye. Ursula hesitated. He asked her if there was anything
else she wanted to say. No, she replied.

The last page and a half of 'The Monument' need no mental
transposition from fiction to history, beyond that of the name
Ali for Ibrahim:

The house belongs to a Coptic merchant who moved to the
capital some years ago. It has all the qualities that my
shadow side demands – it is decaying, it has the elegance of
a ruin. The overgrown garden is full of birds. Inside there
are a few pieces of heavy furniture in a pale tropical wood, a
double bed, a few chairs, and a sideboard with a big misty
mirror behind it. I bought some mats. I hung a long
snakeskin (given to me by Ibrahim) above the bed. Through
the netted window I can see a tangle of trees and creepers,
illuminated at night by the lights of a neighbouring house. I
spend the days behind half-closed shutters, waiting. I am
still capable of moments of pleasure, even though it's a
decadent pleasure, doomed. I still have one more thing to
wait for besides my death. Noises from the town penetrate
faintly – a passing car, drumming, scurrying children. A
dusty little boy brings me food from a nearby eating-house.
I don't go out because Ibrahim knows too many people in
Nyala.

Much sooner than I had expected, only four days after

leaving Zalingei, I heard a stealthy rattling at the door. It was seven in the evening. Ibrahim was standing there, serious and unsmiling. He asked if there were anybody else in the house. He complained about the road to Nyala – he had arrived at midday and was staying as usual with Hashim. I was beginning to think that nothing more was going to happen, when he suddenly got up and asked to see the rest of the house. When we were in the bedroom he said, 'Shall we do it now?'

Energy and the absence of the slightest superfluous gesture. After an hour he said that he must go back to Hashim's where a baccarat party was in progress. 'It's better that you don't come – nobody knows you are here. I will be back at ten.' The beauty of his naked body breaks my heart.

He returned at midnight. He was only moderately drunk. We made love and drank and talked in turn. Yes, he had thought about it right from the beginning. 'But here sex is never serious and there is no such thing as love.' He said this categorically. 'What is serious then?' I asked. He arched one perfect arm above his head and answered, 'Nothing is serious.' So we have something in common after all. 'You can't stay here long,' he said then, 'in the end people would find out.' So we made love all night on the assumption that there would be no other chance.

In the morning he left, grave and sleepy, saying that he would be back at seven. He appeared at eleven, dead drunk, fell into bed and was instantly asleep. He woke at dawn and made love to me with the sort of grim energy one uses for cutting wood.

When I asked if he couldn't, just for this short time, drink a little less, play cards a little less, he replied, 'They are suspicious anyway. It is immoral, you see.' He didn't come back that night. At two I locked the door and settled my accounts. I will wait till tomorrow night, and if he doesn't come the pills and the razor are waiting. Not because of him in particular. I dimly knew all along that his mystery was unreal, unworthy of being explored. If I decided to attempt the exploration, it was so that the final disappointment would play its part in finishing me off. I once heard an

Amazonian boat-hand declare that a man dies 'cuando es hora', or when the time is ripe. The time is now ripe. This is a good house for it. A dust storm is blowing outside. Technicians are toiling away to make this country ready for industry, for democracy. My race has long been extinct. I have no contact with the world, and my appetites are exhausted. *Es hora*.

Ursula's suicide, far from being the sombre and considered conclusion that you'd expect from the last sentences, was miserably messy and long-drawn-out. The journal records her last days with a degree of exhausted dispassion that is astonishing in the circumstances. Between March 5th and 9th she made three separate attempts using razor blades, a dagger and a large quantity of tranquillisers. On the 9th she still had the physical strength and moral determination to go out into the town and buy the revolver with which she finally killed herself on the 18th. That it was Justin's birthday she must surely have forgotten.

Justin waited for Ursula at the airport on the day of the final flight, the 22nd. When she didn't appear he went to the agricultural consultancy firm. After making a few calls they informed him that she was dead. He flew to Nyala to find that she had already been buried.

This letter, smeared with blood and clearly written with the greatest difficulty, was the first thing to catch his eye in Ursula's house:

What I have done could only have been done alone – calmly, that is. I don't know what went wrong. I shed enough blood to flood the *hammam*. Enough pills to kill me seven times over according to the doctor . . . If I get into the clutches of the hospital you must help . . . It is the last thing you must do for me.

Why did I deceive you? I had no strength for argument and certain things are beyond words. I knew I was doomed. You have been more to me than anything in life. I think of you and feel you and speak to you now . . . A good house for it. The sort of house I've been looking for all my life, the

sort I intended to end up in. You held me up so long . . . To
crucify oneself for the useless thing . . . One makes up one's
fate as one goes along . . . Sell Greece. Simplify life. It was
beautiful once but it won't remain so . . .

Justin spent a day going through every scrap of paper he
could find in the house. These consisted almost entirely of
versions of 'The Monument', which Ursula had revised
considerably since Ali's visits, and the last notebook of her
journal, which I shall quote from a point equivalent to the end
of 'The Monument':

March 4th, 1981
Slept with the aid of Valium and got up at dawn feeling
peculiarly calm. Imperceptibly my mind has been made up.
I dressed and went out for the purpose of buying blades.
　　Washed my hair, polished my legs, filed my nails, and felt
better for it. Who was it who said there was no earthly reason
why one shouldn't die with one's face properly painted?
Ancien régime no doubt . . . the snakeskin levitates very very
slightly in the half-light and the birds rustle in the creeper.
Darkness slowly descends allowing for a last-minute postponement. I lie down and wait for the hours to ebb away. I
don't think about the past very much . . .
　　Will I be like Kirilov? I don't think so – haven't enough
metaphysical imagination. Also there is really no reason to
make such a big thing of it all. Not one trace of desire to get
drunk in all these days of waning physical control.

March 5th, 1981
I have had enough of everything, sex included. There is
nothing more. I am too tired. Four gashes on a once
beautiful arm. I did it with detachment. The Mongol blood
perhaps. May it serve me tonight.

March 7th, 1981
I have had enough of blood on the whole. A constant pain.
Began to clean up the premises. So weak I bruise myself on
the corners of the furniture.

March 9th, 1981

Lying in the dark. The smell of blood and the *arak* I disinfected the knife with, cleaned the knife with, downed the pills with, thinking: How apt, Allah, how apt. The pistol has to be mended and will be delivered on the 13th. A ropy little seven-shot ·22 revolver. It will have to do. I can't cut anything else – my knowledge of anatomy is far too elementary. Four shots. I tested it out of town into the empty sky and it works, so three remain.

At the bottom of the final page was scrawled the following note to Justin:

Don't write or have anything to do with him [Ali]. He is too confused and more sinned against than sinning.

Justin however did contact Ali, who, being in the police force, had already heard about Ursula's death. Justin's ostensible reason for getting in touch was to retrieve two pieces of Ursula's jewellery, which she had left in Adem's house. But he must also have had other, and mixed, motives for the meeting. He wanted Ali to know that he considered him blameless – there would have been a hint of patronage in such an exoneration. On the other hand, he wanted to show by his manner that, being fully in control of himself and of the situation, he was in no need of condolence.

Justin had deep reserves of pride, and now that he needed them as never before, they didn't let him down. The first thing to be seen to was the inquest. Ali attended as the friend of Justin's that he believed himself, first and foremost, to be – he wasn't called on to give evidence. Justin himself gave evidence briefly. It was established that Ursula had killed herself while the balance of her mind was disturbed. Then he took a room in a random hotel. In imitation of Ursula's method, he slashed his wrist repeatedly with an open razor. When, after nearly an hour, he was still conscious and the flow of blood seemed disappointingly slow, he took seventy-two Valium tablets, which he had prepared in advance for the eventuality.

* * *

Before she met Justin, Ursula knew that something had to change if she were to survive. When she met him something did. Having started off as the catalyst, Justin progressed into being the guardian, the maintenance man of that change, which put a brake on her despair and added seventeen years of great intensity to her life. But from having been gregarious, hilarious, cynical and all-questioning, she became reclusive, serious, mystical and omniscient. Happiness put a frown on her face. My brother went with her, and Hugo Stewart's cry from the heart could have referred to either of them in the years of their marriage. When I asked him what he'd thought of Justin after the change, he answered, 'I couldn't get through to him at all. I thought: What the hell's happened to him, where's all his sparkle gone?'

Happiness turned Ursula inside-out. In many ways she was happier unhappy than she was happy. Happiness, being a by-product rather than an objective, should never have been pursued in the first place. Her guilt – for being alive, for being female, for being happy – became so generalised that it was virtually inextinguishable. With Justin she fashioned a fine container for goodness – but meanwhile she never lost the conviction that she herself, the content, was bad. And this 'good' life accommodated her guilt far less comfortably than the 'bad' one she had exchanged it for.

There's a thin descant to the melody line of the journals that sounds like the uncharitableness of the newly pious – Ursula developed a convert's rigidity. She became so oppressed by the continual necessity of living 'well' that the slightest lowering of standards demanded punishment by death. She wanted to die. The death by act of God that she dreamed of refused to materialise. That meant she must kill herself, but to do so she needed some truly shocking motive. She found it in the brutal destruction of the 'goodness' she had been so assiduously cultivating.

When I outlined these rather harsh conjectures to Ursula's close friend, Eve, she deflected me back to the tragedy in its more immediate context. Ursula's dependence on Justin was based on the coincidence of spiritual recognition with sexual compatibility. Justin had taken her to a peak of sexual fulfilment that she had never approached with any other man. But with the first symptoms of the menopause the magic stopped working. It was a devastating shock. She had come to regard sex as a life-support drug – in the absence of a pure supply from Justin she looked elsewhere rather than admit that she had become immune.

Ursula confided most of this to Eve before leaving for Sudan. When she met Ali she was already prepared. She subscribed, although her pride wouldn't have allowed her to admit it so baldly, to the myth of the sexual superiority of the black man over the white. The same mythology in reverse was directing Ali – black men commonly believing that white women are more enlightened sexually. Eve assumed that it was only the tenacity of this belief that bamboozled him against his better nature into infringing one of the great taboos of Muslim convention – sex is admissible with anyone, man, woman or dog, except the wife of your friend.

Justin gives another, more suggestive reason for Ursula's choice of Ali – that he reminded her of her father. The horror of the incestuous urges implicit in the idea certainly lurks in her writing. And in the course of my investigations I was told by someone who asked not to be identified (but whom I have reason to trust) a detail of further-reaching significance: Ursula's father was a high-ranking officer of the AVO in Budapest. If this is true she might as well have been the daughter of Heinrich Himmler. At once many things would be explained – her systematic apoliticism, the mendacious impression she often gave (simply lying by omission), her need for an ivory tower, her horror of (and efforts to escape from) twentieth-century civilisation, her obsessive hatred of her father, her refusal to have children, her love of fiction and parallel dislike of history as the word is generally understood, but above all her self-disgust and her guilt. Seen in this context her death could be viewed as an atonement.

Bruce Chatwin found Western Darfur a highly understand-able choice as a death-place: 'Thorn country is terminal country, the beginning and the end – that landscape was the original home of man. It's completely natural that having once seen it you should want to go home there to die.' And when I put it to him that Ursula was anachronistic he corrected me: 'No – she was futuristic.'

9

Justin

Justin came to on the verandah of a hospital in Nyala. He asked someone the date – it was the morning of April 4th, and he had been discovered in his hotel room on the afternoon of April 2nd. He later told Eve that conditions in the hospital were extremely primitive, a fact which corresponded to its area of specialisation – nearly all his fellow-patients seemed to be suffering from wounds inflicted by camels. Some had been bitten, others kicked or trampled. The observation shows a lucidity which is strange in the circumstances. He told me that, finding himself not only alive but apparently unharmed – apart from the deep cuts in his wrist, now stitched and bandaged – his first conscious reaction was: Ah well, this means a delay. Realising that it was essential for him to get on top of the situation, he proceeded to make himself useful in the understaffed hospital.

Meanwhile the story had been exciting the concern of the expatriate community. Letters from well-wishers, few of whom he had ever met, began pouring into the hospital. Everyone was treating him with astonishing kindness. He received a visit from the old Sheikh, Adem's father and Ali's father-in-law, who had always taken a paternal interest in him. The Sheikh, without showing any knowledge of his son-in-law's involvement in the affair, told Justin that a court case was being prepared against him, attempted suicide being a crime under Arab law. He assured him that he would use his influence to get the proceedings dropped.

Among the letters Justin received was one from the Greek wife of the manager of the British agricultural consultancy firm, asking him to come back to Khartoum and stay in their house until he felt ready to travel to England. Again he was amazed by this kindness and accepted gratefully, flying back to Khartoum as soon as he was discharged from hospital. The generous couple, Christopher and Riri Howse, took Justin into their family. It was the beginning of a close friendship that lasted until his death.

Riri Howse described her first meeting with Justin the day he learnt of Ursula's death: 'Chris had to tell Justin that his wife was dead and had committed suicide. He was amazed at how calmly Justin took it. He wasn't even surprised. Then he went back to his hotel, the Grand Hotel on the banks of the Nile. I was absolutely shocked at the story and felt that we couldn't leave this man alone in a hotel room at such a tragic moment of his life. He might even try to commit suicide himself. Justin had said he was going to ring Chris in the evening, and when he did we asked him over and he immediately accepted. I was expecting a hippie-type tourist, scruffy and dirty, and I was very surprised to see Justin looking fresh and cool and cleanly dressed. The only native thing he wore was a pair of *markoups*. He was very polite and reserved, but when we started talking Greek he relaxed. Outwardly he showed no signs of distress. He told us about a house he had in the Mani. We said that we were looking for a place to buy in Greece but that we never had the time to make a proper search. He said he would not want to live there now that his wife was dead and that he was thinking of selling the place.

'He wanted to go to Nyala although he knew that Ursula was already buried. The custom here is to bury the dead the same day, before sunset if possible. We heard that after she was found the police had a problem about who was going to carry her to the cemetery, because she was a Christian and Muslims refuse to do it. Eventually they got a couple of Southerners from the jail – the Southerners are mostly Christians. The Sudanese don't use coffins, so I suppose she was buried in a shroud.

'Justin left two days later for Nyala. The next thing we heard (from Chris's people there) was that Justin had tried to commit suicide by cutting his wrists. I wrote him a letter telling him to come back to Khartoum, because we were afraid he would try it again. I told him in Greek, "Your hour has not come yet." He was very struck with that phrase and would repeat it several times later on.

'He came to Khartoum and prepared to leave for England. In the meantime we made arrangements to meet in Kotronas to look at Nysi when we went on leave. He gave me a black and white bead necklace that had belonged to Ursula. I gave him a small pharaonic mummy in porcelain. He thought it was a very appropriate present. He said, "C'est un cadeau d'outre-tombe." We used to speak French sometimes.'

Justin arrived at my parents' house straight from London airport on Friday April 17th, 1981. Unfortunately they had weekend guests staying. He had purposely not warned anyone in the family beforehand, preferring to break the news face to face – but he hadn't anticipated the possibility of this social difficulty. He handled it with dignity and aplomb. He said what had to be said to my parents. When everyone else had gone to bed he talked at length to my mother. Next morning he left, saying that he would be back in a few days. He packed some of Ursula's clothes into his Renault, which he had left in my parents' garage before his departure for Sudan, and drove away.

He drove to Eve's house near Slough. She was shocked to see him standing there on the doorstep carrying three large bags – she knew at once that something was wrong. She asked where Ursula was. 'She's dead,' he replied. He stayed that weekend, in the course of which he told the story of Ursula's death in great detail and at astonishing length. Eve had previously known Justin less intimately than Ursula, but she quickly understood that listening was the only thing that she or anyone else could do for him. From then on, whenever he needed her, he was sure of an affectionate, intelligent listener who had also been Ursula's closest friend.

Justin states in *Style* that it was only to Eve that he recounted the entirety of what happened in Sudan. But when

he visited me a few days later in London, the version he gave
me was also very detailed. I was stunned not only by the
infinite sadness of the news but also by the sheer length and
weight of his monologue. Although this was in the form of a
continuous, if rather staccato, narrative, it was peppered with
names, Arabic terms, quotations, and theosophical concepts
of which I was quite ignorant. At first I tried to stop him
whenever I needed elucidating on some point or other, but,
finding that the elucidation confused me more than ever,
I realised that he wasn't really interested in a precise
communication – it was simply, as Eve said, that he needed a
listener. After the sixth hour of this, I caught myself thinking
miserably that I had never understood him – and that, as a
result of the appalling backhander that fate had dealt him,
there was very little hope of my ever being able to do so in the
future.

Justin went back to my parents' house with the idea of
establishing himself in a stable retreat, where he could start
the book he was planning and still be within easy reach of Eve
at Slough. Once the book was under way he would deal with
the selling of the flat in Rome. I had the feeling that
everything had been arranged in his mind before he got back
to England. There was a kind of inner certainty about all his
actions that you were afraid to question. But his state of spirit
was still more or less mysterious to most people who saw him
at the time. His ability to talk for hours at a time gave a
paradoxical impression of loneliness, almost of alienation, not
less noticeable for his manifesting no outward symptoms of
grief. On the contrary he was sociable, almost gregarious. Eve,
encouraged by this, introduced him to several of her friends,
including Mark Peploe.

'Mark knew at first glance,' his wife Louise told me, 'that
Justin was somebody to whom something extraordinary had
happened – but he couldn't guess what it was. Eve told him
the story in private afterwards, and of course it explained his
intuition. When Mark came home, full of this fascinating man
he'd just met, I wanted to meet him too. I think it was Eve
who arranged it again. We both felt an affinity for Justin. He
had this strange sort of detachment, but on the other hand, he

was all pumped up with adrenalin. He was absolutely obsessed
with his book. When we saw him later in Rome, he was
working on it till four or five in the morning. I don't know
when he ever went to bed.'

The vision that he had conceived of my parents' house as a
'stable retreat' failed to materialise – he was far too restless.
Carmen and Manuel Vazquez, who work for my parents and
live in the house, developed an affectionate admiration for him
that bordered on hero-worship. I remember Ursula, years
ago, explaining why the English upper classes have got it all
wrong about domestic servants – because they're frightened of
them. Her argument was that if you must have servants, an
unthinkable and preposterous proposition, the relationship
can work only when the master is masterful enough for
the servant to respond – face to face, that is – with a
complementary servility. Justin now set about putting this
theory into practice: 'Manuel, polish my boots', or, 'Ugh,
Manuel, you make the worst coffee in this world', or, after a
display of tears from warm-hearted Carmen over the poor
boy's plight, 'Carmen, it's high time you grew up'.

Manuel described, with an awed tenderness, the twelve-
hour stretches when the typewriter clattered from the childhood room at the top of the house, accompanied by the
wailing, tribal music that Justin had recorded in Sudan. But at
night he drank with them, usually whisky or vodka, in
quantities that would have been inconceivable at any time
since his adolescence. Alcohol made him excited, almost
ecstatic, but remoter still. At a certain stage he would put
some Arabic music on the record-player and dance, an
impressive performance, both wild and controlled, during
which he would become so oblivious of his audience, Carmen
and Manuel, that they gradually felt obliged to withdraw from
the room – it was as if the dance were intended for Ursula's
eyes alone. The next day he would announce that he was going
abroad.

A precise chart of Justin's movements between his arrival in
England after Ursula's death and his final departure in
December the same year wasn't easy to plot. He hopped
between Rome and Paris and Greece and England in a jerky

rhythm that seemed to be trying to re-create, in disjointed quick-motion, the measured intervals in space and time of the whole of his seventeen years with Ursula. Although this frenetic activity was dictated in part by restlessness, he had two objectives which gave it an ostensible justification: the disposal of material and emotional links with the past – Nysi and the flat in Trastevere – and the writing of the book, whose subject-matter was so closely bound up with both places.

In June he went to the Peloponnese and met Christopher and Riri Howse in Areopolis, where he had arranged for them to stay in a beautiful hotel – he himself was sleeping at Nysi. Riri said, 'We didn't know what to expect of Nysi and we were pleasantly surprised. Justin always said that the rock looked like an icon, which is true. With every visit we loved the place more, and in the end we decided to buy it. When it was known in the village that he was selling Nysi to us, there was quite an uproar from the original owners, who had discovered the value of the place and wanted it for themselves. I don't know if they had the £30,000 cash (one of the five brothers, a sea captain, claimed he had), but Justin didn't hold this family in much regard and didn't want to sell it back to them. So the preliminary deeds were given to us.

'There was one man, a mason called Stathis, whom Justin appreciated very much. He was one of the workers who had helped build the house. Justin sometimes used to go hunting rabbits or birds with him. Stathis would say to me in Greek that Justin was "a correct man". All the people in Kotronas liked Justin and Ursula, although they kept a respectful distance. Justin was always very helpful, and whenever they were going to Areopolis or Gytheion, he would ask the villagers if they needed anything. They appreciated that very much. Once a fire broke out on the opposite side of the bay of Kotronas, and when Justin and Ursula saw the flames they went across with their fishing boat and helped put it out. The villagers were very impressed at these two foreigners helping with something that didn't concern them. But Justin led a healthy life at Nysi and did a lot of underwater fishing. That led to rumours that they were looking for antiquities to take away and sell.

'Justin was terribly sad when we were at Nysi with him. The whole place reminded him of her, he felt her absence there more than anywhere else. He rented a fishing boat and took us round the coast all the way to Porto Kayou. It was a pilgrimage and farewell to the places he and Ursula knew so well. We would stop at some little creek and he would go ashore. He would climb the rocks or go up a goat-path and stay immobile for a few minutes, as if in prayer. He was just looking at the beautiful, barren Mani scenery for the last time and saying goodbye.

'He showed us a point just across the bay of Nysi where Ursula used to go swimming and then lie on the rocks. According to Justin a large section of these rocks broke away and slid into the sea after Ursula died. (All the rocks around Nysi are black – in the old days they were used to make black mosaic floors.) It really gave us the feeling that for him the chapter called Nysi was closed.

'From what Stathis told us the next summer, he went to the village before leaving and said farewell to everyone in a very emotional way – he told them that they would never see him again. He told them that Ursula had died of a heart-attack. Some believed him but some thought that he had killed her because she was old (many of the village women commented on how much older she looked). It was only to Stathis that he said that she had committed suicide. When he said goodbye to Stathis the tears were running down his cheeks – he said how sad he was to leave this place that he loved so much, knowing that he would never come back. People wondered why he could not come back, and the more cunning villagers deduced that Justin and Ursula were spies and that something must have happened. They still try to corner me into admitting that they were spies, and I can't help laughing in their faces and asking them, "Spying on *what*?" The twelve fishing boats in the harbour?'

Justin visited Tom Hilton in Glasgow twice, once before and

once after his farewell to Nysi. Each visit lasted at least a week, so Tom had plenty of time to form impressions. 'The first time he came he was radiating a powerful energy. He was centred in himself and certain of his approach. He said that he'd given himself a year, and that if he couldn't find a justification for going on living, then . . . He didn't finish the sentence. Our talk was usually jerky, we'd approach a subject and then bounce off it. But even though most things were too painful to be talked about, we still did talk about them elliptically and spasmodically, mixed into other conversations. There was nothing oblique or melodramatic about his announcement of giving it a year. His plans for selling the property and writing the book were firm and to be proceeded with. Though aware that I was in the presence of someone who had suffered an almost mortal blow, I found that so much of his charm and confidence remained intact that it was a pleasure to be with him. The only awkward moment was when he showed me a photograph of Ursula taken just before her death. He said with tears in his eyes, "Look, she was beautiful, how could she possibly say she was too old to go on? That couldn't have been the reason." But I saw a very tired woman wearing a headscarf for concealment, ill, tired eyes, downcast demeanour. Of course I kept my mouth shut, but looking at that photo and then at the very fit, handsome man in front of me, I felt that that was exactly why she had killed herself.

'The second time he came he was burning – there was real fire and irritation and impatience showing. We used to drive about Glasgow a lot, usually in his car. If the traffic lights were red he was incapable of waiting for them to change, he'd just roar through, often overtaking a whole queue of stationary cars. He did this at every set of lights in Glasgow and there are a lot. Like the first time, he only slept about two hours a night. But now his tiredness was more obvious. The way he talked for instance – he'd start a sentence in English, but go off into Arabic or Greek or Italian without any desire to be understood or any awareness of not being understood. I found him more tiring to be around – all that controlled hysteria. I was conscious then that he'd missed out on some sort of learning

stage and that that was connected to his sense of having failed
Ursula in some way . . . '

I asked Tom if he thought that the speeding and the
sleeplessness were a technique for cramming as much as
possible into that last year. 'Perhaps. But the paradoxical thing
was that the second time he didn't mention the "one more
year" thing. Of course he had an underlying self-discipline, a
code of gentleness and kindness that the wildness never
overshadowed. But I did have a feeling that maybe he was
changing his mind.'

Carmen agreed, but added that his attitude changed again
before he left England for the last time in December. 'He tried
everything to be happy – he drank, he danced, he laughed, he
had girl-friends. He pretended to be happy, but he needed too
much love to make up for Ursula – and he didn't get it,
because she left an emptiness that nobody could fill. Nobody
understood him, nobody understood his need for love. When
he left at the end I kissed him, crying. He said, "Carmen don't
cry for me – look after my mother." Manuel said, "Why you
going to Sudan, why you going?" He said, "I have to go, I
have to finish something."'

Justin had already announced that he was going back to
Sudan. Before Ursula's death the two of them had agreed that
one day they would embark on an extensive research into
Sudanese history and ethnography. His plan was to return
there in the New Year and begin this labour, thereby
redeeming some kind of pledge to his love. How realistically
he anticipated actually working on the project is open to
doubt. In view of what happened when he finally reached
Sudan, it seems more likely that he thought of the country in
general terms, as the scene of work in progress cruelly
curtailed – just as he was obliged to turn his back on Nysi,
where Ursula had been alive and happy, he was irresistibly
magnetised by the place of her death.

In August the old Sheikh, Ali's father-in-law, flew to
England for a periodic medical check-up. Justin had previously
invited him to my parents' house. He arrived, a truly awe-
inspiring figure, tall, venerable, virile and handsome, dressed
in a long white robe. Carmen and Manuel thought he was a

supernatural apparition, and someone else remarked, 'He makes the rest of the human race look like a lot of rabbits.' He spoke no English so Justin had to interpret. The Sheikh, my mother and Justin went on a tour of the property. As they stood in my mother's bedroom, looking out over the undulating landscape, uninterruptedly green except where bisected by the dull silver of the Thames, the Sheikh clasped Justin's shoulder, gazed into his eyes, and spoke to him in tones of evident tenderness and belief. 'What is he saying?' asked my mother, and Justin reluctantly translated. 'He says that, although I am like a son to him, I belong here among all this beauty, and that I should not go back to Sudan.'

When in London, Justin usually stayed with Jonna and his second wife Beverley in their house in Putney. The two brothers, so close in age, who had shared with a reasonable amount of harmony what Jonna describes as the happiest of childhoods, had lost touch completely at the time of Justin's elopement. 'It sounds a terrible thing to say,' said Jonna recently, 'but I wasn't tremendously upset when he died. It was as if he'd already died, years ago, when he got together with Ursula. After that he was a closed book. But I'm grateful to have seen a lot of him in that last year. He used to stay with us for two or three days at a time. He was staggeringly generous. For instance, he insisted on giving us £1,500 to mend our roof. I was worried about it and didn't want to take it, but Justin swore that if I didn't he'd just send the money to my bank. Of course I now know that he was distributing his wealth.' 'How do you think he had so much money?' 'He was clever with money, not like you and me. And then they lived so moderately, they didn't have children, their house cost nothing to build . . . Anyway I was talking about his generosity. He was always taking us out to dinner. It was impossible to pay, he just wouldn't hear of it. The only trouble was that he was terribly embarrassing with waiters – you know, always ticking them off and talking Italian or French to them. Somehow it didn't come off, perhaps because he could sense our embarrassment. But probably, in the old days, he and Ursula felt the same way about that kind of thing, so it was okay. But, you know, it's really Beverley you should be talking to – she loved Justin and her feelings weren't so complicated as mine.'

'I remember it very much as Jonna does,' said Beverley, 'except that you've got to imagine us, completely broke, when along comes this glamorous, tragic brother-figure, loaded with money. I loved the times when he took us out to dinner. He had this observant, dry sort of humour. He'd point to some total stranger in the restaurant, and mutter some absurd comment about them – we laughed non-stop. But meanwhile he was drinking a lot. At a certain point, when he'd had enough to release it, I suppose, he'd start talking about Ursula. By this time we were usually back home. And then he'd begin to cry – which made me cry as well. The whole thing was so unbelievably sad. They were very strange evenings. It was as if we were all high on a mixture of drink and drama and tragedy. I think Jonna and I were also flattered that he should have chosen to seek us out.'

In 1976 Eve had introduced Justin and Ursula to Caroline Dawnay of A. D. Peters, the literary agents. In July 1981 Justin renewed the acquaintance, thinking that he'd need an agent to find a publisher for his book. He visited Caroline at her office several times during the progress of the writing, and once took her out to dinner. I asked Caroline whether the relationship had remained on a work basis.

'Yes, in a way, but there was also a real sympathy between us, an alliance. I felt that he liked me.' 'Were you attracted to Justin as a man?' 'Yes, I was. For a start he was extremely good-looking. He was also hypersensitive in a heterosexual way, not that he ever showed any sexual interest in me. I was attracted by his seriousness, even his arrogance, the way he laid down the law. I think women often find dogmatic men of that sort attractive, in the same way that men like women with long blonde hair.' Long blonde hair made me think of Ursula, and I asked what impressions Caroline had of her. 'It was the two of them as a couple that interested me when I met them at Eve's. They had a sort of fierce gentleness towards each other, an unusual degree of respect and carefulness. I don't mean just his helping her on with her coat, but the way they continually watched each other in conversation, without much reference to anyone else in the room.' Here Caroline cupped her hands to mime a ball or an apple. The gesture shocked me, because it was precisely the one that Justin himself had often used to symbolise his marriage. She went on, 'But it was a bit frightening, such dedication. They seemed poised on an edge. And their certainty was somehow alienating – perhaps they weren't really of this world at all . . . '

Later Caroline talked again about the book. 'My God, how I agonised about it. I felt that I owed it to him to make it happen, because it was almost as if he'd already died, as if he had sufficient faith in me to be able to afford now to lose interest. From now on it didn't matter what happened to him, because I was going to look after *her*, Ursula I mean, the book, her memorial. Did you ever get the feeling that Justin was a bit crazy? Surely any ordinary person would have said, "Look, I know I'm laying a tremendous burden on you, but . . . " You know what I mean? Because after that last dinner at Chez Victor I was certain, absolutely certain, that I was never going to see him again.'

Nobody knows quite how, but Justin got it into his head that he should send his typescript to Graham Greene. He was already talking about it before he was half-way through the work. I tried hard to dissuade him. I thought that there was no possible chance that an old, reclusive, hard-working, much-solicited master would find the time to read, let alone commend, such a document, and that for Justin, in the condition he was in, the consequent silence would be discouraging, even destructive. Caroline Dawnay, with professional experience reinforcing common sense, also thought it a bad idea. But when Justin wanted to do something, nobody but Ursula had ever been able to stop him. Harriet, by now my ex-wife, arranged for him to meet her cousin by marriage, Caroline Hill, who had painted Greene's portrait at his flat in Antibes. Caroline wrote him a letter of recommendation, and at last, in December, the huge bundle was posted from Rome to the south of France, with a covering note from Justin on the headed paper of A. D. Peters.

Style, the book that Justin washed his hands of on the day
he sent a copy to Graham Greene is huge (nearly 500
typewritten pages often in single spacing), chaotic and
misshapen. It's exhausting, maddening, but sombre and well
worth the effort of reading. The story is told by an accountant,
who meets Justin (always referred to as O.) in Khartoum
immediately after Ursula's death. Ursula herself is invariably
called Helena. Apart from these two devices, the use of an
invented narrator and the changing of the names, the book
makes no attempt at fiction. It's simply (or rather compli-
catedly) a work of homage to Ursula, incorporating a
biography of her life before he met her, and including a great
mass of her own writing. The biographical section, which
covers about a hundred pages, is written subjectively,
investing the heroine with a sweeping overall purpose and a
continuous and goddesslike dignity. It celebrates not so much
a human being as an ideal – when you can understand it, that
is. For pages at a time Justin's meaning is hard to grasp,
almost as if he thought that Ursula's spirit was beyond the
reach of the ordinary reader, and that was the way he wanted it
to stay. Nevertheless, this section does communicate, and very
movingly, his overwhelming love, his contained grief, and a
furious impatience with the rest of mankind. Next comes a
250-page selection of excerpts from Ursula's journals and two
of her stories, including 'The Monument'. The book ends
with Justin's own commentary, as related to the accountant-
narrator, on her death in Nyala.

Justin's daring choice of Graham Greene as the first
objective critic of his work turned out to have been intuitively
correct. On January 23rd 1982 Greene wrote this letter:

Dear Caroline Dawnay,

I have received from Justin Behrens the copy of his book
Style. He asked me to send my opinion to you.

It's a very difficult book to judge. I found parts of it very
moving indeed and one of the two short stories of his wife I
thought brilliant. I can't see any English publisher in the
present bad state of things giving it the time and thought
necessary for publication. If I had still been a publisher I

think I would have been ready to embark on a long discussion with the author or rather, as Behrens is more the editor, the editor. I would have proposed a simplification and removing the disguise that the book is prepared by an accountant. I would have proposed altering the title. I would have proposed very severe cuts in the wife's diary quite apart from the obvious necessity to remove some of the quotations in modern Greek etc. that the ordinary reader can't possibly understand. There are a great many mis-quotations and misspellings but those could easily be put right. Somehow I think it would be possible for an able editor to cut the diary in a way which would enable the sad story to proceed towards this tragic end with a certain sense of inevitability. Somehow there is a most moving book struggling to get out . . .

In September 1981 Riri and Christopher Howse went to England to meet Justin and complete the sale of Nysi. Justin invited them to my parents' house. Riri described his guided tour of the place. 'He was very casual and had his usual air of disdain, but underneath that I could sense his pride. All the time he was in England he seemed aloof from the natives [the English] as if he could barely tolerate them. I went to his room in the attic because he wanted to give me some clothes of Ursula's. The walls were covered with photographs of her – it was the first time I had seen her. I asked him if she minded growing old, and he said she did very much. In all the photographs she was extremely serious, but then so was Justin. Even in a photo I saw of him as a little boy he was deadly serious. The ones of Ursula looked somehow very old-fashioned. To this day I cannot imagine Justin with her.

'We made an arrangement to meet a few days later in London to sign the papers at the Greek Embassy. It was the last day of our stay in England. After a couple of hours we finished our business, and Justin took us out to lunch in a famous French restaurant in the heart of London. After lunch we went to Fortnum and Mason's to buy cheese and chocolate for a friend of his. I was amused to see that he behaved in a typical English upper-class manner. It was not put on, he

switched to it automatically, without realising it. I told him
about it, and he laughed and shook his head.

'We stayed the night at this friend's house and Justin and I
talked all through the night. This time he wasn't talking about
Ursula but about the book he was beginning to write. It didn't
sound like a good commercial venture, but Justin said that the
point was to *write* the book – what happened to it afterwards
was not of the slightest importance. I could not accept that
and we argued about it for some time. But very often Justin
would talk in riddles – he would say things that could be
interpreted in two ways. I sometimes thought it was because
of his stiff Greek – he spoke the language perfectly but had a
peculiar turn of phrase. But Chris said it was the same when
he spoke English. So in the end I thought he meant that he
didn't care about money, and that he had more important
things on his mind. To chase up the sale of his book would not
be a dignified enough undertaking.'

In preparation for his trip to Sudan Justin bought a new
Land Rover. That he should do something so forward-looking
tended slightly to dispel the anxieties of everyone around
him.

Carmen and Manuel mentioned several times that while
living at my parents' house Justin used on occasion to stay out
all night, without giving any warning or explanation. It was
only at the third mention that I grasped what was behind this
reiteration. 'You mean,' I asked Manuel, 'that he had a girl-
friend somewhere in the neighbourhood?' 'Maybe more than
one, maybe here, maybe in London.'

If this was a guess, Tom confirmed it by saying that in
Glasgow Justin had been more or less indiscriminately in
search of sex. It didn't surprise me – I'd noticed myself that at
times of extreme grief the need for physical contact with some,
almost any, female person was abnormally pressing. I'd always
attributed this to the fearful cold breath against my heart – I
assumed that the warmth of another body, another heart,
would rehumanise me and so lessen my suffering. I suggested
to Tom that Justin might have felt something of the kind. He
replied, 'Any big shock acts as a threat to the organism, and all
the genetic programming will then drive for sex. There's a

trick gardeners use to make flowers come out – they starve the plant of water. The threat of extinction is enough to intensify sexual activity.' Then what was at work in Justin was the reproductive instinct at its most primitive – as if he were trying to father the child that it had not been within the limits of Ursula's love to bear him.

But he was also on the look-out for something more. Justin had lived with one woman, in isolation and without a break, since adolescence. To say that he had become addicted would be an understatement – the constant companionship of a woman was the only way of life he knew. Justin had given himself one more year, which wasn't much for finding a replacement for someone so irreplaceable as Ursula – but that, whether consciously or not, was what he seems to have been trying to do.

Rosanna Castelletti was the daughter of the solicitor whose services Justin used in May to negotiate for the sale of the flat in Trastevere. They started an affair which lasted on and off from then until the end of December when he finally left for Sudan. Justin took Rosanna seriously. She wanted to go to England, so he invited her to stay at my parents' house in July. Carmen and Manuel were impressed by his attentiveness to her. He would pick a rose from the garden and take it to her with her breakfast in bed, which was exactly what he had done with Ursula. He photographed Rosanna – the poses he asked her to assume, the clothes he dressed her in, again suggested an attempt to remould her in Ursula's image. When he went to Rome in August they saw each other continually, as they did again in December. And it was Rosanna who saw him off from Venice on the boat to Alexandria.

In June, while clearing up the flat in Rome prior to putting it on the market, Justin telephoned Eve – he could hardly speak for the fresh violence of the grief which ubiquitous memories were making him suffer. In August, however, he wrote to her in a very different spirit – Rosanna was a delightful person and he was sure that Eve would like her. But he felt the need to apologise for what might appear to her as a betrayal of Ursula. He needn't have worried – Eve was only too relieved that he had found someone who might help reattach him to life.

In the end Rosanna turned out not to be that person. Probably he was scared off by the strength of the feelings he touched off in her – feelings whose reciprocation he knew could only be coaxed out of him very gradually, if at all. I'm guessing, but then so was everybody I talked to on the subject. For a time she comforted him at a heavy price to herself.

The boat from Venice to Alexandria passed by the southern tip of the Peloponnese in the middle of the night. Justin told Riri that, in spite of atrocious weather, he went on deck to strain his eyes for the lights of Kotronas. This ghostly glimmer was his last sight of Europe.

It was in early January, the exact time of year when he had always launched his African trips with Ursula, that Justin landed in Alexandria. He then set off on a journey that he knew was extremely dangerous – he was planning to drive the Land Rover all the way up the valley of the Nile. The stretch from the Egyptian frontier to Khartoum is notorious, a sandy track that no sensible person would dream of negotiating without a convoy. But he managed it somehow. On the way down, by a nasty stroke of irony, he discovered the very house for sale – a kind of Sudanese Nysi – that he and Ursula had searched for in vain for the previous three years.

As soon as he reached Khartoum, Justin visited Riri and Christopher. He explained that he was staying only a short time because of his eagerness to return to Darfur. He had met an old friend from Zalingei who had agreed to travel with him as guide and mechanic – but first there was the problem of finding diesel fuel for the arduous six-day drive, not an easy assignment in Khartoum. It was during this interim, which would otherwise have exacerbated Justin's by now chronic impatience, that the Howses introduced him to a friend of theirs.

Ruth Salan was the daughter of a husband and wife team of cabaret performers who happened to be in Khartoum at the outbreak of the Second World War. In the circumstances they decided to settle and open a night-club there. After the war the club did well enough for Ruth's mother to be able to give up performing and dedicate herself to a life of retirement in style. At the same time she felt that she owed her daughter advantages she herself had been denied – she sent Ruth to boarding schools in England. This education caused Ruth to react against the racier values of her early upbringing – she grew up withdrawn and wistful with Pre-Raphaelite looks and a talent for flower-arrangement.

Justin was in no condition to take feminine vulnerability into account, and if he caused Rosanna and now Ruth to suffer inordinately he can hardly be blamed for it. Leaving aside the distortions of personality caused by grief, he had no experience of the various ways that pain can be inflicted – from the age of sixteen he had lived with Ursula in a state of continuous emotional harmony, by which I mean that they loved each other equally. His feelings towards Ruth became warm, fraternal, protective, and he didn't have any precedent for supposing that her own could be anything very different.

Justin arrived in Nyala at the end of February. By the end of March he wrote to Rosanna that he had rented a house, bought furniture, and moved in. His purpose there was to take care of Ursula's grave. In the Peloponnese he had designed a white marble slab with a low pedimented upright, which he had then had carved by a local monumental mason. This stone he conveyed in the Land Rover from Greece to England, back to Rome, down to Khartoum, and finally across the desert to its resting place.

When he had sunk it into the earth he couldn't bear to leave the little cemetery, where he was still in some way in touch with Ursula. It was a forlorn square of land, with dusty thorn trees, a family of wild cats, heaps of rubbish lying about. He took on the task of turning it into the sort of setting she would have wanted. Her place of burial had always preoccupied Ursula – now she was in a graveyard which he had played no part in choosing. To atone even slightly for what he saw as his negligence over such a long-prepared-for duty, he tried to re-create the graveyard in the spirit of Nysi. He dug and weeded

and pruned. He rebuilt entirely the stone surrounding walls.
He bought a new iron gate and set it in its place.

Riri corroborated the view that a woman might have saved
Justin, and that he himself was close to admitting that this was
the case. 'I knew by instinct that he needed a relationship with
a woman and I thought that would have been the best thing
for him. I am convinced to this day that had he found a
woman who was sexually attractive to him, who wanted him
and *needed* him – physically, emotionally, financially, in any
possible way – but one who had a strong personality
compatible with his, with a big dose of mystery and
mysticism, he would certainly have started a new life with her.
The trouble was that any woman, in order to captivate Justin,
would have to have been an Ursula and a half.'

Riri herself, although (or possibly because) she was sexually
unavailable, seems to have come closest to providing Justin
with the insight that such a thing were possible. She was
Greek and had an English husband. Justin's position in the
household, as a male who didn't go out to work, must have
been a little ambiguous. I wonder if it also dimly reminded
him of the position he had occupied in Kenelm's household so
many years ago.

'Emotionally my relationship with him was very close,' Riri
said. 'We would always speak Greek or French, whoever was
in the room with us, and that gave us a sort of complicity. I
also had enough snobbishness to make him feel at ease,
understand his class jokes, etc. At first he did not totally
approve of Chris, for the simple reason that he was English.
The English and England were something to be avoided at all
cost. But later he came to appreciate him, especially when he
understood that Chris had no social hang-ups.'

I quoted Jonna as saying that Justin was clever with money,
far cleverer than Jonna himself or I. Without ever having done
a stroke of gainful work in his life he increased his initial
patrimony until in the end he was in pretty comfortable
financial circumstances. He achieved this by a canny mixture
of moderation, understanding of the exchange laws and good
investment. Jonna and I blundered through a series of
manoeuvres, very different in detail but parallel in essence,

whose obscure purpose seems to have been to get rid of every penny and start again. But because Justin, unlike us, had rejected the concept of a career, he found himself short of an outlet for his energy once Ursula, his *raison d'être*, was no longer there. At this crucially balanced moment it would surely have been better for him if he'd been obliged to use his brains for securing his material survival.

Riri's thoughts on the subject show poignantly how, from sheer force of habit, he tried vainly to occupy his time by working for the pleasure and betterment of women. 'Justin had no purpose – such an active and intelligent man had nothing to do. He was looking for something useful to do. After Ruth's father died she had to clear out the stores of the cabaret – Justin was more than happy to go along and help her. Of course he joked about it to me, but he was happy to feel that he was needed. He often took Ruth to sunbathe by the banks of the Nile. But it wasn't enough for him.

'In his search for something useful to do he decided the only thing left was to help someone else. The British Council in Omdurman gave a small party to which we went with Ruth and Justin. There he met a youngish Sudanese girl who was very liberated. She didn't wear the *tob* but dressed in Western-style clothes, mini-skirts, etc. Justin looked very interested. Ruth came home with us but he stayed on at the party. I think he went to bed with her, but when I asked him how serious he was, he said she was not at all his type. He said he felt sorry for this girl, who was suffocating in the narrow-minded Sudanese society, who wanted to be free, to travel, to settle somewhere like London where she could do whatever she wanted.

'He decided the only way he could help her was to marry her, give her a British passport, and then divorce her. But because she couldn't have married a Christian he went to a school and studied the Koran for a few days, passed a test on it, and became a Muslim. One day he came to lunch with us as usual and announced that he was a Muslim and was going to get married. I told him that he was oversimplifying the whole affair – suppose she wouldn't give him a divorce or couldn't get the British passport as quickly as he thought. He said that nothing mattered except that this girl should get the chance of a new life.

'In the end it was she who didn't want to marry him. She must have first light-heartedly said yes, but when she was faced with the real thing she must have sensed that something was wrong and refused. I must say I respected her for that. Some of those girls are very honest with themselves, and I think they are real women. So that was a disappointment for Justin, although he was relieved at the same time.

'In Chris's office Justin got to know a Coptic secretary girl – he went there sometimes in the morning to see Chris. He went out with this girl and proposed her the British passport deal, but she didn't want it either.'

Justin was disheartened by these rejections. He was also dismayed by his inability to make the same kind of easy contact with the Sudanese that he had made in Darfur – in Khartoum, where there are substantial numbers of whites, people were more suspicious of his approaches. Yet another source of depression was his failure to sell the Land Rover. He had met someone in Darfur who was so close to buying it that Justin went to the lengths of having the man's cattle brand painted on the car – but at the last moment the deal fell through. He went on trying to dispose of it in Khartoum, but in August, with still no sign of a buyer in the offing, he gave up. The Land Rover's licence as a foreign vehicle was on the point of expiring anyway, and then he'd have to pay a large import duty. One night he told Christopher that he wanted to give it to him.

The same evening he announced that he had nothing more to do in Sudan. In some ways this came as a relief to Riri. 'We were glad he had made up his mind to go. We thought that Khartoum wasn't doing him any good, and that it was a waste of time his endlessly rushing about here and there with no real aim or purpose. I asked him where he was going and he implied it was Italy. I wanted to know where he was getting his ticket – foreigners aren't allowed to buy them locally. He said he would get one somehow, and we thought maybe Rosanna was going to send him one. I kept on asking him about these details, but his answers were always vague. We should have been more intelligent and realised what he had in mind. But the awful thing was that none of us did.'

I have chosen to end the story in Riri Howse's words because of the disinterested love, the honest indignation, and the unflinching regard for the facts that they conveyed to me.

'The day before his death he came late for lunch. I went to greet him and told him that his place was waiting at the table. He smiled sadly. He looked so sad that day I cannot describe it – I tried to cheer him up but it was impossible. He ate very little. I insisted he should take more, because he usually ate a lot. He was obviously hungry but he didn't feel like eating. I think it shows that up to the end he would gladly not have done it. The physical side of him was not ready for death.

'After lunch we talked about Nysi. He said he was very happy that we liked the place – he had done the right thing selling it to us. I asked him if he would consider going back to help us build some more bedrooms. He was so surprised at this idea that it took him several minutes to answer. Then he said that it was impossible for him to go back.

'Immediately after coffee he left. He said he had things to do for his trip. I said we would expect him for lunch tomorrow. He said not to wait for him, but I replied that of course we would, we couldn't have lunch without him. He smiled and kissed me, and that was the last time I saw him alive.

'He knew the kids were due to come back from their holidays in a week's time, so he planned his death for a time when they wouldn't be there. I suppose once he had made up his mind one day more or less didn't matter.

'That evening, from what we learned later, he went round saying goodbye to his friends. He told the secretary at the office that he was leaving early the next day for Nyala. To others he said that he was leaving Sudan. Unfortunately we were invited out that evening, so when he came to our house he didn't find us. Wherever he went he had generous amounts of whisky, and by the time he reached the secretary's house he was quite drunk. She said that her father and Justin drank nearly a bottle of Scotch. The office watchman told us that Justin went round there at 3 a.m., left his car in the yard and some documents in Chris's office, and then took a taxi to his hotel.

'Earlier he had paid his hotel bill and collected his passport, which he left with the other things at the office. When he got to the hotel, he spread out all the photographs of Ursula that he had. They were all over the place on the extra bed, on the dressing-table, etc. One was a black and white photo of her in which she appeared to be sleeping – or dead. She looked peaceful. All his things except the photos were packed in suitcases. He burnt some papers in the bidet of the bathroom.

'I think those minutes before he pulled the trigger must have been unbelievably terrible, because I am convinced he did not really want to die. He must have heard the birds singing in the trees outside his room, because it was 5 a.m. by then. He must have thought that if he didn't do it right then he wouldn't have the courage once the sun was up. He went to a corner of the room, put the pistol in his mouth, and pulled the trigger. The bullet did not go straight but to the left of his skull.

'At 7.30 Chris was surprised to find Justin's car at the office, and even more so when he saw the brief-case on his desk. There was a letter from Justin asking Chris to forgive him for all the trouble he was going to cause, and to take the brief-case with its contents to the British Embassy, who were to send them to his lawyer in England. There was a second letter to Chris, but he didn't find it till later, because it was underneath some office papers. It said that life without Ursula was nothing to him, and that he wished to be buried next to her in Nyala. He left Chris the money to pay for the charter to Nyala. He had foreseen everything. Chris came immediately to pick me up and we went straight to the Grand Hotel.

'At the reception desk we asked the manager for a spare key to open Justin's door. He told us that Mr Behrens had said he was leaving for Nyala at 5 a.m., so probably he had already gone. Chris explained that we thought something might have happened to him. He said we needed someone to come with us, as we didn't know what to expect. The minutes trickled by like hours. For ages they looked for the key. Then they decided to call in a policeman who happened to be on duty in front of the hotel. It was 8.15 before we finally got up to the room.

'The big surprise was that the door was slightly ajar. Why did he leave the door open? Did he hope people would hear the shot and come to his rescue?

'The policeman went in first, then Chris, then me. The room was in darkness as the curtains were drawn. Chris was the first to see him in the corner. We realised that he was still alive, he was still breathing. Then the policeman panicked – he thought it was murder, and didn't want us to touch anything in the room.

'I was getting hysterical, because my only thought was to save him. I was desperately trying to find the Arabic word for suicide, so that I could tell the policeman. Then he might have let us help him. But he pushed us out of the room and locked the door. He went to call the police station but I told him to get an ambulance.

'Outside the room Chris, who had had a good look at Justin, said that although he was still breathing it was only a matter of seconds before he died. There was nothing we could do. We had arrived too late. Those were the worst minutes of my life – sitting outside that room not being able to help him in any way.

'At last an officer arrived who could speak English. We quickly explained that it was suicide and not murder, and begged him to take him to hospital as soon as possible. He wanted to know why we were so sure, but when he saw I was about to have a fit, he ordered some servants to put Justin on to the bed and carry him in a sheet to the police station-wagon.

'When they brought him out his eyes were half-open and he was still breathing. His face was unrecognisable, it was so disfigured. They put him in the station-wagon rolled in the sheet. We followed them to the hospital. The roads are bumpy and dusty.

'Have you ever been in an African hospital? You wouldn't believe the disorder, the dust and dirt. They put him in the emergency ward. There was only a metal bed – no drip, no oxygen, nothing but flies. Eventually a doctor appeared, examined Justin, and told Chris that he was dead. I asked him to look again, to *try* to do something, but he said there was no point – Justin had died.

'The rest of the day we spent with the police. They found the note explaining the reasons for his suicide. They also found that his pistol had been smuggled in from Italy, which made things easier for us. There was not too much questioning.

'When we got away we went to see Ruth Salan who didn't know what had happened. She took it very badly. She was extremely upset, poor girl. It was as much of a shock for her as it was for us. Why didn't we guess what he was going to do?

'Chris arranged for the charter. We found a special lead coffin and in a few days we all left for Nyala – Chris and I, Ruth, an Anglican priest, the office secretary, and Ayoub, a Sudanese from the office who liked Justin very much.

'Have you ever read a book by Nikos Kazantzakis called *Freedom and Death*? I was reading it during the three and a half hour flight to Nyala, because it was from that book that Justin got the idea for the inscription on the plaque. In the plane Ayoub produced a bottle of gin and handed it round. Everybody refused, so he sat at the back quietly drinking. Needless to say by the time we landed at Nyala he was completely sloshed.

'Chris's people in Nyala met us and took us to the little cemetery, where we got a shock. On Ursula's grave there was the marble plaque that Justin had brought from Greece. The inscription was in Greek and said, 'Ursula and Justin – one'. Justin's place was waiting for him next to hers. The English priest, who was an extremely good and gentle person, said prayers for both of them.

'Ayoub sat on Justin's coffin and started singing in Arabic. When someone tried to take him away he refused and nearly fell into the grave. I am sure that Justin would have been very amused.

'We had a little fence made around both graves to show that they are one, as the inscription says. So now he lies next to Ursula for ever in a small cemetery in the heart of Africa.'

Glossary

SUDANESE ARABIC TERMS USED BY URSULA

arak	an alcoholic spirit
Baggara	a tribe of cattle nomads
Beni Hashim	a nomadic Arab tribe
bhang	a tree whose leaves are chewed as a stimulant
Dimengawa	tribe
Dinka	tribe
Fellata	tribe of cattle nomads, originally from Senegal
Forawa, Fur	native of the province of Darfur
gabbana	very strong spiced coffee
ghautiyya	hut of mud or straw
hadj	someone who has made the pilgrimage to Mecca
hakaama	literally, a judge's verdict. Used by Ursula in the sense of licensed commentator
hammam	public Arab bathhouse
haraz	kind of acacia thorn tree
haris	guard
jellabah	long Arab shirt or robe
kisra	dried pancake
markoups	sandals worn in Darfur
mawlana	respectful title for lawyers and Koranic teachers
m'hafiz	provincial commissioner
mimm	tree with thick foliage

mughliz	the faithful
'semi semi'	'lovely, very nice'
stiraha	rest house
tob	veil worn by the women of strict Muslim families
zariba	thorn fence, enclosure for livestock